"Susan Jean Mayer has managed to distill a vast and complex literature into accessible, even economical, prose. It couldn't be clearer that teaching is attending to 'what and how a person knows' (as Mayer explains), that intellectual authority is established not bureaucratically through protocols, but intersubjectively, grounded in social-psychological knowledge. Brilliant and clear as a bell, this book is, as Mayer describes great teaching, 'meaningful, powerful, and transparent.'"

—*William F. Pinar, Canada Research Chair, University of British Columbia*

"Susan Jean Mayer has given us a timely and elegant book....Mayer cleanly separates the chaff of a host of reductive, hierarchical, pseudo-scientific education policy prescriptions from the wheat of the human relationships, imbued with desire and need, claims and counter-claims for voice and attention, and the call to understanding, which comprise teaching. ...This lucid, grounded, well-argued book gives us a chance to re-orient our policy debates. It does this in part by teaching us about teaching and learning in the real world. It is at once deeply informed by good classroom practice and deeply informative about good classroom practice. It is a model of an especially attractive form of research: Rigorously empirical but with its head well above the sand, in quest of understandings that matter. Never polemical, it is animated by a deep, even a fierce, sense of urgency, as we may all now find ourselves to be."

—*Dirck Roosevelt, Associate Professor of Education;*
Director, Master of Arts in Teaching Program, Brandeis University

"This is an important book. It draws on both Piagetian and Vygotskian traditions and provides an original synthesis that will be of value to a wide range of readers. If ever there was a moment to enhance discussions of classroom discourse and democracy it is now!"

—*Harry Daniels, Professor, Centre for Sociocultural and Activity Theory Research,*
Department of Education, University of Bath

"Whether one's interest is in the broader realm of philosophy of education, in the micro world of utterance-level meaning, or at the frustrating intersection of the theoretical, empirical, and applied study of learning through discussion, this book will be of value. My own encounters with Susan Jean Mayer's superb and learned writing, and with her informed commitment to democratic education, have been of great value in my own work. I want to express profound gratitude to her and to the publisher for making this work available to all of us who continue to puzzle over classroom discussion and its potential."

—*From the Foreword by Catherine O'Connor, Professor and Chair*
of Educational Foundations, Leadership, and Counseling, Boston University

CLASSROOM DISCOURSE
and democracy

Educational
PSYCHOLOGY

Critical Pedagogical Perspectives

Greg S. Goodman, *General Editor*

Vol. 13

———————

The Educational Psychology series is part of the Peter Lang Education list.
Every volume is peer reviewed and meets
the highest quality standards for content and production.

———————

PETER LANG
New York • Washington, D.C./Baltimore • Bern
Frankfurt • Berlin • Brussels • Vienna • Oxford

SUSAN JEAN MAYER

CLASSROOM
DISCOURSE
and democracy

MAKING MEANINGS TOGETHER

PETER LANG
New York • Washington, D.C./Baltimore • Bern
Frankfurt • Berlin • Brussels • Vienna • Oxford

Library of Congress Cataloging-in-Publication Data

Mayer, Susan Jean.
Classroom discourse and democracy: making
meanings together / Susan Jean Mayer.
p. cm. — (Educational psychology: critical pedagogical perspectives; v. 13)
Includes bibliographical references and index.
1. Interaction analysis in education. 2. Democracy and education.
3. Civics—Study and teaching. 4. Authority. I. Title.
LB1034.M39   371.102′2—dc23   2011047736
ISBN 978-1-4331-1286-7 (hardcover)
ISBN 978-1-4331-1285-0 (paperback)
ISBN 978-1-4539-0544-9 (e-book)
ISSN 1943-8109

Bibliographic information published by **Die Deutsche Nationalbibliothek**.
Die Deutsche Nationalbibliothek lists this publication in the "Deutsche
Nationalbibliografie"; detailed bibliographic data is available
on the Internet at http://dnb.d-nb.de/.

The paper in this book meets the guidelines for permanence and durability
of the Committee on Production Guidelines for Book Longevity
of the Council of Library Resources.

© 2012 Peter Lang Publishing, Inc., New York
29 Broadway, 18th floor, New York, NY 10006
www.peterlang.com

Printed in the United States of America

For Madeleine and Zoe,

who have taught me much and made this all matter more.

Table of Contents

Foreword

In a democratic society, we might expect that one of the aims of schooling is to provide all students with the chance to acquire *intellectual authority*. As Susan Mayer points out, intellectual authority concerns not just "what and how a person knows," but also that person's willingness and ability to understand the sometimes divergent views of others. This gives rise, however, to the inevitable question: how do we accomplish this aim?

One of the approaches to this question, instantiated in various ways through the history of education, revolves around the use of talk. In this view, classroom discussion is a place where all students might take up the work of externalizing their thoughts, clarifying them, and responding to the thinking of others. Through this, learners may construct productive understandings of important concepts, processes, theories, and facts and might even jointly forge new knowledge. But in addition, the hope is that through engagement in this process, students will also forge for themselves personal identities that include the desire and the capacity to exercise their own intellectual authority in collaboration with others. In the end, we hope that they will see it as their right and responsibility to contribute to the larger social enterprise in this way.

At various times and places in the last century, a commitment to engaged talk as a tool for democratic education has deeply taken hold in a classroom or a few schools through the concerted efforts of one or more teachers. Many more profess to value it. Researchers, however, have found again and again that *discussion* is generally rare within classrooms and difficult to sustain. Applebee et al. (2003) found that even in English language arts and social studies classrooms in middle and high schools, the average amount of discussion is less than two minutes per hour! Those of us who spend a great deal of time studying and reflecting upon classroom discourse—talk between and among teachers and students about academic content—find this unsurprising. We repeatedly find ourselves flummoxed by the complexity of classroom discourse at every level.

The dimensions that contribute to this complexity are various. We ponder talk as a vehicle for learning specific content—an ineluctably complicated amalgam whether one is looking at math in first grade or literary studies in high school. We ponder the complexity of talk as a socializing practice, inducting students into the ways of thinking that characterize particular disciplines. Then there is the puzzle of talk as a threat: a threat to the teacher's sense of control and to students' positioning within the social hierarchy of the classroom. When open discussion is practiced, one cannot predict what ideas will emerge or how those who voice them or respond to them will be subsequently viewed. At the level of linguistic structure within utterances, there is endless complexity, for those so inclined. And finally, there are the challenges of implementation: given the interpersonal, cultural, and social class freightings of particular discursive forms, how should one approach bringing these into a particular classroom, or into teacher education more generally?

So while many people share the intuition that the thinking of an individual student can be deepened or made more robust by engaging in conversational interaction with others, it is not easy to reach consensus, or even a general framework, for how this should be done in actual classrooms. Many seem to fend off the complexity by forming strongly held, even adamantine, positions on this. Some hold that the only goal worth striving for is student-led discussion, where the teacher principally stands to the side in appreciation. Others feel strongly that this cannot work: in order to convey the intellectual content in a way that preserves its integrity and prepares students for further study, the teacher must invariably lead. Those who attempt a middle position are buffeted by the challenges of balancing and managing the social, intellectual, and practical dimensions of combining varying degrees of so-called dialogic and monologic discourse.

We can see the same pattern across the recent history of education. Progressivist educators reacted to the perceived rigidity and limitations of traditional 'teacher-centered' lecture-driven classrooms. The resulting range of more 'open' pedagogies created a backdrop for counter-reaction, this time by those who construed the valuing of student discussion and exploration as a denial of the importance of content. Rarely in the heated exchanges about the philosophy of pedagogy does one find a systematic and detailed consideration of the instructional actualities, with all their challenges and rewards. Perhaps the relative absence of empirical foundations for this debate can be found in the bewildering complexity of classroom discourse in all its dimensions. Its potential may be enormous, but we have not yet succeeded in finding a common ground for wider consideration.

It is thus a great relief and pleasure to turn to this deeply thoughtful and powerfully written book. The reader finds that its author, Susan Mayer, does not choose a position on the student-centered vs. teacher-centered continuum. Nor does she shrink from the complexities mentioned above. Rather, she addresses many of the oppositions by transcending them: she places the entire set of puzzles within the larger framework of intellectual authority, its sources, and its development within a system that is committed to human equality and intellectual liberty. Yet this is not a treatise that trades only in abstractions, holding itself aloof from the messy realities of real students, real teachers, and real classrooms. Mayer knows that only in those realities can one find answers that will truly serve our loftier commitments.

Based on close analyses of classrooms where discussions are long and fruitful, Mayer calmly and insightfully examines the affordances and constraints of *teacher-led*, *student-led*, and *co-led* classroom discussions. These three 'types' are not facile reductions of the gradient interactional forms we find in actual classrooms. Rather, each is treated as an opportunity to consider the benefits of the relative weightings of teacher intellectual authority, textual authority, and student participation in the process of reading, understanding, and interpreting. Each one is scrutinized with a clear-sighted yet sympathetic view. Mayer deeply understands that the character of classroom discourse is emergent—it is a product of all the dimensions that constitute its particular species of complexity: the content and the specific textual forms within which it is represented; the teacher's commitments and capacities; the students' backgrounds and expectations; and the relationships of all of these to one another through the unpredictable course of face-to-face interaction.

One of the many valuable elements of this book lies in Mayer's ability to present a clear and sophisticated picture of potential development within the messiness and imperfection of classroom discussion. She takes on the question of how students might develop *intellectual* authority within the settings she describes by introducing the construct of *interpretive authority*. This construct allows us a systematic way to consider the varying degrees of scaffolding afforded by teacher-led, student-led, and co-led discussion. In a sense, student engagement with interpretive authority is the fulcrum on which the effects of a classroom discussion depend.

The core of the book consists of analyses of these three types of classroom discussion in terms of how they might support the development of student intellectual authority. Central to Mayer's description of constraints and affordances of these three pedagogical arrangements is the notion of *participant frameworks*. Originating with Goffman, this idea allows her to examine how the teacher, the students, and the text are put in relation to one another, utterance by utterance, episode by episode. Her skillful use of this tool allows her to plumb the complexity of classroom talk by tracking its critical strands as they weave in and out. What are these strands? One involves the academic *substance* being addressed in the utterance— what is being said about the text, or about comments upon it? One is *interactional*—who is talking to whom, following what interactional history? One we might call *positional*—who is being intellectually positioned as a knower, a questioner, a critic, a creator? And finally, one that Mayer refuses to ignore, the *interpersonal*, where caring-for and caring-about are conveyed and constructed, a dimension that Noddings and others have deemed central to intellectual growth within the democratic ideal.

Whether one's interest is in the broader realm of philosophy of education, in the micro-world of utterance-level meaning, or at the frustrating intersection of the theoretical, empirical, and applied study of learning through discussion, this book will be of value. My own encounters with Susan Mayer's superb and learned writing, and with her informed commitment to democratic education, have been of great value in my own work. I want to express profound gratitude to her and to the publisher for making this work available to all of us who continue to puzzle over classroom discussion and its potential.

Catherine O'Connor
Boston, Massachusetts
October 27, 2011

Acknowledgments

This thinking has grown through conversations with countless committed educators who share many of the concerns that organize my work and who have contributed immeasurably to my own ideas about democratic classroom practice. In professional communities large and small, practitioners and scholars at every degree of remove have helped me to develop and hone these thoughts. In addition to the American Educational Researchers Association, these communities have included the John Dewey Society and Jean Piaget Society and three curriculum theory conferences: Bergamo, Curriculum & Pedagogy, and the American Association for the Advancement of Curriculum Studies.

My mentors in this work have also been many. The four who have read and commented on phases of this work most extensively are Eleanor Duckworth, Kurt Fischer, Howard Gardner, and Catherine O'Connor. The perspectives and insights of these scholars, generously shared, provided a vital context for the thoughts I present here. In particular, I want to thank Catherine O'Connor, who read a full draft of this book and whose penetrating questions and concerns sharpened my thinking in any number of places.

Special thanks also goes to Scott Barksdale and Jonas Jeswald, both of whom found time in their busy schedules as teachers and as fathers of new babies to read these chapters as they were written and to review them most thoughtfully for their import and clarity. Other people who have read and commented on sections of this book include Cynthia Ballenger, Courtney Cazden, Sally Klingel, Lisa Schneier, and my husband, Ken Parsigian. Each of these readers has helped to sustain and advance the deliberations reflected in these pages.

My graduate students have asked many of the questions that are addressed in these pages. Their insistence that I speak about issues that matter to them in terms they find meaningful has led me to be able to speak in the voice I have employed here. In particular, I want to mention the five passionate novice teachers who served, in effect, as my workgroup as they finished their graduate research projects and I finished writing my final chapter: Janice McKeown, Farisha Mohammed, Katherine Reed, Roberta Udoh, and Megan Whitaker.

I must also thank my editor, Greg Goodman, for believing in this book before any of it had even been written and my publisher, Peter Lang, for having the vision to devote a book series to the critical examination of educational psychology—truly a topic for our time. As mentioned in these pages, the journal *Language and Education* published a complementary section of my research in 2009 that provides additional methodological detail for those readers who share my fascination with all that can be gleaned and gathered from attending closely to the language of classrooms.

INTRODUCTION

Intellectual Authority for All

Upon what grounds might teachers in today's ever more diverse classrooms establish a pedagogical authority that reflects and represents democratic values? Shall a teacher's ability to improve students' standardized test scores be thought central or a teacher's mastery of disciplinary content and contemporary pedagogical theory? What about a teacher's ability to relate to students and to appreciate something of their often complex relationships with learning and school?

Today, educational administrators and teachers are under tremendous pressure within many school systems to raise students' test scores by specified margins within specified time frames. Some administrators therefore likely look to their teachers primarily to raise those scores. Educational theorists have proposed professional expertise in subject matter and pedagogical theory as the valid grounds of teacher authority. Others have suggested that teachers must also be able to relate to their students' lives.[1]

People defer to other people's *authority* when they are bound together by a social code that suggests, not only that such deference is appropriate, but also that it is morally right.[2] While each of the above capacities is likely to bolster a teacher's stature in the eyes of some, none clearly distinguishes a democratic pedagogical authority from other forms, as none of these capacities directly references the moral commitments to human equality and intellectual liberty that define democracy as a social and political form.

I propose characterizing democratic pedagogical authority in relation to yet another kind of capacity: the ability to orchestrate meaningful, powerful, and transparent 'knowledge construction processes' within one's classroom. Each of these adjectives—meaningful, powerful, and transparent—represents an organizing line of thought within the world of democratic learning theory. I specify *meaningful* because we now understand that ideas take root and grow only when they are linked to a student's concerns, understandings, and conceptual frames; *powerful* because all citizens in a democracy need to master the languages, ideas, and practical tools required to become fully participating members of the broader society; and *transparent* because transparency is essential to the democratic construction of publicly held understandings.[3]

To be interested in 'knowledge construction processes' means to be interested in how knowledge is created and used by people to make sense of their worlds. The phrase suggests that one sees knowledge as located within people who are working to understand each other and the world around them in order to be able to behave in useful and satisfying ways. In this view, knowledge does not reside in books, although authors may successfully represent aspects of their knowledge within books, and knowledge is not seen as information that can be handed unchanged from one person to another, such as a phone number. Rather, knowledge is viewed as an ever-evolving matrix of cultured impressions and understandings that each of us continually constructs as we apprehend and interact with the beings, contexts, and objects in our lives. Knowledge, as employed here, determines the ways in which each of us views, and acts upon, the world.[4]

Meaningful, powerful, and transparent knowledge construction processes support the development of what I term 'intellectual authority' among all who participate in such processes. Intellectual authority has to do with what and how a person knows *and also with the ways in which a person attends to what others know*. To possess intellectual authority means to be able to represent one's own knowledge in personally and culturally meaningful terms and also to be willing and able to understand the divergent views of others.

Each of us holds intellectual authority to varying degrees, depending upon how much we know about a matter and the extent of our ability to consider alternative points of view on that topic. To hold intellectual authority in relation to a particular issue or area of concern, then, one needs to know something about how different people have thought about that issue. To establish intellectual authority within a professional or academic field, one must both become versed in the assumptions, methods, and shared understandings of that field *and* be able to weigh the relevant strengths and weaknesses of competing lines of thought in a principled and fair-minded fashion.

These conjoined capacities—developing and articulating an informed perspective and appreciating the divergent perspectives of others—are best learned in tandem within a respectful and caring learning environment. In requiring students to maintain a discerning attention towards their own contributions and the contributions of others, teachers can help to foster a classroom community within which all feel free to speak their minds without fear of ridicule or neglect. This quality of learning environment allows each student to view his or her perspective as a valued asset in the work of the classroom, even when that perspective diverges from the perspective of the teacher or from those of other students. Such divergences come to be seen as opportunities for all to work toward greater transparency by clarifying the assumptions, experience, and reasoning that lie behind those different ideas and claims.

Nurturing everyone's sense of emotional safety and personal worth is particularly important within the world of Pre-Kindergarten-12 (PK-12) education for obvious reasons. Children are impressionable and vulnerable; their relationships to learning and knowledge are shaped in lasting ways within the primary and secondary schools they attend. In order for our schools to inculcate valuable cultural resources and cultivate a commitment to democratic values and methods, educators need to create learning environments in which everyone appreciates and respects the significant challenges that can accompany any effort to build new understandings. It becomes as important for students to value their own and each other's thinking as it is for the teacher and students to understand and value each other.

Rather than speaking of 'teacher-centered' or 'student-centered' teaching styles, I will speak here of teacher-led, student-led, and co-led learning experiences, *all* of which can advance the intellectual authority of both teachers and students. When well constructed, each type of learning experience can therefore contribute to the creation of a richly realized democratic learning environment. As the philosopher John Dewey long ago argued, there can be no choosing between teacher understandings and student understandings within democratic schools.[5] To the contrary, teachers and students must continually strive to engage with the content of their studies in ways that deepen understanding, extend cultural literacy, and increase intellectual clarity for all.

In providing children and adolescents with the resources to represent their own experience and understandings in literate and cogent terms, teachers prepare their students to assume their rights and responsibilities as active participants within their democratic society. In enabling their students to grapple with cultural understandings in a meaningful and rewarding manner, teachers nurture a sense of social integration within those students and a propensity toward lifelong growth and learning. In these ways, accomplished, democratically minded teachers establish principled grounds for the responsible exercise of their authority.

In contrast, a teacher's convincing mastery of prescribed content knowledge and current pedagogical theory means little if that teacher cannot inform the lives of the students who enter that teacher's classroom each day. And a teacher's ability to relate to students' beliefs and perspectives means little if that teacher cannot empower those students to make sense of their greater worlds in culturally fluent terms and to build constructive attitudes toward and relationships with those worlds. Finally, the currently widespread pursuit of high test scores will provide meager returns indeed if, in the end, students feel diffident towards the competencies they have mastered in order to earn those scores.

Should teachers prove able, however, to harness their content knowledge, pedagogical expertise, and interpersonal resources to orchestrate meaningful, powerful, and transparent knowledge construction processes, then each of these capacities could mean a great deal. And should high test scores be seen to represent an appropriately conceived (and so, modest) share of students' expanding sense of intellectual authority, then the capacity to generate those scores among one's students might also be made pedagogically valuable.

These claims are based upon a theory of democratic education that aims for every student's willing intellectual engagement within the classroom, leading to their eventual responsible and personally satisfying participation within the broader society. Such willing, responsible, and personally satisfying participation is seen as essential to vibrant democratic life and is believed to rest upon both a sense of membership in one's surrounding communities and a sense of personal liberty to believe as one chooses in many areas and to shape one's experience according to those beliefs. These feelings of social membership and individual liberty are seen, in turn, to result reliably from particular forms of shared experiences and the consistent nurture of democratic commitments, sensibilities, and methods.

These ideas regarding the dispositions and capacities that democratic schools must foster are supported by a considerable amount of scholarship from a number of relevant fields. I have mentioned the philosopher John Dewey, who investigated the defining characteristics of democratic education throughout his long career. Although some have seen Dewey as a moral relativist, Dewey believed that democratic relations imply and entail a distinctive moral outlook, one that underlies the character of classroom discourse advanced here.[6]

Of the many philosophers who have engaged and advanced Dewey's insights regarding democratic school practice, this work references, in particular, the scholarship of Amy Gutmann, Nel Noddings, and Maxine Greene. As a political philosopher, Gutmann has focused on the essential role that principled deliberative processes play in all democratic relations, pointedly arguing that children therefore need to be apprenticed into such processes throughout their school years. Gutmann's development of the notions of liberty and justice in relation to democratic school practice also supports the emphasis readers will find here on providing opportunities for personal meaning-making throughout a child's primary and secondary school career.[7]

Noddings is well known for her thoughtful deliberations on the broader aims and interpersonal character of democratic classroom practice, again based upon organizing democratic commitments to human equality and intellectual liberty. For example, Noddings has investigated the roles that human care and happiness play in sustaining democratic relations and has situated these considerations in relation to the daily rhythms of elementary and secondary schools. Within Noddings' writings, one finds studied explication of the ways in which intellectually curious and emotionally attentive school environments help to develop motivated, socially engaged, and fair-minded people.[8]

Much of Greene's work has focused on the possibilities and responsibilities of freedom. Greene's lifelong study of the arts and of arts education is rooted in her interest in how human creativity and moral human transaction serve to advance human growth and development. As discussed further when we return to these philosophers in chapter six, Greene's work builds upon Dewey's contention that the responsible cultivation of every child's creative vision works hand in glove with the project of socializing them to the demands of democratic living.[9]

Contemporary educational psychology also proceeds from a consonant set of assumptions regarding how children should learn in democratic schools. Neo-Piagetian theory, one of the two major strands of developmental learning theory, provides a vision of learning that is rooted in children's creative engagements with conceptually significant materials in concert with their peers.[10] Vygotskian, or 'sociocultural,' developmental theory places a complementary emphasis upon children's increasingly sophisticated capacity to employ the linguistic, conceptual, and material resources of their culture.[11] All of developmental—and cognitive—learning theory stresses the crucial place of active and original thought in any child's intellectual growth as children must continually integrate *all* new understandings into their developing conceptual frames.[12] As we will see, opportunities for this kind of 'intellectual agency' are also needed for a student to develop any sense of intellectual authority.

Classroom discourse analysis and theory now also provide a wide range of analytic and investigatory means designed to support the close consideration and theorizing of democratic knowledge construction processes.[13] Many educators and educational researchers have employed these resources to study classroom discourse in ways that pertain here. For example, classroom discourse analysts have focused on the opportunities that exist for students to ask and explore their own questions and to speak and reason in their own terms—two basic forms of intellectual agency.

Research shows that students are more likely to be granted such opportunities if they attend school in economically privileged neighborhoods or if they have been placed in advanced academic tracks within tracked schools.[14] I will argue that there is no pedagogically sound reason to distribute intellectual agency on these bases and that this practice, perhaps more than any other within our schools, undermines the intellectual purposes that democratic schools should serve.

Any large-scale shifts toward greater intellectual agency and authority for all students, however, will require thoughtful study and support, as classroom practice has not historically included models upon which teachers can draw. Many educators today also find that the institutional pressures that have accompanied pervasive federal, state, and local testing have complicated existing efforts to rethink classroom practice in the necessary ways. Unfortunately, no one can craft a simple set of guidelines, guaranteed to democratize classroom discourse while improving test scores by prescribed margins. Orchestrating collaborative knowledge construction practices within classrooms is delicate and complex work that always implicates a teacher's personality, professional interests and priorities, and developed repertoire of teaching approaches and strategies.

This book is intended to support teachers and classroom researchers as they study and strive to enrich and diversify the discourse of classrooms. Despite new and persistent challenges, democratic theorists and practitioners are called upon to continue the work of articulating, explicitly and in practical terms, the character of a school pedagogy that responds to the demands and promises of democratic living. Only by providing recognizable markers of democratic pedagogical practices and by theorizing their implications for our children's lives can today's educators expect those beyond our field to understand and support our aims.

Chapter one offers an approach to conceptualizing the inter-penetrating dimensions of what I call 'democratic knowledge systems.' This discussion provides a platform for considering the several kinds of understandings that all children continuously need to construct within democratic learning environments and the various ways in which these different kinds of understandings can be fostered. Specifically, the *personal* understandings of individual students and teachers are placed into relationship with contemporary *expert* understandings and theories and with *foundational* cultural understandings and resources. Each of these three kinds of understanding has a crucial role to play in democratic classroom practice and can be most effectively nurtured when drawn into explicit relationship with the other two.

As further developed in chapter two, these three "kinds" of understandings can also be conceptualized as interrelated dimensions of all human knowledge: our personal experiences and perspectives, the claims of the experts we recognize, and the character of our cultural context all continually shape what each of us knows. In this sense, no understanding is ever *exclusively* personal, expert, or cultural but is always, in some manner, informed by each set of influences. Although it can be confusing to view knowledge and knowledge construction from more than one angle, today's more sensitive findings and theory about human knowledge and knowledge construction require educators to think in more complicated ways.

Social scientists are therefore beginning to shift towards a conception of social, psychological, and cognitive systems as dynamic and interconnected. Nowhere is such a shift more necessary than in the study of democratic classroom life and learning. Multiple dimensions of human need, desire, capacity, and difference must be continually negotiated if democratic classroom communities are to live up to their intellectual and social potential. At the same time, there are important claims to be made and considered regarding the underlying character of democratic classroom practice.

Chapter two therefore ends with a proposal for methodologically pairing structural and narrative-based research lenses in order to address the implications of all of this human complexity for the purposes of advancing democratic classroom practice. Comparative classroom researchers need to balance structural analyses—such as the one provided here of three different forms of learning experience—with some kind of narrative portrayal capable of conveying a sense of the situated character of classroom life.

The next three chapters present the three forms of learning experience mentioned above—teacher-led, student-led, and co-led—and characterize both the pedagogical possibilities and constraints of each of these forms. Valuable educational aims can be achieved through a teacher's capable enactment of any of these three approaches to organizing classroom experience. Throughout this section of the book, I place these three pedagogical forms, which are based upon my own research within secondary language arts classrooms, into relation with related classroom research and theory.

As we will see, the teacher/student/co-led analysis classifies learning experiences according to the extent of 'interpretive authority' that is granted to students.[15] The concept of 'interpretive authority' provides one useful way of thinking about intellectual agency within any learning environment: students need to be granted *interpretive* authority in order to able to develop *intellectual* authority. While some analysts, in responding to the constraints of traditional practice, have focused solely on increasing the amount of intellectual agency granted to students, it is equally important to recognize the purposes served by learning experiences that systematically prioritize teacher viewpoints and established cultural understandings. As in the case of the student-led form, teachers need to appreciate both the affordances and constraints of effective teacher-led and co-led forms of learning experiences.[16]

For each form of learning experience, I also present and discuss illustrative transcript excerpts based upon my reading of transcript content and of subtle interpersonal cues noted at the time. Although the manner in which a teacher organizes any significant aspect of classroom practice is likely to affect student learning, no single dimension of practice determines the overall character or quality of a learning environment. Rather, a masterly mix of mutually supporting structural and contextual features always shapes the work of any successful learning community.

For example, some classroom research, including my own, suggests that the interpersonal dynamic within a classroom—which can be more sensitively and comprehensively characterized through narrative-based research forms—may more pervasively affect student learning than any other variable. If students feel that their teacher and others genuinely care about their ideas and learning, this idea goes, students will be more likely to invest in the academic challenges before them, whatever their form. As Noddings has argued, central interpersonal features of intellectually generative classroom dynamics can be identified, but these features generally cannot be usefully isolated, as the effectiveness of any one feature invariably relies upon its interplay with a host of others.[17]

In chapter six, I review the implications of everything I have discussed for the greater intellectual growth, personal well-being, and material prosperity of democratic citizenries. Against the drumbeat for higher test scores now heard within public schools across this land, the profound professional discourse from which high quality classroom practice must always grow has, in many corners, grown faint. Yet serious and dedicated practitioners require the time, support, and conceptual resources for professional study and collaboration more than they require anything else educational administrators and policy makers might provide.

Fortunately, committed scholars and practitioners have been investigating what many in this field have always thought of as the 'democratization of school practice' for more than a century. For nearly half of that period, linguists, anthropologists, and educators have worked together to study and theorize this process in order to provide the sort of grounded conceptual tools and resources that democratic teachers require. This scholarship is methodologically diverse yet is bound together by a shared interest in making primary and secondary school practice more intellectually accessible and compelling for all.[18]

Any person's sense of intellectual authority can only grow when that individual is able to hold open the possibility of learning from others, whether this be by learning to see some aspect of the world in a new way, by being pushed to express one's own thoughts more lucidly, or simply from coming to realize that others understand some matter of interest in a foreign and startling fashion. All democratic teachers and students should regularly experience such opportunities to extend their thinking about themselves, each other, and the larger world in these ways.

The orchestration of meaningful, powerful, and transparent knowledge construction processes within classrooms creates conditions within which all students can grow to appreciate, contribute to, and feel connected to the greater purposes of their society and so provides a generative conceptual basis for organizing the purposes of democratic schools. By providing opportunities for all students to make sense of their immediate experience in a culturally literate manner and in relation to broader social realities, teachers help to democratize the world.

We know that such valuable learning experiences can only be made available when classroom language inspires and sustains them. This book therefore primarily considers the ways in which educators and students talk with each other in schools. In studying the content, patterns, and tone of classroom discourse, researchers can discern the parts that teachers and students are assuming in the construction of content understandings or, in other words, the ways in which—and the extent to which—classroom life is nurturing the intellectual authority of all.

CHAPTER ONE

Democratic Ideas about Knowledge

Throughout recorded history, philosophers have offered different approaches to characterizing human knowledge and to proving that ideas are true. Even today, those who consider questions of human knowledge and truth continue to disagree about the extent to which, and bases upon which, any of us can construct reliable understandings about any aspect of the world. Such disputes are natural given the philosophical nature of the premises involved and are therefore to be expected within an intellectually open society. Democratic educators do need to appreciate, however, that some of these visions of knowledge and of knowledge creation are more compatible with the commitments of a democratic society than are others.

For example, within traditional cultural hierarchies, such as medieval monarchies or institutionalized religious orders in the Western world, public knowledge is sanctioned by those positioned at the top of those hierarchies and passed down to all other members of that culture. Those at the lower levels of such hierarchies are not invited to participate freely in the construction of these under-standings or to disagree publicly with those who are positioned above them.

Western nations' gradual embrace of democratic political systems has, over time, conferred intellectual and religious freedom to a progressively greater share of all those living within these societies. Today, in the democratic world, people are free to believe in or agree with the pronouncements of those who hold positions of political and religious power or not, as they choose. Culturally powerful people arguably do exert a greater influence on how others come to understand many issues, but in democracies, people with little cultural power are also entitled to think for themselves and to speak their minds freely.

This universal freedom to think and believe as one chooses is now viewed as essential to the very notion of democracy. Yet a full appreciation and acceptance of the implications of this ideal can remain challenging. People holding a wide range of religious and political beliefs protest virulently against exposing children to the divergent beliefs of others—in print, on television, and in our schools. Even many public figures evidence little interest in exploring what the divergent views of others may suggest for the workings of our pluralistic society, seeking instead to silence or demonize perspectives they view as threatening.

Yet the ideals of democracy demand more of us. Democracy's commitments to intellectual freedom and to reasoned deliberation are not incidental to the concept of representative rule, but rather comprise its foundation. A reluctance to recognize and to grapple with competing perspectives and beliefs diminishes democratic aims by reducing the potential of democratic processes. This direct link between granting others our thoughtful attention and achieving democratic relations remains in place even when the perspectives of others confuse or disturb us: to the extent we remain willing and able to express our own thoughts clearly and to take in the divergent thinking that troubles us, we move toward democratizing our relationships with others.

Learning how to enact meaningful, powerful, and transparent knowledge construction processes within classrooms supports all class members in incorporating the "values, purposes, and practices" that underlie democratic knowledge construction processes.[1] At the same time, achieving a practiced familiarity and comfort with such processes provides children and adolescents with the intellectual resources they will need to sort through the challenging conflicts they are certain to encounter in today's world despite any efforts that may be made to shelter them from diverse values or points of view. All adults demonstrate their commitment to democratic means and purposes when they teach the children in their care how to sort through complex and uncertain matters themselves and then, gradually, trust them to do so.

Any Number of Possibilities

Embracing the ideal of intellectual freedom and working toward realizing this ideal in our daily lives can be undertaken from various perspectives on knowledge: people do not need to share all of the same beliefs about knowledge or about how people come to know what is true. Reflecting upon these various viewpoints can provide clarity when educators face controversial subject matter in their classrooms or divisive issues in the greater school community. One need not choose between moral and intellectual relativism, on the one hand, and dogmatic certainty, on the other. Indeed, neither of these extreme positions is particularly well suited to furthering the purposes of democracy. The ideal of democracy entails specific moral commitments, such as to the worth and equality of all, and requires that citizens engage with each other fairly and in an open-minded manner across intellectual differences of every kind.

John Dewey, America's most famous and prolific philosopher of democracy and of democratic education, was a Pragmatist. Pragmatists vary in the extent to which they believe in an ultimate reality that informs human understanding, but all Pragmatists believe that no human being can represent any aspect of the universe in final terms—that is, in terms that are clearly best for all people in all cultures for all time.[2] Yet Pragmatists do believe that human understandings can be shown to be better or worse in relation to specified contexts, situations, and goals. Theoretically, those holding Pragmatic commitments will welcome the opportunity to engage with those holding diverse views as a lively exchange of ideas generally stands to increase the understanding of all involved.[3]

This set of beliefs about knowledge can therefore be seen to be quite compatible with democratic knowledge construction processes. For if one believes that no one culture or person should ever be seen as possessing the final word on any topic for all time, one is more likely to participate willingly in collaborative deliberative processes even though such processes typically demand greater time and thought than more hierarchical relations and decision-making procedures.[4]

It is by no means the case, however, that only Pragmatic beliefs about knowledge are compatible with the claims of a democratic society. Many people in democratic societies do believe that people can come to understand at least some aspects of the world in final terms. For example, many religious people believe that their religion provides final answers to the most important questions people ask about how to think and act in the world and that these answers should be seen as true for all people for all time.

In addition to those who believe that their religion provides at least some final answers, there are also those who believe that scientific investigation combined with logical and mathematical reflection will likely eventually provide some final answers. Some of these people, for example, believe that physicists might one day generate a final mapping of an underlying universal order, possibly unlocking mysteries about the universe that cannot even be imagined today. Some of those who believe in this possibility are also religious and identify that elusive universal order with their idea of God. It seems Albert Einstein, for example, thought about God in this way.[5] Other scientists do not believe that any final scientific discoveries can ever be made, but rather commit to the idea of formulating increaseingly efficacious, elegant, and comprehensive theories about the world.[6]

There are also religiously observant people who do not believe that people can formulate final and culturally independent truths. These people may nonetheless find that their religion offers understandings that do feel true to them. Some may view their religious understandings as one valid way of representing larger universal truths; others may simply find that their religious practices support them in reflecting upon important questions and in investigating these questions in ways that are not available in the secular world.

Many religious people also consider scientific insights and information when reflecting upon what they know and believe. This kind of open-mindedness toward diverse fields of intellectual inquiry can be seen to serve the purposes of a democratic society. Science, as a field of endeavor, provides greater practical transparency than fields such as religion, philosophy, and the fine arts possibly can. Scientific investigations and deliberations focus on readily observable phenomena and are based upon evidence that can be replicated and is available for public review. All reputable scientists strive to articulate and to justify the purposes, assumptions, and methods of their work based on established modes of practice and theory.

Scientists investigate matters that are of relevance to all and their findings therefore inform the direction of democratic societies in many ways. All members of a democratic society therefore need to understand basic scientific perspectives and methods. Although nobody is required to believe what particular scientists or other types of experts claim, everyone should more or less understand how various kinds of scientists and other types of secular experts have come to settle upon the understandings that they share.

So there are many different ideas about the possibilities and parameters of human knowledge that people in democracies hold today. How any of us chooses to think about the relationships between personal experience, science, philosophy, spirituality, and truth raises questions of belief that are very much at issue in our time and promise to remain so. Although these large questions are rarely addressed directly in schools, they profoundly influence our understandings about the world and therefore our interactions with others, creating differences of interpretation that will naturally surface from time to time within any intellectually vibrant classroom. As we will see, teachers can support their students' satisfying negotiations of such differences by teaching them how to work together toward the intellectual transparency that democracy demands.

These questions regarding the nature of truth and knowledge within democratic societies provide a backdrop for the vision of knowledge construction that will be discussed here. Regardless of what one believes about knowledge or about the possibility of formulating final truths, in democratic schools, all students need to learn that there are matters that will legitimately divide members of their democratic society and others upon which everyone must more or less agree in order to be able to work together and to maintain their society's democratic character.

Foundational, Expert, and Personal Understandings

Although democracies legally guarantee their citizens' intellectual freedom, anyone's capacity to think "for oneself," as we say, is naturally constrained at a number of levels. Human minds develop in relationship with the demands and resources of the surrounding culture: all learning and thinking unfolds in response to the material and social conditions within which people are raised. At the most basic level, if a child does not feel safe or has not been adequately fed, the child's ability to think cogently about topics other than the need to address these pressing challenges will be limited. Beyond essential material considerations, if a child does not feel accepted and valued within a social context or is not encouraged to express his or her thoughts and feelings, the child's natural inclination to connect intellectually with others will be suppressed.[7]

Assuming a child's basic material and social needs have been met, his or her emerging thought will also be organized by the cultural resources and expectations of the surrounding community. All children must learn some set of practical and communicative skills in order to be recognized as capable participants within their social worlds. Such resources both constrain and enable children's attention and behavior in ways that allow them to play increasingly mature roles within the worlds they inhabit. Social approval and acceptance will generally rest upon a child's capacity to behave in a manner that is considered culturally and developmentally appropriate.

Throughout this process, growing children absorb the beliefs, values, and manners shared by members of the families and communities in which they live. To a certain extent, these beliefs, values, and manners do not even need to be explicitly articulated. Children acquire many of the behaviors and attitudes of their elders and peers through observation and imitation.[8] Once one learns to view any situation or relationship in an established fashion, one becomes less likely to view that situation or relationship in an entirely new way. Over time, all people settle into relatively stable, culturally inflected perspectives regarding the central features and phenomena of their worlds.

Within today's increasingly diverse democracies, the values, perspectives, and skills that children learn at home are likely to vary in some respects from those they will be expected to learn at school and from those of some of their classmates and teachers. Some students will need to learn the nation's official language or the standard dialect of that language at school. For all, a broader range of beliefs, values, and manners will, over time, need to be understood and respected, even when these differ from the ways in which one has learned to think and behave at home.

Due to a growing awareness within the field of the ways in which traditional school practice has historically favored students who come from certain backgrounds and who think and act in particular ways, many educators have begun to attend more systematically to the diverse understandings, capacities, and interests of their students and how to build upon these resources to promote learning.[9]

All children enter a new culture when they arrive at school for the first time: all must learn to navigate the expectations of a foreign and less intimate institutional setting. All will need to learn new ways of approaching common challenges and of interacting with those around them. Democratic educators therefore need to reflect thoughtfully upon how best to negotiate the relationship between school and the students' lives beyond school so as both to safeguard each student's emerging sense of self and to acculturate all students into the foundational understandings of their society.

Below, I present one way of thinking about the balances that democratic teachers need to achieve between the *personal* knowledge all children employ when learning and two kinds of school understandings: *foundational* and *expert* understandings. Foundational understandings include the values, purposes, and practices that organize recognized fields of inquiry within our society. *All* students need to develop a command of basic foundational understandings in order to appear and act as educated members of our society. Some share of expert understandings is also required in order to be seen and to function as an educated person, but schools in different areas of the country, or within the same city but with different academic foci, may require and develop different kinds of expertise.

Foundational Terms of Engagement

All of the understandings and performances that serve to define a culture and that are required in order to be able to participate fully as a member of that culture, I will call *foundational* understandings. The official language and established values of a society are not open to negotiation (as much as they may vary within a range and do evolve with time): they create the context within which practical activity can be coordinated and the construction of further meanings can occur. For example, Standard English is this nation's official language, making the capacity to read, write, and speak Standard English a foundational set of skills. Similarly, commitments to human equality and intellectual freedom serve to define a society as democratic, making these commitments foundational values.

Although the notion of categorizing different kinds of understandings may seem esoteric, it is actually helpful for teachers in democratic classrooms to be able to distinguish in rough terms between the foundational understandings that they are charged with imparting, the expert knowledge that they may choose to teach (as an integral part of the prior project), and the personal understandings that serve to organize their own and their students' worldviews. All three of these categories of understanding have necessary roles to play in democratic knowledge construction processes, although the salience of any one of the three within a given lesson or class period may vary based upon factors such as field of study, specific pedagogical aims, and the students' developmental levels and achieved expertise.

I specify that educators need to distinguish 'in rough terms' between these categories because it is actually not necessary or even possible to distinguish precisely between them. As with other analyses that readers will find in this book, this analysis of classroom understandings into the categories of foundational, expert, and personal is meant to serve as a heuristic—that is, as a conceptual tool for rethinking the work of democratic classrooms. What must we insist upon from *all* students and why? Beyond these culturally foundational resources and understandings, what else would we want our students to learn about, or to learn to love, and why this particular content? How can we incorporate our students' existing understandings, characteristic interests, and creative visions into the work of our classrooms?

These are the kinds of questions that this heuristic is meant to raise. The proper administration of any type of democratic authority requires clarity in regard to one's purposes and transparency in regard to one's demands and designs. School-based educators should be able to respond with clear, cogent, and principled arguments when queried as to why they believe some understandings and capacities are needed by all. (While educators today are also required to treat the performances required by high-stakes tests as *necessary*, this does not mean they will also always view those performances as *foundational*. School-based educators do, however, need to have made this analysis and be able to explain the ways in which they are working to ensure their students' mastery of what they view as essential capacities and content.)

Democratic teachers (who are like democratically minded parents in this way) need to insist upon a certain set of values and performances, to turn other matters and decisions entirely over to their students, and to learn how to wrestle productively with a large set of matters in the middle. Foundational understandings are those values and performances upon which we insist—at times for reasons we can readily justify and, at other times, for no other reason than that our society happens to work that way.

While different groups of educators are likely to characterize even so basic a set of skills and understandings differently, the notion of *essential* cultural tools and resources should provide the grounds for deliberation.[10] Educators at the district, school, and department levels should work together to achieve clarity about what they find their students need in order to be able to function as educated citizens. The resulting sense of shared purpose can then inform and inspire other members of their school communities.

Academic subject areas, such as mathematics, the sciences, and the humanities, are all comprised of values, purposes, and practices that participants within these fields must incorporate into their own perspectives before they can adequately grasp the concerns and issues of those fields. Some specialized concepts and terminology may also be required in order to be able to participate in the work of a field at even the most basic level. It is important to distinguish, however, between mastery of the needed concepts and of the terminology that may be used to describe those concepts. For example, 'metaphor,' as a concept, represents one valued aspect of what can occur for people when they read and reflect upon literature. Educators may therefore consider metaphorical thinking to represent a foundational literary understanding.

On the other hand, a student's ability to define 'metaphor' as a term (or to pair it with a brief definitional phrase) probably cannot be considered a *foundational* understanding: many educated adults could not provide a ready definition of metaphor. Yet these are the kinds of performances that students who are facile with standardized testing strategically master for a limited time and that students who are not at all facile with standardized testing must increasingly strive to master anyway. The key point to be made is that such performances do not demonstrate whether *any* of these students has had enough experience with metaphorical thinking to develop a personal appreciation of the opening that concept can provide into their experiences of literature.

The set of foundational understandings one needs to incorporate in order to function expands as one takes on new kinds of challenges. A student may need to learn how to operate a graphing calculator in order to transfer into algebra. Third-graders may need to learn how to take care of small plants before they can be trusted to take them home and study them. Shop students may need to learn how to handle the power tools safely before they are allowed to build anything. To some extent, the tools and understandings a school needs to teach will depend upon the kinds of knowledge the school seeks to foster.

Foundational understandings do change with time: a language absorbs new words while others fall into disuse; understandings about the rights and protections a democratic society must provide to various members of the society have shifted over the past several centuries and continue to do so; new technology arises that can support new kinds of learning. Such shifts in foundational values, purposes, and practices can create controversy in schools, and school communities need to be able to grapple with such controversy meaningfully and transparently.[11] Foundational understandings are, however, the most stable among the three categories of understandings.

Expert Understandings and Theory

Expert understandings are somewhat less certain and stable than foundational understandings; they consist of secular knowledge that practitioners within academic and professional fields currently view as useful and credible—as more or less "true" in relation to the work of their fields. Experts within any field always share some set of specialized content understandings: familiarity with the current thinking within a given academic or professional area is part of how we define someone as an expert in that area.

While foundational understandings can be thought of as the fundamental linguistic, conceptual, and practical means with which cultural knowledge is constructed, expert understandings can be thought of as the understandings that have been built with those resources and tools. Being able to read is a foundational skill; having read and studied Gabriel Garcia Marquez's novels brings a particular form of expertise. While knowing a considerable number of expert understandings is also important to being able to act and to present oneself as an educated person, the need to know *specific* expert understandings will depend upon context. If one had instead read and studied Shakespeare's plays, one would have expertise, but in a different area. One can always learn about any expert works, claims, or theories one chooses if one possesses the foundational cultural resources and tools that make further learning possible.

Expert understandings would include everything from contemporary evolutionary theory to current understandings of the novel as a literary form. Within any field, certain understandings are likely to be viewed as more significant or reliable than others; yet members of a field will generally take all the expert understandings that influence the current work of that field seriously. Particularly in well-articulated fields, such as the physical and biological sciences, such expert recognition will be based upon a widespread appreciation of the problems, interests, and methods that have led to various expert claims and theories.

Expert understandings can also be controversial, generating intellectual divisions and debates within a field. Even within physics, experts disagree about important theoretical matters; literary critics disagree about the cultural import of specific literary works. All academic fields have issues that are contested or remain open to diverse interpretations: such issues act as necessary catalysts, inspiring and organizing the ongoing work of a field. As a result of such efforts, expert understandings continually change, at times rapidly.[12]

Introducing some of these expert disagreements into classrooms can inspire intellectually generative inquiries and debates between students. As discussed further below, controversial matters that students hear discussed at home and in the news can provide a meaningful basis for engaging classroom inquiries. Given that the experts within a field themselves disagree, why not invite students to consider the arguments that they find personally convincing?

Different fields determine what is viewed as expert knowledge in different ways. Textbooks, for example, present content that has been approved through textbook adoption practices, which can, in some circumstances, become highly political.[13] Pedagogical approaches are also increasingly influenced, either explicitly or implicitly, through government-mandated reform efforts. In these cases, divergent stakeholders, including politicians and educators from different fields, often bring competing claims and theories to the table based on differing assumptions, evidence, and lines of reasoning.[14]

The category of expert understandings, then, includes all the understandings that are recognized to be important by various types of authorities at a given historical moment: these are the understandings that members of a field will take seriously, even if they do not personally agree with them. At the political policy level, for example, the idea that schools should be closed or radically reorganized if students' test scores do not increase by a specified amount over a specified period is currently a prevailing policy idea. Some educational policy experts accept this idea and feel as though they can justify this approach to improving education based on what is known about underachieving students and schools. Other educators find this approach counter-productive based, again, on what they believe they know about underachieving students and schools. Both sets of understandings prevail in certain quarters and together constitute one of the major educational issues of our time.[15]

Our Personal Beliefs and Experience

Personal understandings are not directly subject to the social and political forces that serve to sanction expert understandings. As individuals, each of us can more or less believe as we choose to believe, and we all continually make determinations guided primarily by our own judgment and experience. From time to time, we are called upon to make significant decisions based upon our personal understandings; at such moments, we may solicit the viewpoints of our closest family members and friends.

Personal understandings include deeply held beliefs and commitments that serve to anchor our sense of ourselves in the world and also more casual, even ephemeral, thoughts and ideas that are easily altered or replaced. Religious beliefs and observances, which may organize one's life in a profound manner, represent one category of personal understandings; intuitive inklings or hunches that one may not even be able to articulate or to justify also qualify. All cognitively healthy people continually generalize based upon their personal beliefs and experience; such generalizations help us to orient ourselves and to respond to the world around us in ways we often do not even recognize.

Discussions with others—including the kinds of principled deliberative processes we will treat here—may or may not, therefore, alter the discussants' personal understandings. Yet thoughtful deliberation regarding contested matters does reliably expand one's sense of intellectual authority. Careful consideration of contrasting perspectives encourages participants to articulate their assumptions, relevant experience or evidence, and lines of reasoning more clearly and broadens their fields of reflection and review. By methodically placing our own commitments and perspectives into relationship with the divergent or opposing viewpoints of others, we can increase our knowledge about a complex topic, as well as learn more about other people and ourselves, without necessarily changing our beliefs or perspective.

The relationship between personal and expert understandings can be seen to be more fluid and reciprocal than the relationship between foundational understandings and either of the other two categories. As we learn about various kinds of expert knowledge, our personal beliefs and perspective may change. Personal understandings also shape expert understandings in several ways. As discussed at further length in the next chapter, all human thought embeds a personal dimension, so even different experts in the same field see the knowledge they share somewhat differently. Personal commitments can also serve, sometimes in dramatic ways, to advance expert knowledge: understandings that may originally be seen to represent unlikely, fringe, or even apostate views—such as Galileo's claim that the earth is not at the center of the universe—eventually come to be embraced as common knowledge with time.

Personal understandings are based upon personal experience, commitments, and beliefs and therefore include ideas over which people will often disagree and about which people may feel passionate. Yet respectful and unprejudiced deliberation regarding divergent beliefs and experiences can nonetheless be personally rewarding. Learning to appreciate the reasons that we disagree with others can help us to uncover interesting aspects of our own identities, learn about unfamiliar aspects of others' life experiences, and give us a greater sense of emotional and intellectual connection to a larger world.

By definition, personal understandings have not been determined to be valid and useful by the experts of any secular field. In some areas, such as religion, this will be due to the metaphysical nature of the assumptions involved. In other cases, personal understandings simply do not merit that level of scrutiny and reflection; as noted, we may barely be able to articulate some of these understandings ourselves.

Other personal understandings may merit broader cultural attention but simply have not received it: Galileo's claim provides an historical example; the introduction of acupuncture to the Western world provides a more contemporary example of new (in this case, foreign) understandings running into resistance due to the constraints of the Western conception of medicine. Although acupuncture has long been valued as reliable expert knowledge in much of the Eastern world, Western doctors did not understand how it could work in terms that made sense to them and so, for many years, considered acupuncture unreliable and unscientific. During these years, many individuals within the Western world came to believe in the efficacy of acupuncture based on personal experience or the reports of others they trusted, even though this belief had not been sanctioned by the experts of their societies.

Psychologists and sociologists have studied many of the dimensions upon which all people vary and now theorize that these differences can lead people to form divergent impressions of and beliefs about the world. Educational researchers and theorists therefore increasingly attend to three dimensions of variation in particular: developmental phase, cultural background, and individual intellectual profile. Students of educational theory will find that each of these dimensions of human variation is discussed in any contemporary educational psychology text, always in relation by now to a significant body of research. We will review some of this research in chapter two.

Whether personal understandings inform public debates in an explicit or implicit manner, personal experiences and belief systems influence everyone's understandings about the world and therefore play a part in the construction of public understandings. Even within well-established academic fields—again, one could cite physics— some authorities will favor assumptions that other authorities do not find likely based on their personal beliefs about their work and their field.[16] These preferences may relate, in turn, to people's beliefs about human existence and our relationship to the greater universe. Such differences of perspective should be seen not only as unavoidable but also as generative within an intellectually open society.

The Relevance of This Analysis for Classroom Practice

Today, expanding cultural diversity within schools combined with a growing appreciation of the role culture plays in framing human understanding has led some educators to question their own pedagogical authority and the final worth of the knowledge they seek to convey.[17] At the same time, the majority of educators continue to work from outdated assumptions about the creation of knowledge and its relationship to culture, leaving themselves open to challenges from those who would constrain open deliberation within schools in accordance with their own personal experience and belief systems.

Some parents, for example, have objected to exposing their children to expert understandings regarding evolutionary theory, which these parents find to contradict their beliefs regarding the biblical account of Earth's creation. Yet all children in democratic societies need to learn why scientists find the evidence for evolutionary theory compelling, even if they ultimately do not choose to recognize that evidence as compelling themselves. Without some exposure to these methods and theories, citizens cannot participate meaningfully in what arguably represents one of the most engaging intellectual issues of our time.

Familiarizing students with claims that remain contested within their society can also draw children into deeper relationships with the foundational and expert understandings that are implicated in the controversy. Open and probing discussions of contested matters— whether between experts within a field *or* between those experts and other members of the society—can bring any academic content to life. Children benefit from being exposed to different viewpoints that they are likely to confront beyond the classroom doors, *assuming* their teachers are able to teach them how to grapple with contrasting viewpoints in a respectful and principled manner.

In some cases, parents may legitimately worry that teachers will dismiss values and understandings that they, as parents, find fundamental to their worldviews. Yet as long as parents' values and understandings can be seen as consistent with this society's commitments to liberty, justice, and equality for all, students should be supported in sharing ideas they have learned at home. Learning to navigate between home and school understandings nurtures a student's sense of cognitive coherence and therefore intellectual authority. Discussing the value and import of evolutionary theory, for example, might open the way for a consideration of the differing roles and purviews of scientific and religious thought within a democratic society.

When controversial matters arise in a classroom, being able to sort issues into their constituent foundational, expert, and personal dimensions can be of practical pedagogical use. In the case of evolutionary theory, such reasoning might take shape in the following manner:

1. Evolutionary theory provides the conceptual framework that organizes all biological thought and can therefore be seen as *foundational* to any understanding of the discipline.[18] No high school student should graduate today without possessing a

meaningful appreciation of the way in which contemporary biologists see the world (although students commonly do, even from Advanced Placement biology courses, which typically focus more on content coverage than on deep understanding).

2. While the *expert* understandings of biologists converge to support all of the basic assumptions and claims of evolutionary theory, they also diverge in some interesting areas. For example, scientists disagree about whether evolutionary processes were gradual and continuous or, at times, rapid and dramatic. In a related area that is not directly covered within evolutionary theory, scientists disagree about the conditions under which life might have first begun. Discussion of divergent perspectives on such compelling questions supports students' construction of enduring under-standings and can inspire their imaginations long after the coursework is done.

3. If one had to generalize about the average citizen's *personal* understandings about evolution, one might only want to say that most people's understandings are not as informed as they should be in a society such as ours.[19] Students in far too many biology classrooms memorize material that means little to them and interests them even less. How might the national conversation about evolution shift if all high school students—college-bound or not—were required to represent and to deliberate together upon their personal understandings of the issues and controversies that evolutionary theory continues to engender?

In drawing students' attention to the conceptual diversity present within the expert category, educators invite their students into a personal engagement with their larger culture. Rather than diminishing the intellectual authority of experts or of expert knowledge, uncovering the uncertainties associated with topical issues such as evolution can help to highlight the value of the foundational values, purposes, and practices that the experts of a field share. Focusing on what is currently at issue between experts within a field can actually promote greater confidence in and attention to the widely accepted methods and accomplishments of the field.

Even within school communities that are relatively homogenous culturally, individual and developmental differences among students will result in divergent thinking that can be leveraged to pedagogically valuable purposes. Teachers can also introduce competing perspectives on critical issues of the day when theoretical diversity does not naturally present itself; debates can be structured so that students represent, without needing to claim, opposing perspectives on an issue, encouraging students to ponder alternative viewpoints in greater depth.[20]

Teachers are generally not taught to notice and nurture students' personal beliefs and intellectual commitments. Yet, as we will discuss further in chapter two, learning theorists all agree that students' personal points of view need to be engaged in order to inspire meaningful and enduring learning. These findings suggest that if students want to take issue with the assumptions of biologists, they should be given opportunities to do so—once they have learned enough about those assumptions to be able to discuss them in a literate manner.

Democratic schools, at their best, provide opportunities for people with diverse perspectives to come to understand and appreciate each other and the basic aims and means they share as members of their society. Teaching even young children that grown people often disagree about important matters gives them a basis for appreciating the ways in which personal beliefs and experience serve to shape all people's perspectives. Teaching students how to negotiate such differences fosters intellectual transparency and allows students to understand the generative role intellectual differences are meant to play within democratic societies.

Summary

Intellectual authority relies upon one's developed ability to explain the assumptions, experience, and reasoning upon which one grounds one's claims and upon one's openness to the relevant challenges and experience of others. Democratic pedagogical exchanges therefore need to tutor students in the discursive and intellectual means they will need to represent their own perspectives in a convincing manner and to place their perspectives into relation with those of others in a sensitive fashion.

In order to nurture the intellectual authority of all members of a classroom community, teachers also need to achieve clarity in regards to the matters that can and cannot remain open for discussion in their classrooms. Furthermore, they need to be able to communicate with students, parents, and other educators alike regarding the principled grounds upon which they distinguish between these two domains of understanding. Appreciating the ways in which foundational, expert, and personal understandings interact to create what each of us feels we know can support teachers as they seek to achieve this quality of intellectual transparency within their professional lives.

Although democratic educators must hold themselves accountable for apprenticing children into the effective use of foundational means and resources and with familiarizing them with the significant expert thinking of their day, they are not authorized to demand uniform performances or perspectives beyond those integral to foundational cultural proficiencies and to the commitments and values that all members of any democratic society should learn to hold dear.

A powerful command of foundational resources and expert understandings gives members of a democratic culture the means to participate as equals in the creation of cultural knowledge. A meaningful appreciation of and clarity regarding one's personal views and perspective make such participation feel worthwhile. In democracies, these feelings of personal power and significance are every citizen's due, and the responsibility of developing the necessary capacities must fall, to a great extent, upon the nations' schools.

It is not too much to say that the future of democracy rests upon democratic educators being able to articulate, theorize, and enact democratic values, purposes, and practices within schools. Children's school experiences shape their feelings and understandings about their society and its public institutions. Educators therefore need to take quite seriously their responsibility to accustom all children to the demands and rewards of democratic living.

CHAPTER TWO

Knowledge Building as Interpretation

Distinguishing between what might primarily be considered a foundational, expert, or personal understanding can help educators balance their curricular aims and negotiate the differences of perspective that arise within all intellectually active classrooms. At the same time, it is important to recognize that no human understanding belongs exclusively to any one of these three categories: all of our understandings are organized by the various influences represented by the foundational, expert, and personal categories. This means that all classroom understandings will in some manner be shaped by the organizing commitments and resources of the culture, currently recognized expertise, and the individual perspectives of the members of the classroom.

Even 3 x 4 = 12, which represents what we interpret to be a universal mathematical reality, clearly reflects cultural influences, for mathematical systems have been organized and symbolized differently throughout human history. Mathematical systems have also played varying, though related, roles in the work and imaginations of different peoples.[1] Even within a single culture, people construct relationships with mathematical symbols, and with the concepts such symbols represent, which are in some aspects personal. For example, grown adults have been known to argue at some length about whether 3 x 4 means three groups of four or rather a group of three taken four times.

Recall, we are viewing knowledge as an ever-evolving matrix of culture-bound impressions and understandings that each of us continually constructs as we apprehend and interact with the beings, contexts, and objects in our lives. In reviewing this definition, one can hear the multiple dimensions of influence that are represented by the foundational, expert, and personal categories. Although it is useful for educators to be able to organize their pedagogical aims and content in relation to these three kinds of understanding, these three "categories" are more aptly viewed as dimensions of an integrated system for making sense of the world.

As any child grows older, his or her conceptual means for making sense become increasingly elaborated and nuanced as a result of increasingly thoughtful personal exploration and cultural uptake. These conceptual means represent each child's intellectual responses to a challenging and volatile world, a world nonetheless constituted by reliable social, material, and cultural realities. Each child struggles to comprehend the implications of these reliable patterns for his or her own needs and desires, employing whatever cultural, personal, and interpersonal resources are available.

In a related fashion, the people of any culture collectively interpret the culture's defining aspirations, shared history, and contemporary challenges and organize their personal thoughts and actions in relation to this cultural narrative. The material, aesthetic, and theoretical resources that give cultures their distinctive character represent acts of cultural interpretation just as each of our individual lives represents acts of personal interpretation. Personal and cultural knowledge systems are both always in motion, continually reorganizing themselves in response to shifting demands, possibilities, and influences.[2] At different levels, healthy people and cultures both strive to make the world ever more comprehensible, manageable, and satisfying.

Dynamic knowledge systems therefore tend towards growing increasingly capable over time. Foundational resources are altered by new expert understandings; personal insights inspire the emergence of new expert knowledge. What is viewed as unfamiliar or even objectionable one day can eventually become widely accepted, leading to entirely novel lines of thought and experimentation; new research can render expert understandings obsolete overnight, leading to the emergence or decline of related cultural tools. In general terms, such changes tend to be more rapid within democratic societies as robust democratic knowledge systems continually review and integrate novel and diverse perspectives.

Classrooms as Interpretive Communities

So what does this all mean for classrooms? Effective classrooms function like small cultures populated by any number of young people and usually one or two adults. Over the course of a school year, these people together come to make sense of certain aspects of the world together, employing foundational cultural resources, referencing established expert understandings, and attending to the personal perspectives of individual classroom members. Over the course of the year, shared understandings are constructed, and everyone's conceptual resources expand.

Over the past fifty years or so, psychologists have come to appreciate just how complicated it is to direct so involved a process well. Jerome Bruner, a psychologist associated with the cognitive revolution, has participated in these ongoing efforts to pull disparate research traditions into relationship with each other in order to inform and deepen our understandings about school learning. Bruner's contributions to this conceptual integration began with his involvement in the cognitive revolution itself, which overthrew the reigning associationist and behaviorist conceptions of learning based upon isolated cause and effect relationships.[3]

Bruner went on to embrace Western psychology's subsequent integration of the work of Russian psychologist Lev Vygotsky after this work began to be translated in the 1960s.[4] Vygotskian scholarship focuses on the role that cultural resources always play in human learning and development, with a particular attention to linguistic and literary forms.[5] Along with others in the sociocultural tradition, Bruner has emphasized the central role of narrative in human meaning making, arguing that logical and mathematical thought and narrative thought should be seen as two fundamental and complementary human meaning making capacities, both of which need to be nurtured within schools.[6]

As a philosopher, Dewey had taken a further step toward integrating these two capacities in his treatment of the distinction he made between 'science' and 'art.' Dewey proposed that we think of 'science' as our systematic efforts to survive and prosper and that we think of 'art,' which for Dewey included philosophy, religion, and all else that was not math or science, as addressing a natural human longing for a greater sense of purpose and meaning. In contrast to Bruner's conception of logic and mathematics as more or less distinct from narrative thought, Dewey viewed scientific and aesthetic thought as woven inextricably together within all human meaning making.[7] For example, poetry and dance both draw on rhythm and therefore number, and as Bruner himself has noted, cultural narratives such as President Kennedy's 'Space Race' serve to frame and advance scientific development.[8]

Bruner and Dewey share a vision of classrooms as democratic learning communities charged with the responsibility of constructing understandings in relation both to students' personal understandings and to those of the broader culture. Both scholars have argued that democratic schools must provide opportunities for all students to make personal connections to classroom understandings and to broader cultural perspectives. Each has emphasized that failing to connect students to school aims and meanings risks alienating young people from the culture's larger purposes and values.

From this perspective, classrooms are viewed as *interpretive communities*—as groups of people dedicated to working together to make sense of the world.[9] This project can be seen to entail, in turn, a commitment among all class members to endeavor to understand each other's insights and contributions. The relationship between personal knowing and collaborative knowledge construction can thereby be strengthened, setting the stage for students' lifelong engagement with cultural ideas, projects, and commitments.

Over the years, psychology has had a considerable amount to say about intersubjectivity—this remarkable capacity human beings seem to possess to interpret many of each other's thoughts, needs, and desires. Cognitive scientists now theorize the existence of 'mirror neurons' based on neuro-images that show our brains reliably activating in the same patterns regardless of whether we are performing an act or someone else in the room is performing that same act.[10] Although the relationship between brain activation and human thought is neither simple nor direct, such evidence supports existing theory that positions our capacity for intersubjectivity as basic to all human understanding.

Intuitively, we have probably all felt that we can understand some people better than others and have felt drawn to particular people with whom we share important feelings or aspects of our worldviews. This is as true for teachers as for students: all of us can find it challenging to relate to certain others due to the differences we perceive between these others and ourselves. Yet democratic classroom practice asks that both teachers and students cultivate an interest in, and learn to care about, people to whom they may not be readily drawn.

In learning how to orchestrate meaningful, powerful, and transparent knowledge construction processes, teachers therefore need to learn how to reach across human differences of all kinds. As noted in chapter one, it can be particularly useful for educators to focus upon three dimensions of human difference: developmental, cultural, and individual. Although differences across these categories do not necessarily pose barriers to mutual understanding, experience has shown that such differences can at times obstruct mutual understanding within schools. It is therefore worth considering the research that has been done in these areas and how that work can support teachers' efforts to build a sense of intellectual community in their classrooms.

Developmental Challenges

Nearly a century ago, Piaget spent a decade of his life striving to develop a methodology that might allow him to discern the perceptions, assumptions, and patterns of reasoning that reliably led school-age children to some startling conclusions. Piaget realized that the psychometric tests that had identified these patterns of inaccurate responses could only tabulate the discrepancies between the conclusions reached by adults and those reached by children; they could not access or reveal the character of children's reasoning.[11]

The methodology Piaget developed has since been further refined, and some now fault Piaget for his comparative lack of methodological (and theoretical) sophistication. Yet Piaget revolutionized the study of children's thought and, in doing so, convincingly established that children organize their ideas about the world in ways that have become foreign to adult minds. For this reason, children may often experience a teacher's reasoning, however clear and coherent in adult terms, as confusing or even incomprehensible.

A corollary to the notion that immature minds work in a distinctive fashion is that new conceptualizations are always built from old ones, which need to give way and get reconfigured. New ways of understanding the world cannot be imported whole. Piaget's insights on these issues have since been further developed by many other developmental learning researchers.[12]

Contemporary learning theorists such as Eleanor Duckworth and Constance Kamii, both of whom studied with Piaget and his colleague Bärbel Inhelder in Geneva, have sought to adapt Piagetian method into a pedagogical approach that can uncover and support students' emerging understandings in much the same way as Genevan learning research did. We will look more closely at Duckworth's pedagogical adaptation, called 'critical exploration in the classroom,' in chapter four on student-led interpretation.[13]

Learning researchers—including Kamii who has conducted extensive research in classrooms—have repeatedly confirmed Piaget's observation that peer discussion inspires learning in ways that attending to the thoughts of a teacher cannot. Children are often more able to understand and work through the challenges presented by a peer's thinking. Also, because a peer's claim does not carry the final authority that an adult's claim would, children are more frequently inspired to argue a matter through, which helps them to deepen and clarify the bases of their reasoning. Finally, as Kamii notes, "When peers debate sources of truth, they become sources of truth, and children develop confidence in their own ability to figure things out."[14]

Piaget's research focused on the development of mathematical and logical thought, which he viewed as both an adaptive biological resource and as the preeminent influence in the construction of human knowledge. Piaget's interest in the role of logic in human advancement extended to the future development of the species' moral reasoning, which he saw as linked to the development of logical reasoning. Piaget believed that if people were educated to reason more systematically, they would naturally bring a principled moral sensibility to all their interpersonal dealings.[15]

Kurt Fischer, a prominent Neo-Piagetian researcher, has rightly noted that the greatest limitation of traditional Piagetian thought lies in Piaget's idealization of static logical forms.[16] Sadly, a developed appreciation of logical and mathematical forms does not necessarily elevate a person's moral reasoning; expertise in formal logic does not even reliably ensure a transfer of critical reasoning skills across diverse academic domains. As it turns out, the relationship between logical development and human intelligence—not to mention morality—is considerably more complex than Piaget had hoped.

As Fischer has also stressed, developmental psychologists must concern themselves with both stability *and* variability in any study of intellectual growth. Dimensions of variability that affect every intellectual performance of any kind include cultural resources, experiential background, individual nature, and social context, where social context is seen to include both the support given for a particular task and the emotions associated with its performance. Fischer and other Neo-Piagetian researchers have turned to systems theory in order to represent the interpenetrating relationships between these multiple dynamic variables.[17]

Fischer and others now speak of a dynamic structuralism. Piaget had always theorized that the intellectual structures that allow people to learn and to understand are dynamic and can best be represented as sets of interacting relationships.[18] Along with many other Western scholars of the early twentieth century, Piaget had dreamed that the mathematical systems that modern society was developing might one day represent the natural systems that constitute human reality in final terms. Contemporary scientists, particularly social scientists, are more likely to work from the assumption that all human representations remain partial and contingent, even as they move toward becoming ever more sensitive and comprehensive.

Fischer and his colleagues now substitute *situated skills*, which are always enacted within specific contexts, for the ideal logical forms Piaget studied. Fischer uses the example of throwing a ball, which never happens in exactly the same way twice regardless of how often a player has practiced. Contextual influences such as "temperature, crowd noise, fatigue, having a runner on base, and lighting (to name but a few factors)" always influence any particular throw.[19]

Similarly, the competencies educators seek for their students should not be seen as abstract or as achievable in final terms, but rather as capacities that remain contingent upon the social settings in which they are enacted and are able grow to meet new challenges. Considering the character of these potential contexts becomes integral to envisioning the performances themselves. Where, when, and under what conditions will we want our students to be able to bring what we have taught them to bear?

By attempting to represent the intellectual work that children do in relationship to the nature of the work and the settings in which it is done, psychologists have discovered that they can talk more meaningfully about the governing features of human intellectual growth and function that bind us as a species. These new models provide greater perspective on the conditions that are likely to prove generative for encouraging cognitive growth and can support educators in imagining their way more deeply into children's maturing minds.[20]

Cultural Resources

Shifting to a conception of knowledge construction as an interpretive process organized at multiple levels and dimensions allows one to investigate traditionally Piagetian concerns, while concurrently considering the role played by cultural resources. As Vygotsky theorized in response to Piaget's earliest research, the linguistic, conceptual, and material resources of a culture also always serve to direct and inspire intellectual development.[21] Learning theorists no longer need to choose (if they ever did) between focusing on species-general patterns of cognitive maturation and the developmental influences of culturally specific learning contexts and resources.[22]

Indeed, the most exciting developmental learning research today combines methodological concerns and assumptions that can be traced to both Piaget and Vygotsky. For example, Robbie Case, another Neo-Piagetian scholar, identified the number line as a foundational conceptual structure within Western mathematical thought and, therefore, as a valuable pedagogical tool. In conversation with many others, Case sought to characterize general cognitive structures in more practical, and therefore more culturally sensitive, terms. Rather than assuming, with Piaget, that logical-mathematical thought represents a cognitive platform that constrains and enables all other intellectual performance, Neo-Piagetian researchers have sought out the conceptualizations that lie at the root of valued cultural performances.[23]

Similarly, Israeli psychologist Reuven Feuerstein, who studied with Piaget and now also employs the language of sociocultural theory, has devoted his life's work to attending closely to children's meaning-making in order to strengthen their intellectual capacities through the systematic introduction of specially designed cultural resources. Unlike others who now draw on Piagetian thought without reference or attribution, Feuerstein understands that all of Western developmental theory proceeds from two great Piagetian commitments: Piaget's appreciation of the role of independent reasoning in supporting cognitive growth and the painstaking attention Piaget therefore devoted to charting the character and growth of children's efforts to reason logically.[24]

Different language has been used within different theoretical traditions to describe this process of incorporating cultural resources and understandings. Sociocultural theory speaks of a learner's *appropriation* of a culture's linguistic, conceptual, and material resources, which together are referred to as cultural *tools*.[25] 'Appropriation' has been contrasted with the earlier psychological term 'internalization' and found preferable due to contemporary understandings of knowledge construction as an always active and iterative process organized by a learner's existing understandings and conceptual schemes. Teachers can support students' active appropriation of established cultural understandings through what is known in sociocultural theory as a *scaffolding* process.

In order to understand an aspect of the world in a new way, learners may need to alter their existing conceptual schemes in order to learn to see and experience the world in new terms. In Piagetian language, learners may need to *accommodate* their existing schemes to realities that challenge their current understandings. If the challenge of accommodating their existing schemes is perceived as too great or as threatening for any reason, learners instead *assimilate* their perceptions to their existing schemes, however partially or inadequately, by neglecting or distorting disruptive aspects of reality.[26]

Sociocultural learning theory has therefore emphasized the need for educators to identify each student's 'zone of proximal development,' (ZPD) that is, the sphere within which teachers can authentically engage with a student's conceptual framing of the world.[27] This scholarship has focused on exposing young minds to cultural understandings in a manner that resonates with the child's current knowledge of the world and so serves to enlarge the conceptual means available to the child. As Vygotsky himself was the first to note, the idea of a ZPD builds directly upon Piaget's research into the differences between the cognitive schemes of adults and children, as the notion of a ZPD assumes that any content lying outside of a student's zone of potential learning will not be conceptually appropriated (even if children prove able to memorize and replicate the teacher's language).[28]

The work of scholars such as Case and Feuerstein, and one could mention many others here,[29] extends Vygotsky's efforts to acculturate culturally diverse and academically challenged students into the understandings of the majority culture (although Case did not theorize his work in sociocultural terms). This attention to the tools of culturally powerful knowledge construction is also associated today with the name of Lisa Delpit, a scholar who famously took progressive educators to task in the early 1990s for emphasizing students' construction of personal meaning over the inculcation of basic literacy and numeracy constructs among students who do not arrive at school well versed in these constructs.[30]

Today, Delpit and other sociocultural scholars such as Luis Moll and Carol Lee also invert Vygotsky's emphasis, drawing attention to the intellectual resources that students from non-majority cultural backgrounds bring with them into schools.[31] This scholarship approaches the challenges of trying to connect student and school understandings from a contrasting and complementary angle, suggesting that teachers make space for, and learn from, their students' culturally divergent conceptions of the world. As these scholars—who draw upon ethnographic studies of classroom language among other types of research—have demonstrated, integrating students' culturally divergent intellectual resources into the work of a classroom can serve to extend the cultural literacy of everyone in the room, including the teacher, as well as promote a sense of personal belonging and interpersonal reciprocity within a classroom.

This tension between majority and non-majority cultural resources is primarily a matter of emphasis within the sociocultural research tradition: ultimately, sociocultural scholars seek a meeting of all minds that is facilitated through a joint engagement with shared linguistic, conceptual, and material resources of every available and appropriate kind.[32] As in the case of developmental differences, students arrive with an established set of culturally inflected conceptual schemes that educators need to uncover and engage. As in the case of one's developmental resources, cultural resources can both support and limit people's ability to understand each other, depending on the extent to which these resources are shared or understood.

Individual Variety

The psychologist Howard Gardner, well known for his theory of multiple intelligences (MI), employs eight criteria, from four different academic fields, to ground each of the intelligences he has theorized.[33] A review of these criteria—drawn from biology, logical analysis, developmental psychology, and psychological testing—provides yet another useful angle on the various grounds upon which any two people might find it more or less challenging to make sense of each other's observations, theories, and claims. While Gardner theorizes that all of us possess each of the intelligences he has identified, he finds that we all possess somewhat different mixes of these intelligences, which are then further nurtured or constrained by various social and cultural influences.

As Gardner has sought to characterize the capacities that comprise human thought in general terms, he has naturally turned to criteria that point toward the biological heritage that all humans share. The intellectual capacities and propensities that characterize us as members of the same species allow us to understand each other in meaningful ways across all other dimensions of human difference. Other areas of the research Gardner analyzes point in the opposite direction, toward the ways in which human thought varies on an individual basis.

For example, one of Gardner's criteria from developmental science demands that a number of individuals have demonstrated either special talents or extreme deficiencies in that intellectual domain either from an early age or as a result of dramatic brain injuries. In the latter case, such a shift would suggest a clear link between a particular type of intellectual performance and an area of the brain. Similarly, a criterion from psychological research and testing requires that individual test performances commonly break down along the lines of the intelligences Gardner has theorized. These findings appear to support the contention that each of us enters this world with somewhat distinctive cognitive aptitudes and inclinations.

As a result of this individual variation, a teacher may delight in the way a young student from a different cultural background approaches a particular academic challenge due to the similarities between the ways in which that teacher and that student think. In this case, developmental and cultural differences between the teacher and student have been trumped by their common intellectual inclinations, allowing the teacher and student to appreciate each other's thought processes. While there is every reason for a teacher to enjoy this easy sense of connection with particular students, democratic teachers also need to work on finding ways of connecting intellectually to *all* students across all types of human differences and of intellectually connecting students with each other.

To employ a different type of example of relevance to the topic of democratic knowledge construction, there likely have always been people who were more prone than others to challenge the expert knowledge of their own time and place—one might cite Socrates as a historically prominent example. Even within insulated religious communities or closely identified political subcultures, people also vary based on personality traits of this type. Individual intellectual and psychological diversity, then, can both threaten unifying perspectives within tight cultural groupings and support human connections across the boundaries of such groups.[34]

Although Gardner conceived and expounded his MI theory in the value-neutral language of cognitive science, the concerns that drive his interest in the nature of intelligence derive from humanistic commitments that Gardner has elaborated perhaps most fully in his book *The Disciplined Mind*.[35] Like Noddings, Gardner believes that democratic educators should seek to inspire all students to investigate and ponder the nature of truth, beauty, and goodness throughout their PK-12 experience. These aims, traced to ancient Greece and to Socrates himself within Western culture, would require that students be regularly invited into personal philosophical reflections born of thoughtful engagements with rich cultural resources. As suggested by this brief discussion of his MI theory, Gardner's theory of individual intellectual diversity provides yet another rationale for negotiating the tension between shared cultural and personal understandings with great care within democratic schools.

Considering Complex Relationships

The immense complexity of classroom life and learning has suggested the move some classroom researchers have been making toward a conception of school and classroom cultures as dynamic systems.[36] Systems theory can support educational researchers and practitioners in recognizing and theorizing the variability that characterizes any learning environment. As social scientists from a number of fields have increasingly realized, in studying psychological and sociological dynamics within and *in relation to* situated human contexts, researchers are able to hone their findings and to circumscribe the purported implications of those findings in ways that lead to better social science.

Even a passing familiarity with systems theory can help educators to envision the interpenetrating dimensions of the pedagogical transactions that underlie classroom learning. As ecological theory drove the field of biology toward viewing the natural world as a complex web of mutually constitutive relationships of different orders and kinds, dynamic systems theory supports all similar conceptual shifts. Educators can more readily discern the relationships that exist across the biological, psychological, and sociological dimensions of classroom life, all of which are implicated in our society's contemporary efforts to foster learning.[37]

For example, some scholars have argued that the No Child Left Behind legislation (NCLB) passed in 2001 created pressures that reduced the amount of physical education in schools and that this reduction, in turn, aggravated attention deficit issues in the classroom, issues for which students have been increasingly medicated over the past twenty years. This theorized chain of influence illustrates how a sociological phenomenon—passing legislation in response to a legitimate social concern—might lead to a psychological phenomenon—increased restlessness in classrooms—which then might be treated at the biological level.[38]

A dynamic systems perspective also encourages educators to recognize the many different perspectives from which any pedagogical issue or challenge can be viewed and the value of considering such issues from a number of angles. In our previous example, a dynamic systems perspective invites consideration of whether a rise of disruptive restlessness among a few students might signal broader student agitation and inattention that would be better addressed by rethinking the rhythms of classroom practice.

Activity theory, which arose in Post-Vygotskian Soviet psychology, proposes situated human action as an irreducible object of analysis for many of the same reasons. As the sociocultural scholar James Wertsch has noted, every social scientist carries his or her own disciplinary lens into any field of human engagement: psychologists consider human action at the individual level, neurologists at the biological level, and sociologists at the level of the social grouping. Yet, any one of these perspectives can only consider an aspect or, as Wertsch puts it, a 'moment' within an always multidimensional 'activity system.' No one perspective can be reasonably prioritized over others in explaining a human dynamic or phenomenon absent a compelling rationale that references a more fully constituted social context.[39]

Interpretive Structures and Frameworks

As this discussion of the multiple dimensions of influence upon classroom learning suggests, any student's willingness to engage unfamiliar material and entertain contrasting claims will depend upon a number of factors: although a child's native propensities may well be among them, a child's previous social experience and developmental maturity will also play determining roles. When people feel supported in articulating their own views and find that others respect their personal understandings, they will generally feel more tolerant of, and possibly even interested in, the understandings of others. Children who experience the rewards and challenges of having others attend closely to their observations and ideas more readily learn to appreciate the rewards and challenges of attending closely to the observations and ideas of others. This is just basic human psychology, but it has a lot to do with the ways in which democratic classrooms need to work.

Within the field of education, discourse analysts and classroom ethnographers have led the way in designing research tools capable of methodically studying multiple dimensions of classroom practice and so revealing the content, rhythms, and interpersonal character of classroom relationships. By the 1960s, an interdisciplinary group of researchers had begun combining formal techniques of linguistic analysis with the ethnographic methods of social anthropology in order to characterize pedagogical interactions within schools.[40] Such interactions were investigated for both developmental and cultural influences on students' learning.[41] As we have seen, both sets of influences directly affect the academic success of children. For if a teacher's expectations are mismatched to a student's emerging linguistic and conceptual capacities in either cultural or developmental terms, teacher-student communication is likely to falter, potentially alienating that student from the work and life of the classroom.

Sociocognitive analyses, principally rooted in the work of Vygotsky, originally focused on the ways in which language and other cultural resources construct and mediate understanding at different ages and levels of expertise. This work has called on educators to sensitize themselves to the gaps between what concepts and vocabulary—particularly academic vocabulary—mean to them and to their students and investigates the curricular means by which such differences might be bridged.[42]

Sociocultural analyses of classroom discourse, tied more closely to the anthropological tradition, originally emphasized the ways in which ethnicity, race, gender, and class work to organize discourse both in diverse and in relatively homogenous cultural contexts.[43] By studying the ways in which different classroom conversations presume and require particular kinds of linguistic fluency, these studies have informed a variety of pedagogical concerns. In particular, they have advanced consideration of the ways in which students whose language traditions at home diverge from the American mainstream might be drawn more effectively into the language patterns of mainstream classrooms. Early sociocultural analyses also highlighted the construction of teacher authority within cross-cultural contexts, particularly within Native American classrooms led by Euro-American teachers. This work was among the first to provide conceptual tools for investigating the construction of teacher authority.[44]

A third stream of work has focused more on the general character of school practice, seeking to characterize curricular formats and interactions as these are represented within patterns of classroom language. This work is tied most closely to formal linguistic method and has supported, in particular, research in the areas of primary and secondary language acquisition. Patterns of language acquisition and the pedagogical approaches that effectively nurture emerging language fluency and literacy have been studied.

These three streams of classroom discourse inquiry and analysis—sociocognitive, sociocultural, and linguistic—have increasingly come to merge and to inform each other over the years. In particular, the sociocognitive and sociocultural strands have merged: research that calls itself sociocultural now generally references Vygotskian theory.[45] Other scholars draw on all three methodological traditions, often without citing their specific theoretical heritage.

It will be crucial here to distinguish between discourse analyses that focus on formal structural features of language and studies of more diffuse contextual as well as non-focal structural influences. Formal structural features of classroom discourse can be reliably characterized and quantified employing the type of formal coding approaches developed within the field of discourse analysis. In my research, I developed a method for discerning what I theorize to be structural patterns of interpretive authority distributions. This structural analysis can now be employed to study this one dimension of classroom knowledge construction processes within transcripts from any pedagogical discussion.

In contrast to the spare descriptive capacity and broad conceptual applicability of structural analyses, narrative forms of research can portray more delicate and diffuse influences as these unfold within a specific classroom setting. Ethnographic studies of classroom practice have long served to balance the reductionism inherent within any structural lens. Again, any teaching approach can be enacted more or less appropriately or effectively; by not attending to the character of classroom interactions, comparative researchers risk undermining the validity and significance of their claims.[46]

The need to pair structural analysis with narrative portrayals of classroom life has been emphasized by several prominent scholars within the field of classroom discourse analysis. The social anthropologist Del Hymes, in his introduction to an early edited volume called *Functions of Language in the Classrooms*, emphasized the necessity of pairing structural discourse analyses with the evocative ethnographic portrayals that educational researchers had begun importing from the field of anthropology.[47] Hugh Mehan, in his study of scholar Courtney Cazden's year-long return to urban elementary school teaching, distilled much of this early ethnographic study into a research method he termed 'constitutive ethnography,' which studied "structuring" forces and their interplay with contextual features.[48] As Cazden notes in her foreword to Mehan's book, ethnographic study can also provide opportunities to identify previously unrecognized structural patterns and to consider their significance in relation to other influences of every kind.[49]

By methodologically pairing structural and contextually sensitive research methods, educational researchers can study the structural features that distinguish effective democratic school practice without neglecting the complicating contingencies of classroom life. Such a pairing is particularly valuable for comparative classroom research, as classroom practice must be systematically designed—that is, structured—to promote a particular quality of learning environment, yet must also be responsive to the myriad contextual demands and influences that also always direct the course of lived classroom experience. By evoking classroom life through some narrative form of study, comparative researchers provide means with which their readers may judge for themselves how meaningfully the dynamic under consideration has served to shape student experience.[50]

I refer to this principled methodological pairing of structural and contextual research lenses as 'dynamic structuralism' after the work of Fischer and his colleagues. With this term, I hope to suggest the variable, contextually situated, social and psychological structures the approach is intended to locate and study. As a broad methodological orientation, dynamic structuralism strives to identify and portray structural aspects of human experience and to study the ways in which these forces can be seen to organize that experience within and in relation to specified contexts.

Interpretive Structures

In the mid-1970s, two linguists interested in classroom discourse due to what they saw as its relatively manageable set of linguistic constraints conducted a study of classroom discourse that remains theoretically central to the field today. By comprehensively coding student and teacher utterances based on grammatical features and discourse direction, these two scholars, Sinclair and Coulthard, uncovered a recurring pattern of teacher-student interaction that they assumed would exemplify school practice in general terms.[51]

These linguists had identified the Initiation/Response/Feedback (IRF) discourse move sequence, a construct that was soon taken up by educators who have been investigating its nuances and debating its pedagogical merits ever since.[52] In the tripartite IRF move sequence, the teacher takes the first and third parts: the teacher *initiates*, most commonly by asking a question or posing a problem of some type, a student *responds*, and the teacher then provides some type of *feedback* regarding the response.

Subsequent research has demonstrated that Sinclair and Coulthard were correct in assuming that this sequence characterized most traditional classroom discourse: in many schools, the IRF discourse pattern continues to account for over two-thirds of the talk in classrooms, including face-to-face interactions between the teacher and an individual student.[53] In this traditional discourse move sequence, the teacher generates both question and answer. Students are asked to provide responses, allowing the teacher to build upon, modify, and evaluate those responses. As we will see, the IRF move sequence can also be integrated into more distributed knowledge construction processes in which students are encouraged to frame questions and to evaluate possible responses to those questions based on relevant evidence themselves.

Indeed, all collaborative knowledge construction processes can be seen to enact a parallel version of the tripartite process described by the IRF discourse pattern. For in *any* collaborative negotiation of meaning, one or more people must *frame* some organizing question or issue, the group must then *develop* possible responses to this inquiry, and the group must ultimately *evaluate* the various possibilities that the group has generated. In order for students to learn how to construct reliable understandings themselves, they would need to be given opportunities to participate across all three of these phases of the knowledge construction process.

Coding for student participation within each of these three phases of collaborative knowledge construction therefore reveals an important aspect of the character of these processes—the distribution of what I call interpretive authority. As suggested above, I have termed these three phases *framing* issues, *developing* interpretive possibilities, and *evaluating* these possibilities, resulting in the *framing/developing/evaluating* coding structure, or FDE for short. In the FDE coding system, the elements of the basic IRF discourse *move sequence* the field has historically treated—initiation, response, and feedback—are conceptualized as interpenetrating *stages* of collaborative knowledge construction—framing, developing, and evaluating—that can be enacted in any number of teacher/student move patterns. The traditional IRF sequence becomes one possibility among many.

In the FDE analysis, none of the three stages of knowledge construction is considered to be the dedicated province of either teacher or students. Instead, the coding system looks for all the ways in which any of the three phases of the interpretive process is enacted by either students or teacher. This shift of focus from discourse move sequence to broad patterns of knowledge construction offers necessary perspective on issues of intellectual agency and authority in the classroom. In stepping back and surveying the manner in which teacher/student dialogue functions over time to construct under-standings, one becomes able to see larger and more complex patterns than the IRF lens allows. Most importantly, one can discern *how much* responsibility for framing, developing, and evaluating has been taken on by students and can study the types of teacher contributions that have supported students' interpretive work.

All teachers employ various forms of class discussion in the hopes of inspiring particular kinds of learning. The interpretive balances between teacher and students in these various types of discussion format often differ, as they differ across various grade levels and content areas. It is valuable to characterize and study these patterns of teacher and student interaction as particular patterns are likely to prove more or less well suited to specific pedagogical circumstances and aims.

Structural analyses such as the IRF and FDE coding systems can reliably characterize underlying patterns of teacher and student involvement in the construction of classroom understandings. To understand how a given interpretive structure operates in relation to a specific classroom context and set of pedagogical purposes, one needs to turn to more contextually sensitive means. What might distinguish the interpersonal dynamics inspired by a particular distribution of interpretive authority between teacher and students? Conversely, in what ways might various enactments of the same interpretive authority distribution vary and why?

Participant Frameworks

In the mid-1990s, classroom discourse analysts Catherine O'Connor and Sarah Michaels introduced the sociological lens 'participant framework' to the world of classroom discourse analysis. In their article, "Shifting participant frameworks: Orchestrating thinking practices in group discussion," O'Connor and Michaels argued the need for educators to study the interpersonal nuances of classroom discourse on several grounds.[54] Perhaps most fundamentally, they cited research on language socialization that suggests that schools have an opportunity to socialize students to "interactional routines and practices that will continue to work for them in other settings."[55] As the scholars pointed out, such practices are multidimensional and are represented within discourse in many subtle and complicated ways.

O'Connor and Michaels focused on the manner in which two elementary teachers sensitively positioned their students as theorists and experimenters and nurtured their students' confidence in their ability to help build shared understandings. As their analysis revealed, the work of positioning students in these roles and of acculturating them to academic discourse patterns unfolds on many levels. A structural analysis of student participation absent the researchers' close consideration of the teacher contributions that had inspired and supported that quality of participation would not have adequately represented the nature of the pedagogical resources required.

As any classroom researcher knows, it is generally easier to locate a compelling pattern within a coded data set than to discern that pattern's influence—let alone significance—within a richly characterized social setting. Narrative studies such as the participant framework analysis serve to disrupt a natural tendency for researchers to overemphasize the significance of structural patterns relative to the complex calls teachers must continually make in order to inspire and sustain their students' intellectual engagement and growth.

Simply put, classroom researchers must consider the content and interpersonal tone of a classroom discussion in order to assess adequately the manner in which a particular teaching approach has been enacted. Students will answer a teacher's questions at different lengths and with differing degrees of depth and originality, depending on how interested the teacher seems to be in their thinking and how safe they feel in expressing it. Students will risk pursuit of an inkling of an idea only if they feel that the results might be interesting, that other class members will support them, and that the teacher values such efforts.

A participant framework analysis reveals aspects of a classroom's interpersonal complexity as this complexity is evidenced in language. As an analytic tool, the method considers all cues—implicit and explicit—that have positioned a given speaker in specific relationships to the claims of others in the room at that moment.

Classroom authority relations are constructed over time through the complex transactions that constitute school life. In classroom studies of the construction of any type of teacher or student authority, it is therefore essential to study the content of the interpersonal exchanges through which such relations are created.[56]

Participant framework analyses identify and unpack representative portions of a discussion in order to locate salient characteristics of particular pedagogical interactions. Teachers may seek to establish a specific interpretive structure across several classrooms or within a certain set of lessons in a particular content area. Yet the character of the learning to which such structures will lead will also depend on the unfolding relationships between the people in the room. Learning will depend on the seriousness of purpose with which students entered the room on a particular day and the extent to which they have come to rely upon and take an interest in each other's ideas.

At the same time, different distributions of interpretive authority clearly make qualitatively different intellectual and social demands upon both teachers and their students. It is important to characterize and consider the trade-offs such structural differences imply: such analyses can reveal much about the pedagogical opportunities available in a classroom. Having clarified those opportunities at a structural level, one can then turn to representative transcript excerpts to investigate the character of the learning environments in which those opportunities were made available. Although such an investigation demands careful reflection regarding subtle discourse cues, such study enriches the possibilities of comparative classroom research while providing needed safeguards against the over-theorizing of structural influences.

Summary

The knowledge each of us constructs determines the ways in which each of us views and acts upon the world. Yet this process unfolds in relation to the cultured meaning-making systems within which we live and grow. Cultural and sub-cultural knowledge systems are inescapably implicated in all that any of us has ever learned. Fostering students' abilities to navigate within and beyond their personal and cultural meaning-making systems prepares them for full participation in today's culturally intertwined and rapidly changing world.

As we have seen, contemporary learning and democratic theory both suggest that all students should be continually asked to translate academic content into terms that are personally relevant and meaningful. Developmental, cultural, and individual differences between people cause each of us to see and to understand the world somewhat differently. Unless students are required to represent their emerging understandings in their own terms, there is no way for a teacher to know what students have truly grasped of a lesson or how that material may be shaping students' emerging understandings and worldviews.

All classrooms are diverse classrooms because people vary on multiple dimensions: any grouping of people will represent considerable intellectual and psychological variety, whether or not this variety is readily apparent. While teachers do need to study the major dimensions of human difference that can affect people's ability to understand each other in classrooms, we all must avoid interpreting each other's thoughts and actions based upon generalized understandings of such differences. Rather, teachers need to learn how to access and challenge each of their student's distinctive conceptual and interpretive frames.

Learning how to incorporate students' questions, insights, and observations into all three of the forms of classroom discussion presented here allows teachers to see their students in new ways. Struggling to appreciate students' divergent perspectives and patterns of reasoning can also open up channels of communication between other classroom members who may view aspects of the world quite differently. Such connections provide a real foundation for building strong democratic communities within classrooms.

The framing/developing/evaluating analysis was designed to reveal the manner in which interpretive agency and authority are distributed among the members of any learning community. As we will see in the next several chapters, the FDE analysis can serve as a useful tool for studying classroom discussions, revealing structural aspects of the learning opportunities that those discussions have made available.

Yet in classroom research and research meant to inform classroom practice, one must always complicate the stories that such structural analyses may be thought to tell. Narrative representations of characteristic interactions from a classroom allow readers to interpret the potential significance of structural findings for their own schools in ways than no set of categorical claims, however sensitive or precise, possibly can. As Bruner and others have noted, we humans appear to come equipped with two complementary systems for making sense of the world: we use numbers and logic to analyze and we tell stories to bring a sense of coherence to our experience. Perhaps it should not surprise us, then, if coding tallies and patterns need to be complemented with descriptive narrative in order to represent dynamic social realities in a sufficiently evocative fashion.

The contextually grounded participant framework analysis can help to reveal the interpersonal dynamics that continually shape all meaning making within any classroom. In studying the content and cadence of actual utterances within a specified context, one can access the more subtle registers of a pedagogical dynamic and discern characteristic features of an individual teacher's language. Some of these features may turn out to merit focused structural research themselves, leading to the greater elaboration and sophistication of our pedagogical models.

CHAPTER THREE

Teacher-Led Learning

How are classroom understandings constructed? Who holds the authority to frame the questions and to evaluate the contributions that build toward those understandings? Within most PK-12 classrooms, discussion unfolds within a midrange between teacher monologue and unguided student exploration.[1] Within this midrange, teachers and students interact in order to construct shared understandings: they work together to interpret the world.

Teachers can strategically adopt different interpretive roles within their classrooms in order to support different kinds of student learning. That is, a teacher may at times provide questions for the class to address and at other times ask that students generate those questions. Likewise, teachers may at times choose to weigh in on student contributions and at other times ask their students to consider the value of their classmates' ideas themselves.

The next three chapters describe three different forms of teacher/student interaction based upon the extent to which the teacher participates in framing issues and in evaluating student contributions. In each chapter, I will begin by discussing the pedagogical aims of each of these forms and will end with a review of the principal opportunities that each form provides for learning. The bulk of each chapter will be devoted to exploring the character of that particular form.

Traditionally, PK-12 teachers have employed interactive forms that fall within the category discussed in this chapter, teacher-led learning. In this form of pedagogical interaction, the teacher frames the central questions or issues that are to be discussed and then evaluates a central set of student thoughts, ideas, or answers by the lesson's end. The teacher determines both the content of the questions under review and the content that is ultimately to be viewed as correct or as contributing to the teacher's aims for student learning that day.

When employed well, teacher-led learning experiences can support students in appropriating foundational and expert understandings and in learning to view and to act upon the world in culturally valued ways. In our examples from chapter one, teacher-led learning experiences might be employed to teach students how to use a graphing calculator, care for plants, and employ power tools. In relation to evolutionary theory, a teacher-led discussion might be employed to ensure that students can characterize the basic arguments evolutionary biologists make and the evidence these experts offer in support of their claims.[2]

In language arts classes, teacher-led learning might be employed to teach students the form of a five-paragraph essay or of haiku poetry. Each of these discursive forms provides a foundational set of cultural conventions that can be employed to learn expository writing and to express one's poetic insights, respectively. As discussed in chapter one, foundational understandings represent forms of cultural interpretation. This can be seen in our two examples, both of which reflect the character of particular cultures at particular times.

Teacher-led learning is not particularly well suited to developing personal understandings—though all understandings are in some aspects personal. As we will see in the next chapter, student-led learning is more effective for inspiring and fostering students' personal relationships with content. Teacher-led learning is most appropriate for demonstrating to students how to think about or to accomplish something in close to the same way as others have before them.

Pedagogical Aims and Means

Teacher-led learning can help students to appropriate established cultural forms and understandings and to appreciate the ways in which these forms and understandings enable their participation in their broader culture. As emphasized in sociocultural learning theory, a student's active engagement with culturally powerful language, concepts, and methods serves to expand the verbal, conceptual, and material means available to that student—assuming those resources are positioned in a meaningful relationship with the student's current experience and understandings. When such a relationship exists, students are able to employ established cultural forms and understandings in order to organize and articulate their own experience.

As noted in the last chapter, teachers who seek to impart cultural tools, perspectives, and understandings commonly rely upon the familiar cadence of the initiation/response/feedback (IRF) discourse sequence. IRF exchanges provide teachers with continuous opportunities to shape content and to build upon student thoughts and ideas. As the science educator Jay Lemke discussed in his grounded analysis of what he terms 'triadic dialogue,' the IRF sequence can be used to advance any number of common pedagogical aims. Lemke offers the following examples: drawing out students' existing knowledge of a subject area, confirming that students understand or recall previous lesson content, and eliciting student responses to a shared classroom experience such as a fieldtrip, assigned reading, or scientific investigation. In all of these cases, teachers might ask for their students' thoughts and confusions and then provide feedback that serves to guide students' consolidation of valued vocabulary, concepts, and other cultural resources and to prepare them for new material. For example, Lemke provides the following example of an IRF sequence from the beginning of a high school chemistry lesson: here the teacher is asking for students to recall previously covered content.[3]

Teacher: Hydrogen would have one electron…somewhere in there, and helium would have…?

Student: Two electrons.

Teacher: Two…This is one S, and…the white would be…? Mark?

Mark: Two S.

Teacher: Two S.

While a student's capacity to memorize and reproduce such content has traditionally been rewarded in schools, simple memorization does not ensure that a student has learned to perceive, understand, or act upon the world in a new way. As Martin Nystrand has pointed out, and as Lemke would concur, the IRF sequence still too often is employed in this reductive fashion: students are only and always expected to respond with terms and phrases that are already in the teacher's mind. Nystrand calls this exercise of filling in the blanks in the teacher's narrative with the language a teacher would use 'rote recitation.'[4] To the extent that teachers look for this type of perfunctory student performance in their classrooms, teachers should be employing such exchanges for specialized and limited purposes, such as the review cited by Lemke above, rather than as a general strategy for teaching new material.

A teacher can determine the extent to which students have claimed new understandings or perspectives for their own practical and intellectual purposes only by observing students' personal efforts to wrestle with that content in their own terms. As the literacy researcher Gordon Wells noted in an oft-cited paper on the IRF sequence, knowledge can only be co-constructed to the extent that discourse is meaningfully dialogic.[5] This is as true in the case of teacher-led interpretation as in any other pedagogical form: teachers can only support their students' appropriation of foundational and expert understandings when they are in meaningful conversation with them. Considerable IRF research and scholarship have therefore focused upon how teachers can ascertain that they are truly accessing and influencing their students' conceptions of and understandings about the world.

For example, Wells speaks of the need for teachers to make room for original student thoughts and to query the nuances of students' understandings (and misunderstandings) in order to ensure that teachers understand the language of their students in the manner in which their students intend. Only then will a teacher be able to frame his or her follow-up moves in an adequately sensitive fashion. Once one has ascertained the character of students' thinking, Wells suggests that a teacher might employ the follow-up move to elaborate upon and extend that thinking, to clarify its significance in relation to the aims of the lesson, and to link students' contributions with each other.

Although the formal structure of these suggestions Wells offers is identical in relation to the IRF analysis—each represents a type of follow-up move—the purposes each serves can be seen as distinct in pragmatic terms. That is to say, each of these types of follow-up move accomplishes something distinctive in relation to the meaning-making underway. It is therefore important when studying intellectual agency and authority to consider the ways in which the actual content of teacher comments and questions serves to steer the process of classroom knowledge construction. As shown below, such study of discourse content can be undertaken at both the structural and contextual levels.[6]

Courtney Cazden, another scholar who has long studied the nuances of the IRF sequence, raises another important pedagogical issue in her discussion of "inauthentic questions."[7] Much has been made in some quarters of the fact that teachers often ask questions to which they already know the answers during IRF sequences. As Cazden notes, 'known-answer' questions can serve a variety of important pedagogical purposes, such as introducing background knowledge into the conversation and, as Lemke noted in the work cited above, judging students' recall from a previous lesson. Among other pertinent examples, Cazden cites 'reciprocal teaching,' an approach to teaching reading that advises teachers to ask students the pedagogically valuable question of what students think will happen next in a story.[8]

Students understand that teachers often ask known-answer questions in order to keep everyone on board and engaged with the lesson underway; this familiar type of teacher 'discourse move' can be usefully integrated into any of our three pedagogical forms. This category of question was likely identified as pedagogically problematic only due to its inappropriate use and over-use, as discussed in Nystrand's critique of rote recitation. I would propose that the term 'inauthentic' be reserved for teacher questions that *pretend* to invite students' original insights and interpretations but actually surreptitiously work to drive the discussion toward some set of foregone conclusions. Students readily detect such subterfuges. Good teacher-led learning experiences, frankly presented and pursued, are always preferable to teacher-led learning masquerading as a more distributed knowledge construction process.

In his piece on the IRF sequence, Wells distinguishes between "two prime goals" of education: cultural reproduction (that is, passing one generation's understandings on to the next) and individual development.[9] The IRF sequence, Wells suggests, has been seen as merely reproducing culture and has therefore been embraced by teachers who focus primarily on passing along existing cultural knowledge to their students. As a sociocultural theorist, Wells wants to emphasize the extent to which all children develop *by means of* their ongoing appropriation of valued cultural resources. Wells' construction, while clearly an improvement over placing cultural reproduction and individual development in opposition to each other, still risks underrepresenting the roles of student invention and creativity in learning.

Wells closes his discussion of the IRF sequence with the claim that "when the third part of this structure is characterized as follow-up, rather than more narrowly as evaluation, there are compelling reasons for seeing the IRF sequence as the prototypical Action structure for achieving the overarching goals of education...."[10] Yet, as our discussion of the framing/developing/evaluating (FDE) analysis in the previous chapter suggests, in order to construct *shared* understandings, one always requires an evaluative process of some type. However one conceives of the third part of the IRF discourse move sequence, a pedagogical discussion needs to provide normative direction in some form.[11] In teacher-led discussions, the teacher provides that direction.

The IRF sequence has long served as a conceptual cornerstone for generative analyses of classroom practice, yet it cannot support a comprehensive exploration of the issues of intellectual agency and authority within democratic classrooms that interest us here. Most importantly, it cannot reveal teachers' and students' structural roles in the construction of classroom understandings or track the complex rhythms of knowledge construction in today's more pedagogically dynamic classrooms. To study these phenomena, classroom researchers require different tools: a structural analysis that tracks all teacher and student contributions to the framing of investigative issues and the development and evaluation of interpretive possibilities and a sensitive contextualized reading of the ways in which teachers have positioned their students as participants in the construction of shared classroom understandings.

Analyzing Interpretive Authority

My research focused on discussions of literature within the classrooms of six teachers at three private secondary schools with different pedagogical philosophies. While one of the three schools characterizes its curriculum as 'student-centered' and another as 'traditional liberal arts,' I correctly assumed that the practice within all three of these privileged institutions would be academically serious and that I would not therefore encounter the rote recitation that today's learning theorists disparage.[12] Five of the six participant teachers had been in the field for decades; the sixth teacher had also taught for a number of years and had undertaken graduate study. The teachers all chose their own pseudonyms, which I use here; student names are also all pseudonyms.

I tape recorded between four and six full-period literature discussions in each classroom and asked teachers to choose the two that they felt best reflected what they would consider a good day. I then transcribed those tapes and comprehensively coded student and teacher turns for the role(s) each turn played in knowledge construction. I discovered that the extent to which teachers participated in the framing of interpretive issues and the evaluation of student contributions varied considerably in the different classrooms.[13]

Teacher interviews revealed that all six teachers not only recognized but had deliberately chosen the roles they were found to play in the construction of classroom understandings. As will be discussed in chapter five, one teacher from the 'student-centered' school and one from the 'traditional liberal arts' school grouped together in what became the co-led learning category. This result demonstrates the importance of studying patterns of knowledge construction as they actually unfold within classrooms rather than relying on self-identified or school-based theoretical affiliations.

Again, the distinguishing characteristics of a teacher-led discussion are that the teacher determines discursive content and serves as final arbiter of the content understandings that are to be viewed as useful or correct. Although students are not usually *required* to make framing moves in the course of a teacher-led discussion, in many classrooms, students may ask questions or raise issues that serve to frame the discussion for some period of time. In teacher-led learning, the teacher serves as gatekeeper in such cases, determining which student questions and issues to entertain at what length based on the teacher's goals for the discussion.

Although the IRF sequence was employed at least once in every one of the six classrooms, IRF sequences occurred much more commonly within the teacher-led discussions. This should not surprise us as teacher-led learning places the responsibility for framing issues and evaluating contributions upon the teacher. Again, teacher framing and evaluating moves will not always unfold in the classic IRF sequence, with a single student response neatly sand-wiched between them, but as classroom research has demonstrated, they frequently do.

As we will see, participant teachers who clustered together according to interpretive authority distribution differ in other pedagogically significant ways. Conversely, teachers employing different distributions of interpretive authority shared other significant pedagogical commitments and approaches. For example, one teacher employing student-led interpretation and one employing co-led interpretation both insisted their students work with their texts open and continually reference text passages when making their points, in contrast to the other four teachers.

Reading for Participant Frameworks

The participant framework analysis has its roots in the work of social anthropologist Irving Goffman, who was interested in the ways in which spoken language establishes dynamic and layered relationships between all who hear that language.[14] Goffman noted that any spoken utterance creates an interpersonal framework, however transitory: by speaking audibly in the presence of others, we position those others into relationship with ourselves. Depending upon the circumstances, strangers might even glance up to note who else had heard words spoken on a train platform, perhaps feeling that somebody should respond in some fashion.

In extended conversations between an established group of discussants, such as in a classroom, each remark made positions the speaker and any others the speaker references into ever unfolding relationships with all others in the room. A participant framework analysis considers the manner in which specific discourse sequences enact this process, focusing on the ways in which each participant's words serve to position that speaker and previous speakers in relation to each other and the meaning-making underway.

In addition to what such study can reveal about individual interactions and what these evoke of the interpersonal dynamic within a classroom, close consideration of a teacher's utterances can also help to locate replicable teacher moves that may work to engender positive patterns of student response in general terms. For example, O'Connor and Michaels have drawn attention to the manner in which some teachers "revoice" student contributions, based originally on their study of the language employed by two accomplished upper elementary school teachers.[15]

These two teachers regularly orchestrated lively whole-class discussions, in large part through their sensitive use of revoicing moves to align individual student contributions more closely with the group's interpretive work. In some cases, the teachers explicitly positioned a student's comment into relationship with the previously expressed idea of a fellow student. In other cases, greater alignment was achieved by explicitly articulating an aspect of the student's thought that the student had left implicit, recasting a student's contribution into more academic language or scaffolding a student's incomplete rendering of a complex progression of thoughts (or more than one of these).

Having situated the student's contribution into a clearer and more meaningful relationship with the academic discussion under way, the teacher then always asks the student to evaluate whether or not the teacher had accurately represented what the student was saying. In providing the student with an opportunity to respond to the teacher's characterization, a teacher not only positions the student as authoritative in regards to the character of his or her contribution but also implicitly bestows credit for the teacher's more closely aligned rendering of the contribution upon the student.

O'Connor and Michaels found that the teachers they studied were able, through their use of revoicing moves, to engender particularly lively and generative classroom dynamics. By continually portraying their students—or, in Goffman's more evocative language, 'animating' their students—as ever more capable participants in the creation of classroom understandings, these teachers nurtured their students' willingness and capacity to assume ever more meaningful roles in the creation of such understandings.

Teacher-researchers and other classroom researchers, some of whom spend extended periods of time studying practice within a single room, can augment their study of discourse patterns and meanings with additional ethnographic tools such as long-term participant observation and student interviews. While such familiarity will tend to foster a deeper appreciation of the nuances of classroom exchanges, a great deal of pedagogical significance can be discerned simply by studying a well-wrought transcript.

Classroom transcriptions—rendered with emphases, pauses, repetitions, hesitations, and false starts noted—possess an uncanny ability to transport a reader into a situated classroom exchange. A great deal of a discussant's thoughts, mood, and manner can be read through how that person speaks and what he or she endeavors to say. As a data source, sensitive transcriptions allow readers in on a human exchange from a particular place and time, in much the same way that well-wrought dialogue in a novel does.[16] Such access provides all readers with the opportunity to judge what may or may not have been intended by a particular student's or teacher's contribution and to reflect on the pedagogical import of those contributions.

In addition to producing exacting transcriptions of the chosen class periods, I also interviewed each participant teacher twice, once after the recordings had been made and then again after we had both had an opportunity to review the two transcripts from his or her classroom.[17] Again, any researcher's approach to data collection must respond to the purposes of the research. In this case, I wanted to see how effectively one could study patterns of interpretive agency and authority utilizing only these means. If comparative classroom research is to move past the shallow shores of standardized testing, educational researchers require tools that are reliable, replicable, *and* manageable on a large scale.

I chose to focus my consideration of participant frameworks around two complementary and fundamental aspects of any teacher's

discursive manner: the quality of attention given to student contributions and the manner in which a teacher limits the discussion to
matters of greatest import or relevance. In different ways and to
varying extents, all teachers seek to draw out and, at other times,
constrain the play of their students' verbal contributions for various
reasons.[18] These two dimensions of verbal response work sym-
biotically; a teacher cannot develop all the implications of everything
that students say. Exploring any issue at length leaves other matters
untreated. A close study of the relationship between these two processes therefore provides telling markers of a teacher's interpretive
aims and methods.

Relative to the quality of a teacher's attention, for example, one
can ask whether a teacher seems to be interacting with a student's
thinking on its own terms, seems focused on how the student's
thinking intersects with the teacher's line of reasoning, or is only
listening for a particular response. The extent to which a teacher
sensitively queries—or revoices—students' complex or only partially
developed thinking suggests the extent to which such thinking is
viewed as valuable to the purposes of the class. If a teacher probes
students' contributions in these situations and asks other students to
participate in the work of trying to understand what one of their
classmates is trying to say, confusion and tentativeness will come to
be seen as integral to the work of collaborative meaning-making in
that classroom.

Relative to a teacher's manner of boundary-tending, one might
first identify the reasons a teacher has chosen to interrupt, contradict,
or neglect the implications of a student's contribution. Has a teacher
intervened in order to rule out specific interpretive possibilities or to
shape their direction? Has a teacher insisted on keeping another
student's forgotten insight on the table or sought to connect a
student's current contribution with the prior thoughts of another
student? Does a teacher at times stop students in order to understand
more deeply what they are trying to say or to ask them to provide
evidence for their claims?

In addition to asking why teachers intervene, it is also important
to consider the spirit in which they do so. To some extent, the purpose
of the intervention will inform the spirit in which it is spoken. Yet,

teachers' attitudes and personalities will also be expressed in the phrasings they employ. The emotional register established between members of a classroom community profoundly influences the character of the knowledge construction processes undertaken within that classroom.

A secondary school literature discussion such as the ones discussed in this study differs in many ways from the elementary school discussions that O'Connor and Michaels analyzed. Yet the scholars' analysis of the subtle ways in which teachers locate their students in the learning process stands to inform any consideration of intellectual agency and authority within schools. Classroom researchers interested in such issues must seek to uncover and understand the situated moves with which teachers position individual students as participants in the collaborative construction of meaning.

The Teacher Leads the Way

Although my primary interest in this work is to distinguish between three forms of learning experience and to argue that all three forms belong in all democratic classrooms, my discussion will also touch upon the use of these forms in relation to the classroom context I studied, namely, literary interpretation at the secondary level. A number of language arts educators have long argued that teacher-led discussion is not suited to the work of teaching students how to interpret literature.[19] These scholars and practitioners have maintained that concentrating the responsibility both for framing issues and for evaluating interpretative possibilities in the teacher's hands cannot equip students with sufficient conceptual tools—or intellectual inspiration—for undertaking literary interpretation themselves.

In response, more traditional educators have noted that teacher-led discussion allows teachers to familiarize potential literary scholars with established literary vocabulary, historical background, and broadly accepted readings of the contemporary canon. Such differences in pedagogical outlook intersect with issues of interpretation that have been unfolding within the field of literary theory for over fifty years.[20] During this time, theorists have presented multiple opposing visions of the act of literary interpretation. Commitments to the centrality and contingent nature of the individual reader's response have informed these debates, which have found their way into post-secondary classrooms and from there into secondary and elementary schools.

Of course, even those who agree about the nature of literary interpretation may differ when it comes to determining what this means for secondary school practice, where students are generally introduced to classic works for the first time. Such contrasts will often be even more pronounced between teachers at different schools. Institutional materials, rhetoric, and routines tend to cut across individual differences in pedagogical commitments and emphases to some extent, encouraging (and enforcing) intra-school cohesiveness.

Again, whether or not one chooses to employ teacher-led learning for interpretive discussions of literary works, there are many other challenges for which this approach to teaching is clearly well suited. Of the three forms of learning experience, teacher-led learning most directly positions student thinking into relation with the teachers' own understandings and reasoning, allowing the teacher's perspective to be experienced, and so potentially grasped, most readily.

Interpretive Structure

The one teacher who employed teacher-led interpretation in my research, Randy, worked at the 'traditional liberal arts' school; his tenth-grade class was reading J. D. Salinger's *The Catcher in the Rye*. Randy framed all of the major interpretive issues the class treated and evaluated the ideas students offered throughout each of the class discussions I recorded. As Randy characterized his aims in his first interview, "You teach the text...That is what the job is. So finding ways to explore that particular text...You pick out a few that seem particularly valuable, and important, and essential to that novel, and that's what you're teaching." Randy offered the examples of voice and narrative as particularly generative interpretive angles on *Catcher in the Rye*. [21]

In the two classroom discussions I analyzed, Randy regularly invited student consideration of interpretive issues he had identified and asked a series of related closed questions. These moves helped

Randy to steer the conversation into areas of exploration that he found valuable. Closed questions often served to develop larger interpretive issues, for example, by prompting students to recall and establish relevant particulars of the text.

In the two discussions transcribed, the text was referenced only at Randy's direction. Once or twice each class, Randy directed his students to open their books to a particular page and asked a student to read a particular passage. The ensuing discussion then treated that passage, with Randy introducing a series of interpretive questions for the students to consider. Throughout such exchanges, Randy continually evaluated the accuracy and significance of his students' thoughts as in this excerpt, which discusses the feelings of the main character, Holden, regarding his brother's death.

Excerpt 3a[22]

Randy: Yeah. He talks about how, about how *uncomfortable* he is with the *idea* of, of being buried.

Conner: Actually, he did say that his parents were going to put *flowers* on his grave, like [xxx] --

Steve: He said he didn't like to visit the grave.

Stan: Yeah, he said, he said he didn't like to visit the grave because every time he goes, he thinks about, like, it raining on Allie's coffin.

Randy: Right. Right. He, he, as is typical, he *envisions* this whole scenario, almost independent of *what* it is that he *projects*, he fantasizes, he, *constructs* ah, a *something*, almost scripts it. Can we think of other things, that are *safe*? That are home-base to him? Interestingly enough, *home* is not on the list.

Mirroring the teacher/student role distribution of the IRF sequence, Randy looked for his students to provide responses to his initiations—or framing moves—of various sorts. Throughout the interpretive process, Randy also frequently weighed in with his own developing moves, which helped to move along the developing phase of knowledge construction. The sequence above begins with a brief ratification from Randy that is then followed by an elaboration: Randy first agrees with the previous speaker and then observes that the protagonist feels uncomfortable with the idea of being buried. Randy often either modified or elaborated upon student responses in order to ensure that those responses were developed in accordance with his perspective.

As we see below, Randy employed IRF sequences to build literary interpretations, inviting his students to share any thoughts or insights they may have on the topic at hand. Several students might contribute, at times substantially, before Randy responded with anything explicitly evaluative (although other types of framing and developing moves were often offered along the way). In the coded excerpt below, Randy employs the full IRF sequence to assemble evidence of the protagonist's deteriorating state of body and mind near the end of the novel *Catcher in the Rye*. I have also coded Randy's elaborations on his student responses.

> **Excerpt 3b**
>
> **Randy:** If you recall that scene, what are some *other behaviors* that, that grab your attention to say that he is definitely at risk here? INITIATION
>
> **Nate:** Well, this disappearing thing was a continuation of the first chapter when he's parked across the street from Mr. Spencer's house. And he says, "I better not cross the road. I felt like I was sort of disappearing." That kind of made me feel like disappearing every time he crossed the road. RESPONSE
>
> **Randy:** Good C word, continuation. FEEDBACK Maybe a better C word, culmination. ELABORATION What else? What else? What else? INITIATION
>
> **Nate:** The [xxx] UNCLEAR
>
> **Randy:** What else? … Other behaviors. INITIATION
>
> **Stan:** He's still, sweating like a bastard. RESPONSE
>
> **Randy:** Yep. FEEDBACK
>
> …
>
> **Conner:** It seems like he's, like, having a physical breakdown in addition to his mental breakdown. RESPONSE
>
> **Randy:** And manifestations on the physical side? INITIATION
>
> **Conner:** Well, he has trouble breathing. He's sweating. I mean, he's sort of been, living very unhealthily for about a week. RESPONSE
>
> **Randy:** Yep. FEEDBACK
>
> **Conner:** Just smoking-- RESPONSE

Randy: Smoking, drinking, sleep deprivation. FEEDBACK/ELABORATION

Conner: *Barely* eating. RESPONSE

Randy: Yes. Barely eating. FEEDBACK

In this classroom, IRF sequences were used to develop the teacher's talking points for the day. Though Randy framed all of the principal interpretive issues the class dealt with, his use of the IRF sequence to begin a class or to redirect the class to a new topic allowed him to hear from students and to integrate their contributions into the evolving discourse flow. It gave the process a more collaborative and interactional feel.

Randy's frequent ratifications of his students' contributions could be heard throughout the classroom discussions I observed and created a sense of rolling momentum. This momentum can also be heard in the next two passages from Randy's room. At times, Randy's ratifications could feel like a snowball coming down a hill: the pace was exciting yet provided little opportunity to pause in order to query a remark or to disagree.

Participant Frameworks

Qualities of Attention–In Randy's classroom, students sometimes briefly vetted their tentative thoughts and theories with each other quietly before offering them to the larger group. Here two students, Steve and Nate, come forward with contributions that seem to have emerged from a preceding side conversation between the two of them.

After Steve and Nate have spoken, a third student, Conner, takes the opportunity to develop a thought he had begun earlier. Here, Randy does not simply agree with Conner's contribution but banters with him a little, providing some comic relief. With his ratifications and comic elaborations, Randy has spun all three students' contributions into a single interpretive line that addresses the question with which Randy had begun the exchange.

Excerpt 3c
Randy: Okay. Who else has thoughts on, on where Holden is, and, and why he reacts so *strongly* to the profanity, which repeats itself when he gets to the school? [Note: Nate, Steve, and one other student start talking unintelligibly.]

Steve: [xxxxx] starts at the school.

Randy: Right. So, so there are at least two instances of profanity—

Nate: Then he makes the comment how, on his grave—

Steve: Yeah.

Randy: Right, right, right, right. [Note: background discussions and interruptions have been continuing, but stop here.] And again, he's sort of *projecting* himself as being *dead*.

Nate: Yes. I mean, he does that a lot.

Randy: He does that a lot. Yes. Good. Steve.

Steve: He kind of has a perfect vision of places like the school and the museum. And then all of a sudden, there's this, ah, graffiti on it that just *messes up* this entire thing because it's a change. What's worse is it's a loss of innocence of these places. And then, by, and then it's kind of in contrast with Allie =

Randy: Um-hmm.

Steve: = whose [xx] can't lose it =

Randy: Um-hmm, um-hmm.

Steve: = in a sense. And then he's still worrying about Phoebe, who can still be affected by this.

Randy: Right, right.

Steve: And you *see* that contrast when he pictures himself, his gravestone as being graffitied the same way =

Randy: Um-hmm.

Steve: = when he's dead because it's just kind of a continuation.

Randy: Um-hmm. Good…. [Note: Randy nods to Conner.]

Conner: I was actually beginning it before. Um, I was just going to say, it seems like Holden thinks the profanity is directed at *him*, in a way. So that the world, *collectively*, is saying it to him.

Randy: Right.

Conner: It seems like he pictures it—

Randy: No, no paranoia here at all.

Conner: Right.

Randy: Right, okay, just checking.

Conner: It's like the world is all going to come up, and like *each* person is going to individually scratch it on his tombstone.

Randy: [Note: Randy laughs a little.] Could we get a line. A couple of those police line things. And we get this organized, so that it's at least orderly when they deface my tombstone.

Conner: That's like such a, sort of *bleak* vision. It's like, you're *dead*. He's already gone through the whole thing about he hates the cemetery. And he hates it raining on his brother's grave. And then people come and just scrape [xxx]—

Randy: You know. One more thing. One more *indignity*. One more *way* the world does you in.

Randy has invited students' open consideration of an interpretive issue. Randy asks "who else has thoughts on, on where Holden is, and, and why he reacts so *strongly* to the profanity, which repeats itself when he gets to the school?" He then opens the floor to his students.

Randy's frequent and enthusiastic ratifications suggest that the thoughts that Steve and Nate share are just the sort of responses he had hoped to hear. Although Steve's first comment was not entirely clear on the tape recording, Randy's response that "there are at least two instances of profanity" seems to position Steve's comment as a useful observation from which the class can proceed.

In his third turn, Randy employs a string of ratifications—right, right, right, right—to quiet the class and bring everyone into the conversation he is leading. At the same time, Randy elaborates on Nate's unfinished statement about Holden making "the comment how, on his grave," with which Steve has already agreed, noting that Holden "sort of projects himself as being dead."

In this exchange, Randy and Steve both signal that they knew what Nate was going to say before Nate even finished his sentence, preempting any need for Nate to finish his thought or to develop it further. Just as readily, Nate now seems to grasp what Randy means when he says that Holden 'projects himself as dead' and promptly elaborates on Randy's thought, observing that Holden "does that a lot," drawing yet another ratification from Randy. Steve then returns to address Randy's original question about why the profanity so upset Holden.

As can be seen in this excerpt, Randy's staccato ratifications often serve to carry the discussion forward in his classroom. Randy does not pause here to query any of the claims that Steve, Nate, or Conner have made or to position those claims into relationship with the claims of another student, nor has an opening been provided for other students to query or to challenge these students' ideas or claims. At this point, for another student to challenge or question any of these comments, that student would need to challenge or question Randy's unqualified ratifications of those contributions as well. Even a student request for clarification regarding, perhaps, the passage to which Nate referred or where it is in the text that Holden 'projects himself as dead' would position that student as an outsider, looking in, during this short burst of like-minded collaboration—as having missed something that other students appeared to be following.

One wonders whether Randy fears losing his students' attention should a speaker dwell upon any one set of thoughts for too long. Or perhaps Randy set what now feel like overly ambitious content goals for the discussion and feels the need to move rapidly through a few remaining areas of the text. Perhaps literary interpretation simply feels more engaging to Randy at this pace, and he wants to expose his students to the thrill of building breathlessly toward a shared set of understandings about a text.

Randy's banter with Conner at the end of the passage about a line forming at Holden's imaginary gravesite to deface his tombstone has a fun and collegial feel; again, Randy has seized on Conner's observation as a means of sweeping Conner into the lively exchange underway. Yet Randy's comments also serve to wrap Conner's more complex reflection on the character's vision of life into the interpretive issue that Randy had framed about why the profanity upset him in the first place. Randy positions Conner's observation as responsive to his line of thought rather than as an original and uncharted insight capable of moving the class discussion in a new direction.

Teacher-led discussions, by their very nature, foreground the ideas a teacher wants students to consider over an investigation of students' divergent observations and ideas. The interpretive goals that Randy had established are serving to shape Randy's understandings of and responses to his students' contributions.

Randy wants to involve his students with the work of developing the interpretive stands he has identified, which he views as conceptually significant, and so looks for the ways in which his students' contributions can be positioned as contributing to that process.

Accomplished teachers all learn how to negotiate the teacher-driven dynamic of teacher-led discussions in their own ways. Many books have been written and theories framed about how to inspire one's students to care about material one wants them to come to see in certain ways and perhaps even love. These books and theories represent the field's accumulated wisdom about the craft of teaching. Yet great teaching not only reflects developed craft: it also reflects the kind of developed insight and sensitivity that characterize remarkable creative performances within any field.

Even assuming compelling material and a sensitive teacher, inspiring students' interest and engagement during teacher-led discussions tends to present greater challenges than would opening the floor to, in this case, the aspects of the assigned reading that the students themselves found noteworthy or confusing. After all, the teacher has determined what will be discussed. To the extent that a teacher cares, as Randy clearly did, about students' intellectual engagement with the material, the teacher will need to find ways of inspiring students' interest in that material.

Boundary Tending–Randy did not hesitate to contradict his students when he felt someone had veered onto a wrong track, though this was fairly rare. More often, he simply neglected to follow up on the implications of some student contribution when to do so would have meant straying from the interpretive logic he was following. In the following excerpt, Randy begins by explicitly ratifying and elaborating on a previous student move, drawing a challenge from Joe. As can be seen, Randy does not directly respond to Joe's claim that Holden has continued to pursue an emotional connection with his little sister, Phoebe, in apparent contradiction of Randy's claim that this character is not willing to "let anyone in." In the end, Randy simply acknowledges the complexity of the issue and moves on.

Excerpt 3d
Randy: There's a, you're exactly right. ... If, if you, if you *don't* let yourself feel, then you don't have to feel pain. *That* kind of pain. So don't let anyone

get close. Don't let anyone connect. When you said, *isolated*, it's such a bizarre mix. It's *service*. It's *salvation*. It's *practically messianic*. But it's by himself and outside the conventions. ... And why is that okay? Because he doesn't want to be *hurt*. Because he's hurting so much. How much more hurt can he take? So don't let anyone, in, and then you won't have any more pain. ... Ouch.

Joe: Well, what about Phoebe? ...

Randy: What about Phoebe?

Joe: Well, he's drawn so close to her. He seems to *want* to make a relationship ... but is that because he thinks that it can't happen twice, the same thing?

Conner: I think that's why he protects her so carefully.

Randy: That's why he *protects* her. It's why he whitewashes her flaws. And it's why he goes back and forth.

Conner: He was already close to her. And it's like, he can't really push her away. Nor does he really *want* to, but that's why he gets over-protective.

Randy: And, and get help from a ten-year-old sister? ...

Student: Maybe he thinks he can somehow *control* that.

Randy: I don't know. It's complicated, it's a complicated, because he does, he goes back and forth, even with her. He wanders into the fantasy with her as well. [6 sec] When he's *talking* with his peers... go back to the Sally case now. Do you have a page number for that?

In this excerpt, Conner and an unidentified student seem to take up Joe's query about Phoebe while Randy stays on another track. By actively engaging the interpretive issue that Joe has raised, the two students position Joe as a valued colleague who has identified a matter of interest that can advance their own understandings of the novel.

Although their language intermingles, with Randy picking up on Conner's statement that Holden "protects" Phoebe, the remarks Randy makes about Holden whitewashing Phoebe's flaws and "wander[ing] into the fantasy with her as well" do not directly bear on Joe's question about whether Holden has let himself remain emotionally vulnerable to his little sister. They tie in more closely to an interpretive strand that Randy had introduced earlier about whether or not Phoebe is "safe," in other words a reliable resource for Holden in the character's time of need.

Randy's unwillingness to engage Joe's challenge on its own terms, by furthering querying Joe's argument and by inviting other students to consider the argument's implications, relates to the quality of attention Randy paid to the student contributions in earlier excerpts. Although those prior student contributions could be more easily woven into an interpretive issue that Randy had identified, a consideration of their full interpretive implications and possibilities would have taken the discussion further astray from the interpretive issue that Randy had framed than Randy desired. Here, Randy simply moves on when he fails to connect Joe's observation with either the issues under discussion or with the prior interpretive claim Randy has made.

Opportunities for Learning

Randy led focused investigations of the text, at times pausing to expound upon the text's interpretive meanings. In essence, his students were interacting with and elaborating upon established lines of investigation that had evolved within similar classroom settings over the thirty years of Randy's teaching career. Learning to follow and to contribute to a line of interpretation that a teacher has framed requires a certain intellectual dexterity and attentiveness and exposes students to established modes of literary thought.

In Randy's banter with Conner in excerpt 3b, one could hear some of the playful spirit that often infused the discussions in Randy's classroom. Randy actively elicited his students' thoughts and, to some extent, interpretive concerns. He listened when his students sought to share their thinking and undertook to weave that thinking into an interactive interpretive line that addressed the issues he had framed. To the extent that students follow a teacher's interpretive logic and find the themes the teacher has identified interesting, they may well find such an experience engaging and enjoyable.

As we saw in the excerpts cited, Randy wandered only so far down the paths suggested by his students' more complex and peripheral contributions. In prioritizing his own construction of narrative coherence, Randy provided a convincing storyline without the false starts and uncertainty that would have characterized his students' efforts to do the same. Students were not challenged to identify or to cope themselves with textual complexities and interpretive contradictions. Nor were they necessarily required to articulate their own intimations and intuitions about what the text might mean.

Lively classroom discussions are dense with discursive potential, and transcripts of such discussions therefore always raise questions about interpretive roads not taken and meanings missed. Whether or not a reader agrees with the specific calls Randy made in these brief excerpts—Randy may himself choose differently on another occasion—Randy's moves illustrate a defining challenge of teacher-led learning experiences. In a teacher-led discussion, it is the teacher who must continually determine where to head with the conversation and then strive to bring students along in the chosen direction. The teacher bears the responsibility for interesting students in a line of thought and a set of ideas that the teacher finds valuable.

In addition to the challenges teacher-led discussions can present in terms of inspiring genuine student interest, teacher-led discussions also naturally tend to advantage students who more readily view the material in the same way as the teacher does (for whatever reasons). Although this dynamic can certainly be mitigated by inviting and attending closely to students' thoughts and questions, to some extent, a preferential weighting of these students' contributions is unavoidable as one central purpose of this type of learning experience is for everyone eventually to grasp the teacher's perspective.

Nonetheless, teacher-led discussions can set the conceptual shifts that lead to lasting learning into motion. Again, the teacher models a way of thinking that becomes available to the students through their repeated exposure to his or her reasoning. Randy's use of IRF sequences to stay close to what the students found in the novel and to place their observations into relationship with his thinking likely increases the chances that his students will be drawn into seeing both the novel and the act of literary interpretation in new ways. As Randy himself noted in an interview, this approach also allows students to place their own ideas about the book into relation with themes that the teacher has identified as significant and to gather their teacher's and classmates' responses to them.

These opportunities for student learning are made available through a knowledge construction process that can be seen to be more unilateral than those we will consider in the next two chapters. Here, the teacher offers not only an established means of investigating the world but also an established perspective upon some aspect of the world—in this case, a novel. The worldview that challenges the students' own is primarily that of the teacher, who has learned to view the content at issue in a manner that more or less aligns with the manner in which other knowledgeable people within the culture view that content.

For this reason, teacher-led learning is less likely than the other two forms to cultivate personal insights or a sense of intellectual daring among the students as a group. As we have seen, this teaching approach asks students to follow the teacher's line of reasoning and, to the extent a student seeks to depart from the teacher's interpretive claims, to challenge the teacher directly. While a couple of students were willing to challenge Randy's understandings of the book in the two class periods I studied, most did not do so. Particularly in classrooms with fewer verbally precocious students, such hesitancy can serve to limit everybody's learning. Learners need to feel free to air their doubts and confusions about their teacher's understandings and reasoning if they are expected to integrate those intellectual resources into their own thinking.

As noted, students in Randy's class were allowed to confer with each other from time to time in response to a question Randy had posed. If particularly active and widespread, Randy might let this sort of exchange go on for as much as fifteen seconds before pulling the students back into a single conversation. In our follow-up interview, Randy agreed with my observation that these breaks in the whole class conversation seemed to help students become more comfortable with their thinking before sharing it with the entire group.

Regarding his own goals for this type of literary discussion, Randy spoke first of his commitment to generating universal and enthusiastic participation in his classroom. He said that he wanted all of his students to have the opportunity to try out their ideas "with an eye towards what they're going to write on." While Randy's class clearly broke down into more and less active groups of participants, all students did usually contribute at least once per class period. Randy sees his commitment to universal participation as fundamental to the purposes of a liberal arts education, which aims to prepare students for the active intellectual engagement with the broader culture.

Teacher-led learning offers both teachers and students a number of comforts and assurances. Some students tend to prefer the considerable degree of guidance provided. Many will have received such guidance in other classrooms and will have grown accustomed to it; some may simply prefer the feeling of "knowing" more or less what the material is supposed to mean. When integrating more distributed forms of knowledge construction processes into a classroom, teachers often must reckon with initial resistance from some students for these reasons.

Across the disciplines, teacher-led discussions are suited to teaching established content, processes, and perspectives. This category might include teaching students how to reenact historically significant scientific experiments, how to employ a common mathematical algorithm, and how to behave in the halls. Teacher-led discussions can also be employed for sharing relevant background material such as a conceptual framework or historical overview. Whenever teachers seek to impart a predetermined set of content understandings, teacher-led learning experiences allow them to do so in a more direct and less time-consuming manner than either of the other two forms of learning experience we will consider.

In my own graduate teaching, I employ teacher-led learning for a number of purposes. In my learning theory course, for example, I use this pedagogical form to familiarize prospective teachers with the intersections and contrasts between the worldviews of developmental psychologists Jean Piaget and Lev Vygotsky and to provide a sense of the historical circumstances that organized these scholars' methodological commitments and aims. Throughout these discussions, I strive to scaffold my students' understanding of Piaget's and Vygotsky's perspectives on the growth of human knowledge as I have come to understand these. It is not unusual for my students, later in the term, to categorize other learning experiences in the course as Piagetian or Vygotskian in emphasis as they have learned to recognize the complementary sets of concerns that these two great scholars represent within developmental psychology and have begun to view the concepts of learning and development through their eyes.

Summary

While all members of a democratic society possess the right to disagree with the theoretical claims of teachers and with those of other experts in any field, democratic societies also have a legitimate interest in ensuring that the children of these societies understand the ways in which recognized experts from various professions and disciplines view, investigate, and interpret the world. Teacher-led learning serves to impart a teacher's developed understandings and perspectives to his or her students through sensitive questioning, explication, and modeling. In such cases, the principal aim is for students to learn how to see, think about, or manipulate some aspect of the world in roughly the same way as the teacher does.

When a teacher takes responsibility for organizing the content of a discussion, the teacher will generally need to take more turns and longer turns, and these turns will tend to occur fairly regularly. The Initiation/Response/Feedback discourse move pattern may be more commonly employed in order to provide students with opportunities to share their thoughts and questions, while maintaining the arc of the teacher's reasoning. Teachers have likely been employing this basic discursive pattern since schooling began (although most have simply called it 'teaching').

Good teacher-led learning experiences can expose students to culturally powerful understandings and methods and to examples of transparent and well-supported reasoning. However one may feel about employing teacher-led learning for discussions of literature, teacher-led learning remains a powerful teaching tool appropriate for many common pedagogical purposes. In particular, teacher-led discussions can be usefully employed to scaffold students' appropriation of foundational and expert understandings and resources.

To the extent that a teacher's thoughts and language exist in a living relationship with thoughts and language that students understand and find relevant or interesting, students are likely to appropriate the intellectual resources a teacher offers. This condition, of course, is a challenging one—one that is likely to be met unevenly even among the students of a single classroom. When scaffolding students' learning of foundational and expert understandings, teachers must therefore bear in mind that all knowledge possesses a personal dimension—each of us learns about and comes to see even very basic tools and understandings in a somewhat distinctive manner.

The overall character of a learning community always influences the extent to which students are willing to involve themselves in the work of that community. In the case of teacher-led learning, students must feel engaged and safe enough to question and even challenge the teacher's understandings and lines of reasoning. Teachers, in turn, need to provide continual opportunities for students to represent their own emerging understandings in order to discern where those understandings have begun to connect and to overlap with the teacher's own.

CHAPTER FOUR

Student-Led Learning

The teacher-led and student-led forms together represent the two ends of the conceptual spectrum of interpretive authority distributions that we are considering here. In contrast to teacher-led learning, with which most of us are familiar from our own schooling, student-led learning remains uncommon in most schools even today. Yet this form of learning experience has been developed throughout the twentieth century, originally inspired by practitioners who sought to increase access to educational opportunities for the primarily Southern and Eastern European immigrants who were pouring into America's industrializing cities in the late nineteenth and early twentieth century.[1]

In student-led learning, students learn how to employ foundational cultural resources and methods in order to investigate and interpret the world. Here, the teacher's role is not to familiarize students with the established thinking of experts, but rather to enable students' meaningful participation in culturally established forms of knowledge building. Learning experiences are designed to invite and sustain a quality of intellectual engagement that in many ways mirrors the activity of professionals and scholars within a particular discipline or field. Students publish articles, investigate natural and mechanical phenomena, interpret art, derive mathematical algorithms, and study historical artifacts and documents.[2]

This parallel with mature disciplinary, multidisciplinary, and professional practice extends to the materials under consideration. Student-led learning experiences rely on students' exposure to and consideration of the same kinds of objects and phenomena that experts study and manipulate, although these are often adapted in some way in order to focus attention and to provide manageable levels of academic challenge. For example, elementary and secondary students would not generally be expected to identify significant historical artifacts themselves, but rather would be provided with a cluster of such artifacts designed to inspire observations, queries, and insights regarding a targeted area of study.[3]

Close attention to these materials in relation to a governing purpose or challenge provides the grounds upon which students themselves determine the relevance, validity, and import of each other's observations, queries, and claims. For example, in my research, students faced with the challenge of understanding a novel were continually referred back to the novel itself. Rather than frame interpretive issues and evaluate interpretive possibilities as in teacher-led learning, the teachers of the student-led discussions supported students' work by eliciting students' thoughts and confusions and strategically introducing the types of challenges and clarifying queries that characterize literary scholarship within the adult world.

Literary interpretation may seem a particularly good fit for student-led and co-led learning experiences due to its arguably more open-ended interpretive aims even among scholars.[4] As noted in the last chapter, many language arts teachers have long argued that elementary and secondary students need to be invited into a direct engagement with the complexities of textual interpretation on multiple pedagogical grounds.[5] In many schools, humanities teachers have historically experienced more freedom to encourage student reflection and collaborative meaning-making than their counterparts in the math and science departments.[6]

Yet significant aspects of all content areas can be effectively taught through any of the three pedagogical forms. Students of all ages can uncover mathematical and physical regularities and conduct biological research, as has been emphasized by Piagetian learning theory. Indeed, many American educators and psychologists first read Piaget after his close colleague Bärbel Inhelder attended the Woods Hole Conference convened as part of a broader national response to the Soviet Union's launch of the Sputnik satellite into space.[7] This response resulted in the development of considerable federally funded curricula that placed students in the role of young scientists.[8]

Although most content can be taught through any of the three forms of learning experience, students' *relationships* to that content will vary, depending on the nature of the learning experience. Successful student-led learning experiences create conditions within which students are able to develop deeper and more personal relationships with the curricular content, which is always represented in the form of a challenge paired with some type of proving ground against which the students themselves can test their ideas. In asking students to interpret the world themselves, teachers empower students to locate personally meaningful points of entry into that material proving ground. And by allowing student-framed questions and issues to remain open for ongoing peer debate and deliberation, teachers can help to set the stage for sustained student curiosity and inquiry.

Student-led discussions and learning experiences are therefore particularly well suited for exploring conceptually central issues, matters students may find particularly intriguing, challenging, or controversial, and material that causes students to respond in ways a teacher does not understand.[9] In all of these cases, learning experiences that focus entirely upon revealing and advancing *student* understandings provide teachers with greater clarity and perspective regarding students' ways of approaching and making sense of the material and encourage students to cultivate a heightened sensitivity to the intellectual implications of the object or phenomenon of study.[10]

Many people today use the term 'inquiry-based instruction' to refer to learning experiences that include opportunities for student investigation and discovery.[11] The current call for inquiry-based curricula is based upon well-established findings that all learners need to be active participants in their own learning. Yet students can be invited to explore aspects of the world to different ends and to varying extents. One must consider *who* is constructing *which* content understandings and on *what basis* in order to evaluate the character of the learning experiences that have been made available through inquiry-based lessons.

For even in many 'activity-based' lessons, children reenact scripted investigations in order to arrive at anticipated conclusions—certainly by the time they enter middle school.[12] This sort of lesson might be designed in order to demonstrate the material grounds for historically significant theories and ideas. While such classroom activities can be pedagogically valuable, any lesson that is designed to teach students about established theories or lines of thought (or that is enacted to this end) would not classify as student-led learning. Students participating in such lessons are not invited to reflect at length upon their unanticipated observations or ideas or to pursue original lines of reflection and exploration.

In student-led lessons, students construct understandings themselves by pursuing investigations that are framed by their own observations, questions, and theories. In mathematical and scientific investigations, students may well achieve a compelling consensus as a group, though generally not before they have had to consider matters from any number of angles. Although literary and historical scholarship generally remains more open to diverse interpretation, a broad consensus regarding particular interpretive questions might also emerge. In cases when this does not occur, students are left to explain and justify their own perspectives.

Pedagogical Aims and Means

In student-led learning experiences, students' relationships with a phenomenon or object of study are intended to be as direct and unmitigated as possible. The teacher's role is to ensure that students observe carefully, articulate their thinking clearly, reference relevant evidence continually, and attend and respond to their peers' questions, observations, claims, and arguments. Students then learn both about the matter being studied and about the character of different types of knowledge construction processes through their efforts to enact those processes.

The nature of these processes will vary in some ways, depending upon the disciplinary, multidisciplinary, or practical context: literary interpretation, historical research, artistic expression, mathematical reasoning, and scientific discovery all possess their own languages and methods. These disciplinary contexts also vary from the kinds of knowledge building students would need to undertake to organize a school garden, for example, or learn to repair cars. Yet across all of these contexts, the teacher in a student-led learning experience helps to keep students focused upon the organizing challenge, the proving ground(s) at hand, and the contributions of their fellow students.

Opening and sustaining meaningful student-led inquiries within any area requires that a teacher possess a number of capacities that are not as essential to the successful enactment of teacher-led learning experiences. Yet these very capacities can also inform teacher-led learning and, importantly, can help a teacher to link different forms of learning experiences effectively in the service of expanding students' intellectual authority. For example, student interests and quandaries that arise during student-led learning experiences can lead to focused teacher-led learning experiences. As will be discussed in chapter five, this dynamic movement between student and teacher understandings takes place within a more condensed timeframe during co-led learning experiences.

As Cazden points out in her discussion of what she terms 'non-traditional lessons,' teachers who undertake student-led and co-led learning experiences need to have developed a personally meaningful relationship with the content they are teaching. Of course, within *any* form of learning experience, the greater the teacher's comfort with the content being taught, the more able the teacher will be to pick up on student insights and confusions and either to revoice these thoughts or to respond to them in the students' own language and conceptual terms. In contrast, teachers who rely heavily upon the authority of their teacher textbooks are forced to employ content, framings, and sequences conceived elsewhere, leaving them less able to respond sensitively and creatively to their students' thinking.[13]

While never ideal, a teacher's tentative grasp of content can pose greater challenges during student-led and co-led learning experiences, which require that teachers be able to locate and pursue conceptually significant student observations and questions *in the students' terms*. Feeling confident with a subject area generally makes it easier—intellectually and emotionally—for a teacher to view the material they are teaching through a student's eyes. Conceptual leaps into the minds of one's students require a cognitive agility that can only come with sustained interest in a subject area and a curiosity regarding the thinking of others.

Although more challenging in some ways than teacher-led learning, student-led learning experiences reward teachers with generous opportunities to build new insights and understandings.

Cynthia Ballenger, a scholar who has taught Haitian preschool and elementary school students for many years, has written eloquently of the personal growth and learning to which her devoted attention to the meanings of her students has reliably led.[14] Ballenger's work continuously evokes the sense of delight she experiences when learning something new about her content area or about her own assumptions and perspective as she seeks to view the world through her students' sharply observant eyes.[15]

In a tribute to the personal importance of Lisa Delpit's book, *Other People's Children*, to her own journey as a teacher, Ballenger titled her 1999 book *Teaching Other People's Children: Literacy and Learning in a Bilingual Classroom*. Ballenger's book rests within a growing collection of work that addresses the ways in which students' culturally divergent perspectives and resources can blind teachers to the intellectual strengths and capacities their students bring with them to school. Along with others who work in this area, Ballenger emphasizes that teachers need to learn how to learn from and about their students through their daily interactions with them.[16] Most of what a teacher needs to know about his or her students simply cannot be learned from others: authentic interpersonal understanding must always be constructed on the ground.

Ballenger was a founding member of the Brookline Teacher Researcher Seminar, which began in 1989. The members of this seminar were all interested in opening up new kinds of interactions and investigations in their classrooms, particularly in situations that these teachers had come to view as problematic in some way. Michaels and O'Connor, the two scholars who introduced the participant framework lens to classroom research, soon joined the seminar, strategically contributing their expertise in response to the emerging methodological needs of the group.

In their introduction to a book that recounts this work, Ann Phillips and Karen Gallas spoke of six "values and practices" that seminar participants had constructed together and come to share.[17] I review these briefly below as related 'values and practices' are often claimed among practitioners who strive, as these teachers have, to position their students' understandings and meaning-making as central to the ongoing construction of knowledge in their classrooms.[18]

- **Silence**—To listen more and more sensitively to the thoughts of students, teachers need to say less. This, in turn, means that teachers need to accustom themselves to verbal hesitations and silences of various lengths.

- **Stopping Time**—Members of the group came to appreciate the power of classroom transcripts to 'stop time,' allowing a teacher to revisit and consider isolated moments of practice at length and in an iterative manner.

- **Exploratory Talk**—Intended, in the words of Phillips and Gallas, "to develop knowledge, not to display what the speaker already knows," exploratory talk is fundamental to all genuinely collaborative constructions of meaning.[19]

- **The Puzzling Event**—A term the group coined for a moment of practice that "is amazing, doesn't make sense, or wasn't predicted from our past experience."

- **Valuing Confusion**—Uncertainty always accompanies the construction of new understandings and conceptual frames. Group members came to embrace confusion as integral to the process of original knowledge creation.

- **Big Ideas**—Group members also came to value the power of any number of established theoretical constructs, ranging from work on narrative to sociocultural theory, to inform and extend their practice-based insights.

As this list suggests, student-led and co-led learning experiences rely on the willingness of a teacher to suspend judgment and to listen to students with care. While a teacher's content knowledge continues to organize the pedagogical encounter, the aim of the encounter is no longer that students come to view particular content in approximately the same way that the teacher does. Rather, the teacher strives to understand the meanings that students are constructing, positioning the teacher as learner in relation to how students are thinking and what students know.

Many of these same themes are also treated in Eleanor Duckworth's books on attending to the thinking of children, particularly the value of silence, puzzlement, and confusion.[20] As noted in chapter two, Duckworth has adapted a method of Piagetian learning research called 'critical exploration' into a pedagogical method, which Duckworth calls 'critical exploration in the classroom.'[21] As Piaget himself did, Duckworth has stressed that the required quality of listening can only be learned through extended experience and reflection.[22]

Over the years, Duckworth's teaching and writings have inspired many teachers to integrate more distributed forms of knowledge construction into various types of learning environments. This group includes two of the participants in my study, both of whom studied with Duckworth as graduate students: Grace, whose work is discussed below, and Malcolm, who employed co-led interpretation and whose work is therefore discussed in the next chapter.[23]

In contrast to Ballenger, Duckworth has not specifically treated the ways in which cultural differences can limit teacher/student understanding in classrooms. Given that critical exploration originated as a tool for developmental learning research, Duckworth began by focusing primarily on how her training might help her reveal and study children's developmentally distinctive thinking in the context of curriculum development work such as the Elementary Science Study curriculum and the African Primary Science Program.[24]

Later, as a professor of graduate students at the Harvard Graduate School of Education, Duckworth created opportunities for her adult students to grapple with the considerable individual variety uncovered during critical explorations conducted in class and then again as her students turned to teaching those same learning experiences to others outside of class. Duckworth's work with critical exploration provides a well-developed example of the student-led learning experience: materials and challenges are provided, and students must endeavor—perhaps individually for a while, but then eventually as a group—to make sense of some aspect of the world. Duckworth has characterized her organizing convictions about human growth and learning in these terms:

That is the fundamental point. The way to move a person's thoughts and feelings is not by trying to excise them and replace them with other thoughts and feelings. Rather, it is to try to *understand* the person's thoughts and feelings, and to work from there. It means having the person articulate his or her own thoughts in different areas and in different ways and see where they run into conflict with themselves. That usually means acknowledging complexity rather than replacing one simple way of looking at things with another simple way of looking at things—acknowledging the complexity and seeing where that leads.[25]

Due to Duckworth's studied respect for and attention to all students' existing conceptual framing, critical exploration opens opportunities for appreciating not only learners' developing understandings, but also the mix of individual, developmental, and cultural influences that have shaped those understandings. In practical terms, Duckworth's broad interest in the character and conceptual bases of individual intellectual variety—whether her students are making sense of poetry, permutations, the reflections of mirrors, or the movements of the moon—moves toward subsuming cultural difference within the broader category of human difference, deemphasizing potential cultural barriers while still actively addressing all barriers that *any* type of intellectual difference can present to interpersonal understanding. While cultural differences should never be ignored and may, from time to time, emerge as focal issues, locating these differences within the broader context of human diversity as a general matter helps to teach children not only to recognize and respect cultural influences, but also to see beyond them.[26]

As in all student-led learning, the pedagogical dynamic of a critical exploration relies on engaging students with some rich content and then building upon their observations, ideas, queries, and confusions. To sustain students' curiosity and interest, particularly in a large classroom setting, a teacher needs to know something about the various kinds of questions that a given challenge is likely to raise and have ideas about how to continue the investigation in whichever of those directions students gravitate toward. The teacher continuously strives to fuel and extend original student insights, ideas, and investigations.

Student-led learning experiences therefore provide continual opportunities for teachers to see both their students and the content they are teaching in new ways. In a student-led learning experience, teachers are only and always striving to open up and complicate student thinking rather than attempting to align student thinking with their own. In practice, this means that discussions may range into unexpected places and that a broader cross-section of students may find something useful and relevant to say. Indeed, students who—again, for whatever reasons—do not as readily follow and appreciate the teacher's reasoning can even emerge as discussion leaders when they are encouraged to follow the train of their own and their classmates' thinking.

Duckworth presents a number of additional arguments for including student-led learning experiences within democratic class-rooms. The heart of the work might be characterized as empowering students to value their own ideas as the necessary beginning of all knowledge and to understand that, with careful observation, sustained study, and unprejudiced attention to the thoughts of others, they can and will come to know aspects of the world on their own authority. As work with student-led learning has also repeatedly demonstrated, students who come to recognize and value themselves as intellectual agents and authorities tend to treasure the learning communities that made such self-knowledge and self-possession possible.

The art and craft of orchestrating a pedagogically powerful student-led learning experience lie in selecting a generative and reliable proving ground *and* in asking the right questions both to begin and as the investigation unfolds. The proving ground must provide students with a reliable basis upon which to test their ideas and theories about the organizing challenge. The organizing challenge must be conceptually rich and provide the right level of intellectual challenge. Subsequent teacher queries need to connect directly and sensitively to students' emerging thoughts.

For example, Duckworth has begun critical explorations with the simple question 'what do you notice?' As Duckworth points out, every student can be fairly expected to find *something* to notice about an interesting work, object, or phenomenon. To encourage broad participation, Duckworth may choose to hear at least one unadorned observation from everyone in the room before allowing any students to offer more complex theories and interpretations. As the learning experience continues, teacher questions are intended to point students into interesting and confused corners of their own thinking and to support students' efforts to articulate the connections they have begun to sense between their own thoughts, the work, object, or phenomenon, and what other students have said. Duckworth, for example, often simply asks her students to 'tell her more' about the thoughts they share.[27]

Turning Matters Over to the Students

Of the six participant teachers in my research, two employed student-led interpretation during the discussions I recorded, Grace and Yale. The novel under discussion in Grace's room was Erich Maria Remarque's *All Quiet on the Western Front*; in Yale's room, students discussed F. Scott Fitzgerald's *The Great Gatsby*. Yale's classroom was one of three participant classrooms that discussed *The Great Gatsby* during the data collection period. (Each teacher chose both the classroom and the book discussion that I observed.)

Both Grace and Yale taught in the school that terms its pedagogy 'student-centered.' Grace had also studied with Eleanor Duckworth in the 1980s after a number of years in the classroom and since then has considered Duckworth's work a central pedagogical influence. The discussions led by the third teacher from this school, Frances, were classified as co-led and so will be treated in chapter five along with those of Malcolm, who had also studied with Duckworth, and the sixth teacher, Jay, who taught with Randy at the school that identified its pedagogical approach as 'traditional liberal arts.'

Interpretive Structure

Below, Grace can be seen beginning her class the way she began each of the class periods I observed. Students had filtered in and begun writing in their reading journals (which Grace does not collect or read) about the previous night's reading. This excerpt begins after about eight minutes of silent writing, with Grace's direction to her students to finish the sentence that they are working on. On some days, Grace might ask a particular student who has not said much in a while whether he or she would like to begin. This morning, Molly volunteers to start the discussion.

Excerpt 4a

Grace: *And* finish your sentence. [20 sec] *And* where shall we start?

Molly: Can we start it from "Mother" where we like, left [xxx]--

Todd: Do you know what page?

Molly: It's right at the end of, it starts like at 182, I think. [4 sec]

Grace: Read to us Molly, and then start us.

Molly: Okay, well it's like a really long par--

Grace: That's okay. We like it.

Molly: Okay, I'll start at the top of page 183. Is that okay? [Note: Grace nods.] All right.

> Ah, Mother, Mother! You still think I am a child—why can I not put my head in your lap and weep? Why have I always to be strong and self-controlled? I would like to weep and be comforted too, indeed I am little more than a child; in the wardrobe still hang short, boy's trousers—it is such a little time ago, why is it over?
>
> "Where we are there aren't any women, Mother." I say as calmly as I can.
>
> "And be very careful at the front, Paul."
>
> Ah, Mother, Mother! Why do I not take you in my arms and die with you. What poor wretches we are!
>
> "Yes, Mother, I will."
>
> "I will pray for you every day, Paul."
>
> Ah! Mother, Mother! Let us rise up and go out, back through the years, where the burden of all this misery lies on us no more, back to you and me alone, Mother!
>
> "Perhaps you can get a job that is not so dangerous."
>
> "Yes, Mother, perhaps I can get into the cook house, that can easily be done."
>
> "You do it then, and if the others say anything—"
>
> "That won't worry me, Mother—"

Okay, so that's like, the main, like, part, and it kind of goes on, but—

Todd: It sounds pretty poetic when it, with the, 'Oh Mother, Mother.'

Art: Yeah. [Note: others students also nod or mumble concurrence.]

Todd: It kind of has like a little rhythm to it. …

Molly: But I thought it was kind of ironic how he was like being so childlike, and he even says that he's nothing more than a child. But then at the beginning, we were saying that, he's not, youth, you were saying [turning to Todd] that they're not youth anymore.

Todd: The thing is, would you even want to be a child? There's like that whole loss of innocence thing. That it wasn't really his choice to go become a man, killing people. He's kind of forced into that role through politics, and just, and just through authority, like Kantorek.

Molly's interest in what a specific passage from the previous night's reading suggests about the protagonist's conflicted coming of age has opened the class; a similar type of student question or issue always began discussion in this room. In the second classroom with student-led discussions, Yale varied the way in which he opened class on different days. He began one day's discussion, for example, by reading a single line of text and asking the students what they thought it might portend for future plot developments.

Excerpt 4b
Yale: That's an *honest* line at the end isn't it? **So we drove on toward death through the cooling twilight.** Not sure I like that. … Who would be your candidate for an [xxxx]? [Note: end of sentence unintelligible, but based on the conversation that ensues it means something like 'early death.']

Ali: Gatsby, because I think that Tom is feeling so violent.

Though Yale's opening query only briefly frames the day's discussion, Yale has set the class down a particular path of inquiry, in contrast to Grace, who passed on responsibility for the day's first question to her students. In his second chosen transcript, Yale read a list of student questions that he had asked the students to write the previous class period and had then collected at the end of that discussion. Although some of the questions had been treated in the previous day's conversation, many of them had not. In the excerpt below, we come in at the end of a much longer list.

Excerpt 4c

Yale: ... Why would a man like Gatsby take an interest in Nick? What did Gatsby enjoy talking about at the party? What happened to Gatsby? Why did Gatsby tell Miss Baker to tell Nick about the thing? Why doesn't Gatsby just tell Nick? Is Miss Baker supposed to tell him? What big favor will Gatsby ask Nick to do? Why is Gatsby so set apart from everyone else? Why is he a loner? What is Gatsby's occupation? Why do different cities *always* want him on the phone? Well we can, ah, some of those may be answered, some of those may, never be. We read to page 107. Where do we want to begin with all of this or any of this? [17 sec]

Linda: Why, do, you guys think that, Gatsby had to tell Jordan to tell Nick about his past with Daisy? Why couldn't he just come out and tell, Nick himself? Why did he have to have like a little messenger there? [6 sec] I mean, Nick even asked him that--

Neither of Yale's opening moves charges students with the responsibility of generating a beginning themselves from the previous night's reading the way Grace's standard opening move does. Yet both can be seen to focus the students' attention on some aspect of their personal relationship with the text. In the first case, the students are asked to notice an ominous line from the previous night's reading and to speculate as to what it might mean. In the second case, they are asked to revisit questions they had generated in class the previous day. Yale's opening moves, then, were somewhat less open ended than those of Grace, who simply asked that the students engage the text in some manner.

Both Grace and Yale then looked to their students to frame the discussion for the remainder of the period and to evaluate the interpretive possibilities they generated as they went. As we will see, both teachers sought to make as few framing moves as possible and generally asked closed questions only when it seemed as though students needed to be brought back on track in regards to the basic action of the book or pertinent details of a particular scene or, at one point, the correct use of a literary term.

Just as Wells and others have distinguished between different types of follow-up move within the IRF sequence, I found that the Framing, Developing, and Evaluating move categories also broke down into a number of recurring move types that were employed in different ways and to different effects in the six classrooms. The manner in which some of these move types were employed appeared linked to the distribution of interpretive authority between teacher and students. At other times, the use of these move types appeared to reflect unrelated aspects of the teachers' approach.

Although these sub-codes emerged from a small set of transcripts and so remain preliminary, I will introduce some of these codes in this chapter in order to discuss a few discourse patterns that did appear to support the orchestration of more distributed forms of knowledge construction.[28] For example, students cannot rule upon or even assume they fully understand another student's ideas in the same way that a teacher often will in a teacher-led discussion. Nor can teachers play this role in student-led learning without risking that their students will begin relying on them to help construct content understandings.

Instead, both teachers and students in the student-led and co-led discussions asked speakers to clarify what they meant or asked speakers to justify their claims with evidence more often, moves I call Clarifying and Challenging, respectively. The queried speakers would then either attempt to explain more about what they meant or to justify their claims with further reasoning or evidence, moves I call Explaining and Justifying, respectively.

Paired 'Clarifying and Explaining' and 'Challenging and Justifying' exchanges appeared in all of the student-led and co-led discussions and were particularly common in certain classrooms. It may be that students had learned to ask for clarifications and evidence from watching their teachers do so. This would parallel a finding of O'Connor and Michaels in their work on revoicing: over time, students began to align their own contributions with the group discussion in some of the same ways their teachers had, for example, by placing their thoughts into relationship with those of another student.[29]

In the following coded excerpt, Grace employs a Clarifying move to slow down the conversation and elicit the students' consideration of the deeper motivations that might be operating for the novel's protagonist. As in the last chapter, where I coded Randy's elaborations on students' contributions, I also code such elaborations here. In these classrooms, though, such Elaborating moves are all offered by students. I have also broken down evaluating moves into

Ratifying and Countering moves, depending on the valence of the evaluation, and introduce the Summarizing move at the excerpt's end, in which a speaker seeks to summarize some shared understanding that the group is developing.

Excerpt 4d

Todd: He's very reserved cause, he's like the soldier, like the classic image being the *strong man*, fighting for, like, the nation. And so he kind of, he doesn't want to, put his emotional burdens on his mother. And when his, when like his mother asks him, *how* is like war, is it bad out there, he basically lies, oh, it's not that bad. Like, he doesn't want to put the burdens on his mother, and how *he's* suffering just cause he knows that his mother will suffer with him, just knowing that he's suffering. ELABORATING

Lily: You see that several times too. It's not just his mother. Anytime anyone asks him about, like what really is happening at the war, he denies it. He says, no, it's not so bad. ELABORATING [Note: Mica is nodding.]

Mica: Kemmerich's mother— ELABORATING

Lily: Yeah, *especially* with Kemmerich's mother. [Note: Mica, Todd, and Molly all nod.] RATIFYING

Grace: And I, I just need some clarification. What, what are you guys thinking is, what are his reasons for not, being able to tell, or not being *willing* to tell them? I don't know whether it's not being able or not being *willing* either. CLARIFYING

Todd: I think it's a combination cause, no matter how hard he tries to describe it, with words, he *cannot convey* what actually goes on out there. Like, to a certain point, adjectives, do not, you know, convey the message. And it's basically a waste of his pre-- like emotional strength, describing his suffering. Like, he's not willing to do that. And there's no … *that suffering* is not worth the gain that the people get. Like, sure, they just hear the story, but, ah, they're like okay, good job, thanks for being patriotic for us. But, it's kind of like Kantorek and his father as being the patriotic guy, that, you're not really comprehending the suffering. They just kind of read it through the news. EXPLAINING

Sean: And there's, he probably doesn't want their sympathy, um, cause even though he probably is, maybe consciously, maybe subconsciously, trying to keep up that, uh, war hero image of don't feel sorry for me, I'm, up there, I'm, doing work for my country and I'm loving it. So, he doesn't want them to feel sorry for him. And it's also probably one of those things where, when somebody says, "How's your day?" you automatically say, "Fine." And like, uh, "What's up?" "Nothing." [Note: Grace laughs.] So, I mean, you

automatically just, you don't want to tell everybody your problems. ...
EXPLAINING/ELABORATING

Molly: On page 181, when he was telling Kemmerich's mom, and she like didn't believe that he died like instantly. He, he says, um, like he would never tell her because to him, it's just, he's just *dead*. It doesn't really matter, how he died. So, um, he, I don't think, he's like really trying to, hold up the image of like the *greatest* -- I don't know, it's hard to explain, my point. But, um, he, he doesn't like explain it to her, because he like feels bad for her. But he also, he doesn't explain it to her just because, he doesn't really think it *matters*, so why should she know? Like, to him, it's just *dying*. EXPLAINING/ELABORATING

Todd: Yes, he's dead, and, describing how he's, how he *died* isn't going to change anything. SUMMARIZING/RATIFYING

Molly: Yeah. RATIFYING

Clarifying moves ask for the repetition or further development of another speaker's prior turn. Although these two purposes may seem readily distinguishable, in practice they often are not. As observed in the transcripts and confirmed in the second round interviews, a teacher's request to hear a student's contribution again may actually be motivated by a desire to have a student's peers attend more closely to what has been said. Other times, a more specific request for elaboration may originate in a simple lack of clarity regarding the claim that has been made. Though Clarifying moves can serve several ends, they always, like revoicing moves, return the floor to the queried speaker(s) and provide an opportunity for the student(s) to elaborate on their thoughts.

In providing a dedicated space for the development of an under-articulated or confused thought, Clarifying moves can elicit cycles of student analysis and explanation as seen above. Students may also choose to employ this move for a number of reasons. In the absence of feeling moved to make one's own claim, for example, a student interested in sustaining the conversation (whether from a sense of interest or responsibility) can always ask for further clarification or elaboration from someone who has already taken the floor.

Left to generate lines of literary inquiry on their own, Grace's students continually wove their thoughts into each other's prior contributions, nudging the topic toward new but conceptually related areas of consideration. In this particular classroom, that meant that student Elaborating moves, which generally imply ratification of the prior contribution, dominated the evaluative structure. A single student's confusion or observation would evolve into an organizing issue for the entire group through the elaborations and replies of other students, who interacted with the topic through the lenses of their own concerns and understandings. Occasionally, one of the students would feel moved to counter some aspect of a previous claim, but generally students focused on areas of mutual concern that everyone seemed to recognize as complex and therefore not amenable to clear and straightforward answers.

Classroom discourse analysts Neil Mercer and Karen Littleton, who have operationalized and studied Barne's notion of 'exploratory talk,' distinguish both largely uncritical knowledge building, which they term 'cumulative talk,' and contentious argument, which they term 'disputational talk,' from the construct of exploratory talk.[30] Mercer and Littleton argue that cumulative talk often fails to make reasoning visible or to hold discussants accountable for their claims and that disputational talk results in limited learning as discussants do not bother to investigate the potential worth of each other's contributions.

Interestingly, Grace's class seemed to lean toward generating cumulative interpretive lines, while, as we see below, Yale's students seemed more prone toward argumentation. In either case, teachers of student-led learning experiences must support students' movement toward an active consideration of contrasting interpretive possibilities. At the same time, it is important to recognize that extended episodes of student concurrence and elaboration or of pitched verbal repartee *can* provide the conditions for meaningful student learning, assuming that these are ultimately integrated into more complex and probing interpretive processes. Indeed, cumulative and disputational talk could be usefully conceived of as interactional sub-types within the broader category of exploratory talk.

In the following excerpt from Yale's classroom, the students seem genuinely invested in working through the issue before them. Here the students engage in one of their frequent lively debates, this time on the morality of Jay Gatsby's clearly expressed interest in Daisy, who is married. While the mood is somewhat disputational, the students' Countering, Justifying, Clarifying, and Explaining moves gradually carry the conversation forward. Like Challenging moves, Countering moves generally elicit Justifying moves, as they express a speaker's disagreement with another's idea or claim.

Framing moves have also been broken down into Inviting moves, which invite students' interpretations of the novel and Questioning moves, which ask a closed question. Inviting moves generally pair, at least initially, with Interpreting moves; Questioning moves generally pair with Answering moves.

Excerpt 4e

Steve: Well, I don't think it's wrong because, well like Tom is cheating on *her*. JUSTIFYING

Kelly: But two wrongs don't make a right. [Note: Linda starts speaking over Kelly, agreeing with her.] COUNTERING

Linda: Well, yeah, that doesn't make it right, like morally. That's, it's still -- ELABORATING

Steve: Like morally, like there's, there's not a relationship between them. COUNTERING

Kelly: Yeah, but it's forming. JUSTIFYING

Linda: *I* would have done it. I'm not saying, they, shouldn't have done it, but it's still, I still think that it's wrong for someone's friend to, have a, like little, tea party for two people who he *knows*, were in love at one point and, like it's *implied* that, Gatsby's, um, intentions could be to, you know, win her back. ELABORATING

Kelly: Wait, you think *Nick* is in the wrong? Or you think Daisy -- CLARIFYING

Linda: I think, *everything* is. I don't really think Nick is, I think he was kind of pulled into this. But, I think that the whole *scenario*, is wrong. I, I don't think it's as wrong as Tom cheating on Daisy but I, still think it's, there are aspects that are, not right. MODIFYING/EXPLAINING

Steve: Well I think that it's more dangerous than wrong. COUNTERING

Linda: Than what? CLARIFYING

Steve: I don't think it's wrong, actually, but I think it's dangerous cause, like, Tom hit that woman who is like 'Daisy, Daisy, Daisy,' and, I don't know what he would do to someone who was, like, setting something up for a girlfriend. MODIFYING/EXPLAINING

Yale: What is that woman's name? QUESTIONING

Several students: [Note: students confer unintelligibly a moment until a few get it.] Miss Wilks? ANSWERING

These students' Countering and Clarifying moves position the previous speaker as valuable in that his or her contribution is acknowledged and taken into account in relation to the ongoing construction of shared understandings. Minimally, these moves evidence a responsible attention to the propositional content of the previously stated claim; beyond that, they can also demonstrate a genuine concern for the integrity of the interpretive process. Such moves therefore evidence a valuable kind of intellectual agency on the part of the students who employ them: by Countering and Clarifying the contributions of others, these students position themselves as keepers of the overall quality and coherence of the discussion.

By providing an opportunity for the repair for tentative, under-articulated, and inadequately supported claims, Countering and Clarifying moves also arguably offer a greater sense of interpretive security to those willing to offer a spontaneous thought or to steer the conversation into a new direction. As we will see below, in modeling such moves in a respectful fashion, teachers can help to encourage students to attend thoughtfully to each other's contributions and to take the implications of other's thinking seriously.

Although Grace and Yale did not offer interpretations of their own or evaluate the interpretive possibilities of their students, neither did they allow incoherent or unsubstantiated reasoning to stand. Should their students neglect to challenge questionable claims, these teachers reliably stepped in to do so themselves. In the process, a number of other discursive standards were also upheld, such as when Yale asks his students above to identify the character they were discussing by name.

Grace initiated only one IRF sequence in the two periods transcribed: during a pause in the conversation, she asked whether students recalled how the author had described the voices of the Russian soldiers when they were singing. Yale, in contrast, more commonly employed truncated IRF sequences in which he provided no feedback, but simply, as in the case of the character's name above, asked closed questions in order to get all of his students thinking in a specific way about some relevant aspect of the novel.[31]

Participant Frameworks

Qualities of Attention–The tone was consistently serious in Yale's classroom (though students could become quite animated when some contentious issue surfaced as we saw above). Here, Linda and Ali respond to Yale's question about whether everyone agrees with a classmate's characterization of Gatsby as arrogant. Three turns later, Yale asks Ali to clarify her use of the term 'confident.' Seven turns after that, he asks the entire class whether they would like to continue the exploration that Allen and Cliff had begun into Daisy's deeper state of mind during the scene under discussion.

> **Excerpt 4f**
>
> **Yale**: Do we agree that he is arrogant, Gatsby?
>
> **Linda**: I don't think that *arrogant*, is the right word because I think that, well, I mean I don't think it's like a *snooty* arrogance I guess, because it's kind of like he's been, it's understandable because he has been waiting, for so long for this moment to impress this girl, um, that he's in love with and, I just think for him to want everything to be *perfect*, shouldn't really be considered arrogant.
>
> **Ali:** Yeah, and it's like he is not being arrogant, it's not like he needs to go around showing everyone, it's just like he wants to impress this one girl and like, he thinks that this is part of the way of doing it is. ... He's confident.
>
> **Linda:** Yeah, and like part of being arrogant is thinking that you have, that everything is perfect and you *have*, like all these really nice things, but everything was *not* perfect for him until, *she* was happy with it. Or until *she*, smiled and said she liked it.
>
> **Yale:** Would you like to define your word confident for us Ali?
>
> **Ali:** Well, I mean when I think of *arrogant*, I think of it, in a bad way. Like, if you're arrogant then you're *overly* confident and, kind of cocky. And I think he's, just confident that like, I mean, it's like less *extreme*, kind of, I don't know.
>
> **Steve:** But do you think showing him, ah, showing Daisy, like, his shirts, that would be over the top of confident?
>
> **Ali:** I don't know, that part, um, it's kind of like what Linda was saying that arrogance is too *strong*, kind of. ... I don't really know how to explain it.

Ken: Maybe that he's, well that he is kind of, he's, like, confident in himself, but that he's not, he's not arrogant in the way that he's not trying to, make others, not like condescend, not trying to make others feel bad, he's just confident of himself.

Cliff: I don't think that he is confident at all, though. Because, when he first meets her, he gets all nervous, and he *almost* goes *home*. And then Nick convinces him to stay. I think that he's just really nervous. I don't think he was confident. …

Ken: I get the, I don't know, I get the feeling when I read on page 98 about, um, how she was, Daisy was crying, about the shirts, that, I mean, it seems like that, I mean she, it seems like a kind of a stupid thing to cry about, and that, I'm sure, I think that there's, there might be something, maybe *more* that she's, I don't know, that she's suggesting, that. And the shirts are just … I mean, maybe just like, if you picture that, if you imagine like someone just going up and just like starting sobbing saying, that these are such beautiful shirts. Like you would think that maybe that's, like an excuse, that maybe she is crying about something else and that, she's just using the shirts as, you know, the excuse. And that, I don't know maybe, I'm just like, guessing, that, I don't know.

Cliff: Yeah, I agree with that. I think, it's been a really emotional day for her. She was crying before they went to her house, and I think she was just, caught up in her emotions. I don't think she was crying about the shirts either.

Yale: Do we want to *speculate* about what we think is going on here? What level she's operating out of?

Yale's first two questions represent two classic kinds of teacher move in a student-led discussion: Clarifying, which we have discussed, and Checking-In, which throws the floor open so that students who have not spoken can weigh in on some matter. This Clarifying move asks, 'What do you mean when you use that term?' and this Checking-In move asks, 'Does everyone agree?' These two queries, which can also be employed by teachers in other forms of learning experiences, are designed to demand a clearer articulation of students' ideas and to place students into relationship with each other's ideas, respectively. Here, Yale has employed them to complicate students' understandings of the terms 'arrogant' and 'confident' and so deepen his students' consideration of the protagonist's personality and character.

That the students have spoken for seven uninterrupted turns, Ken at length, is not unusual in this classroom and attests to Yale's frequently articulated commitment to placing students' thinking at the center of the interpretive process in his classroom. As in Grace's classroom, the students here seem to feel in charge of the interpretive process; everyone has learned not to bother glancing over to see how the teacher is going to respond.

Unlike his first two Checking-In and Clarifying moves, Yale's final turn feels charged with implications that are not entirely transparent. For one thing, Ken and Cliff *had* begun a consideration of Daisy's deeper feelings. Yale's question, with its emphasis on the word 'speculate' could be interpreted to suggest that the class was not moving surely enough in this direction. Also, the question 'what level is she operating out of?' presents a conceptual leap from Ken's and Cliff's shared sense that something more complicated is happening for Daisy. Though both students have expressed their interest in this topic, they may not have conceptualized the matter as a question of psychological levels, possibly leaving them at a momentary loss as to how to respond. Ken does, however, return to the topic again several turns later.

Yale's final question also serves as a kind of framing move: it suggests a line of inquiry by asking students whether they *want* to speculate on something they may now sense is important to Yale, given the nature of his question. Yale's question, then, presents a third possible confusion. Does Yale truly mean to ask about whether they are curious about this, or does he mean to suggest this as the obvious direction in which to take the conversation at this point?

Though such an analysis may seem overwrought, particularly based solely on a brief transcript excerpt, the phrasing of teacher comments and questions carries great weight in student-led discussions. One could even argue that phrasing is more at issue than in a teacher-led discussion, given that students do not receive much teacher feedback and so must rely upon a more limited set of cues regarding how the teacher feels the conversation is going.

Students will generally also need continual reassurances that the investigations underway are truly and entirely in their hands. While Yale's opening Inviting move in excerpt 4b regarding who might be 'driving on toward death' could well have been offered and received in the spirit of simply getting the discussion rolling, his question about whether students want to speculate on "what's going on here" cannot be interpreted as entirely casual.

Students also need other types of sensitive support and encouragement before they are likely to collaborate openly with their peers. Below, Grace seeks to expand one of her student's thoughts that had not received substantive play. The student, Allen, has opened a new topic, and two of his classmates have responded, but not with the metaphorical readings he was seeking. Grace asks Allen to elaborate on the metaphor he seeks and then, when his courage seems to fail towards the end, asks him to repeat his final line more loudly. When six seconds pass in silence, Grace engages him again, revoicing his thought to give it a larger presence in the discussion and to ensure that she has understood him correctly. Having drawn him out on the matter, Grace turns back to Allen's classmates and asks them to respond to his idea once again.

Excerpt 4g

Allen: This is *slightly* off topic, but on page 164, when I was reading this, um, it's at the very beginning of our reading, I found this, what I think is this pretty interesting metaphor. **The glass is half empty, but there are a few good swigs ahead of me, and besides I can always order a second and third, if I wish to**. I just, it was, the first thing that caught me was, how he uses, you know like there's always that, is the glass half full or half empty? And it's, he uses half empty. **But there are still a few good swigs ahead of me.** And the one thing I was confused about, um, is when he says, if this actually is a metaphor, **besides I can always order a second and third, if I wish to.** What does he really mean by that?

Art: I think like, I think it's said like he has *time* to, you know? He has the luxury to now, because he's not at the front.

Allen: Uh-huh. …

Art: I think that's what it means.

Todd: Cause at the front they had these limited rations and that's all you got. It's like he's actually knowing that yeah, I had this much food. But there's always more. It's kind of that *thought's* so *different*.

Art: Yeah.

Grace: Allen, if, if that, if that image struck you, that *moment* struck you as metaphoric, I think it would be interesting to hear, what it, what it *raised* for you.

Allen: Well, it almost, to me, it was just like, at least the first half of the sentence really related, um, in my mind to, his, like his struggle in the war, and like just trying to stay alive. The, the glass is half, half empty, so he's, he's being drained by the war. It's not doing anything for him, but more taking away from him. But there's still a few good swigs ahead of me. So he knows that, his time isn't, isn't over yet. There's still, he still has … I don't know, he still has some time before, before he thinks he might die. [Note: Allen's voice becomes quite soft at the end of this sentence.]

Grace: Before he what?

Allen: Thinks, I don't know, the war will finally, take his life. [6sec]

Grace: So he, so … this feels to you like a kind of, um … what, *appraisal* of his life circumstance?

Allen: I think so. That's, that's what I thought.

Grace: Yeah. What do you guys think about that? Does that work for *anybody* else?

After this last question from Grace, Molly agrees that the glass being half empty could be metaphorical, and Rob remembers another scene in which Paul swears that if what he is telling is a lie (which it is), he will not come home from the war alive. The class begins to discuss whether the author is providing intimations of Paul's eventual death. Allen's topic has been pursued, though no one returns to his original question about how the phrase, "I can always order a second and third if I wish to," might work as part of his metaphor. By taking the time to unpack the implications of Allen's contribution, Grace has positioned Allen as a valued colleague and made the level of her interest in the nuances of his contribution clear.

The content, phrasing, and context of a teacher's questions and remarks reveal a great deal about the quality of attention given to students' thinking in a classroom. What does the content of a teacher's questions suggest about his or her purposes? What do the phrasing and context of the questions suggest about the mood in which they have been asked? Might the question sound frustrated to some? Might it sound tired? Might it seem to express genuine intellectual curiosity about how a given student understands the world? Though it may not be possible to code reliably in response to such questions, the emotional undertone of a teacher's words and gestures influences the quality of student learning to an extent that cannot be ignored—certainly not in any consideration of intellectual authority and agency in a classroom.

Boundary Tending–Yale occasionally stepped in and framed textual explorations in response to students' apparent lack of direction or momentum without always specifying his reasons for doing so. These brief teacher-led episodes seemed to suggest that his students required his assistance from time to time to get the conversation back on track. Yet in situations where Yale's purposes and method were not made entirely clear, the topic could drift a bit uncertainly, as seen below.

> *Excerpt 4h*
>
> **Michael:** What does it mean that he is a regular tough?
>
> **Yale:** What page are you on?
>
> **Michael:** Ah, 84, that quote. [8 sec]
>
> **David:** Well, like I think that I can see, um, an example of how he is a regular tough. After, after, at the end of like, his and Daisy's meeting in his house, when he sort of opens up, and becomes more comfortable and confident in himself, like you see in the beginning that he is nervous and, it says he was pale and kind of trembling and stuff. But later on as he becomes more comfortable you see his other side--
>
> **Michael:** So like, so like tough means comfortable?
>
> **David:** No like, more confident. Like he became comfortable with talking to Daisy, because it wasn't as awkward. And we see a different side of him, that, came out afterward. [7 sec]
>
> **Yale:** Well, let's, ah, go back to the bottom of page, 83. Why don't you, ah, start right there. Someone can read, **"It was a strange coincidence,"** I said. Who wants to start reading right there?
>
> **Linda:** I will.
>
> **Yale:** Go ahead.
>
> **Linda:** **"It was a strange coincidence,"** I said. **"But it wasn't a coincidence at all."**
>
> **Yale:** Do we know what the coincidence is?

Ali: Gatsby buying a house across the bay from Daisy?

Yale: Go ahead. [Note: Direction to Linda to continue reading.]

Linda: "It was a strange coincidence," I said.
"But it wasn't a coincidence at all."
"Why not?"
"Gatsby bought that house so that Daisy would be just across the bay."
Then it had not been merely the stars to which he had aspired on that June night. He came alive to me, delivered suddenly from the womb of his purposeless splendor.
"He wants to know--" continued Jordan "--if you'll invite Daisy to your house some afternoon and then let him come over."
The modesty of the demand shook me. He had waited five years and bought a mansion where he dispensed starlight to casual moths so that he could "come over" some afternoon to a stranger's garden.
"Did I have to know all this before he could ask such a little thing?"
"He is afraid. He's waited so long. He thought you might be offended. You see, he is a regular tough underneath it all."
Something worried me.
"Why didn't he ask you to arrange a meeting?"
"He wants her to see his house," she explained. "And your house is right next door."
"Oh!"
"I think he half expected her to wander into one of his parties, some night," went on Jordan, but she never did. Then he began asking people casually if they knew her, and I was the first one he found. It was that night he sent for me at his dance, and you should have heard the elaborate way he worked up to it. Of course, I immediately suggested a luncheon in New York -- and I thought he'd go mad.
"'I don't want to do anything out of the way!' he kept saying, 'I want to see her right next door.'"
"When I said you were a particular friend of Tom's, he started to abandon the whole idea. He doesn't know very much about Tom, though he says he's read a Chicago paper for years just on the chance of catching a glimpse of Daisy's name."

Yale: Okay, thanks a lot. Anything you want to say about that?

Ken: Well I think this is interesting because it answers all the questions about why, or I think that it answers all the questions about why he's, throwing all the parties, and um, I mean just for the chance to see, just for the chance to see, um, like hope, and hopes that Daisy would come one time. I mean that maybe if she lives across the bay, and sees these parties going on all the time, she's going to maybe, wander over there. And I think it's interesting, there's a line on page 83, **He came alive to me, delivered suddenly from the womb of his purposeless splendor.** So, I mean, that Nick finally realizes, he understands, he understands *why*. I mean everything, it seems like everything, Gatsby does, or I mean, I don't want to say *everything*, but a lot, a lot of what he does might be, *hopefully* to impress Daisy. [18 sec]

Linda: Do you also think that he is afraid that she's, um, she's, maybe, not *forgotten* him but, isn't holding on, to the feelings that she had for him and that he has for her? And he wants to be in a casual spot, in case, that happens? Like close to home like he can *drop in*, or that he can drop in to Nick's house, or kind of be in his house when she gets there and then, he can kind of have an *out* because he is so close. By not making it a formal thing? [Note: Allen nods.]

Yale: [7 sec] What else do we find out there? [15 sec]

Ken: That also maybe the reason why he is always so isolated is that, at those parties, he's just, he's looking for one person. And … he is looking for just that one person, but, they're never there. So he's always, he just separates himself, because, I guess maybe like the, the party would just become, a *worthless* expense of his time.

Linda: And we also find out that, um, *that night* it says, um **Then it had not been merely the stars to which he had aspired on the June night**, on page 83. That night when he was on the *dock*, he was probably looking at Daisy's house, or, something like that. Because isn't *that* where the water is, where the bay is?

Yale has apparently asked for this passage to be read because it contains the line "You see, he is a regular tough underneath it all," which had prompted Michael's question. One might imagine that he was not satisfied with David's explanation of the line, or perhaps he was responding to a lingering sense of doubt from Michael. For whatever reason, he asks for the entire paragraph to be read and then asks, "Anything you want to say about that?" Ken treats central meanings in the paragraph without returning to Michael's question. Eighteen seconds after he finishes, Linda adds a thought about what Gatsby might be feeling as he waits for Daisy to arrive at one of his parties. Seven seconds later, Yale asks, "What else do we find out there?" After fifteen seconds, Ken and Linda again offer thoughts on the paragraph but still do not return to the line about Gatsby being "a regular tough." After Linda's remark, the conversation moves on.

As observer to this exchange, I found myself wondering whether Yale had been looking for a student to voice a specific thought, particularly after the second time he asked "What else do we find out there?" I was not sure whether, if so, this would have related to Michael's question, to which no one had returned, or whether Yale simply felt that the passage merited a closer look. In this context, it is also important to note that Yale's direction for someone to read the passage could be credibly interpreted to cast doubt on David's explanation of the line in question, particularly given Yale's tendency to take students to the text in moments of confusion. The issue is then left open.

More generally, Yale keeps everyone's attention on a particular paragraph without framing a specific issue, a move that could be interpreted in several ways, one of which is that Yale wants his students to notice something that nobody has yet noticed. Yale has temporarily altered the group's rules of engagement, which hold students responsible for framing the course of the literary inquiry, and then seems to hesitate to explain his reasons for doing so, leaving his students at least momentarily absorbed with the question of what those intentions might be.

In the following excerpt, Grace interrupts two students. First, she stops Allen from continuing with his question to the class about what may have caused the change that Allen perceives to have taken place in Paul, the protagonist, to ask whether everyone agrees with Allen's assumption that Paul has changed. Her next move, which interrupts Mica's question to the class, asks Mica to explain what she understands about what Todd had just referred to as Paul's 'clarity.' In her third turn, Grace pushes again on the issue of Paul's 'change' or 'clarity.'

Excerpt 4i

Allen: I think it's really amazing to see the ah, the *change* that's happened and that he's, like after going home, he's lost that numbness that we've been talking about so much. Um, there's a passage on 223. Actually, Aliza read, um, one or two lines from it before **The silence spreads. I talk and must talk. So I speak to him and say to him: "Comrade, I did not want to kill you. If you jumped in here again, I would not do it, if you would be**

sensible, too. But you were only an idea to me before, an abstraction that lived in my mind and called forth its appropriate response. It was that abstraction I stabbed. But now, for the first time, I see you are a man like me. I thought of your hand grenades, of your bayonet, of your rifle; now I see your wife and your face and our fellowship. Forgive me, comrade. We always see it too late. Why do they never tell us that you are poor devils just like us, that your mothers are just as anxious as ours, and that we have the same fear of death, and the same dying and the same agony. Forgive me, comrade. How could you be enemy? If we threw away these rifles and this uniform you could be my brother just like Kat and Albert. Take twenty years of my life, comrade, and stand up -- take more, for I do not know what I can even attempt to do with it now.

Um, so, he, he talks to him, basically, he's, he's calling this person his 'comrade' that, he, looks, like even on the page before he's um, he's *wondering* what his wife was like and looking, looking into his life. And he really sympathizes with him and makes the relationship between him, um, Paul and the soldier, that their *mothers* are both as worried and they're forced in the same situation. And I'm wondering what, what do we think? I mean like it's obvious that, after coming back from his home, that there's this change that is happening, but what do we think, exactly, was it that caused this all to happen? ... Like, can we, uh, relate it back to—

Grace: Are we in agreement with Allen that there is a change in Paul when he comes back? [Note: Several murmur agreement.]

Todd: I don't know if it's a change. I think it's just clarity. Like on 201, um, it says, **I can hardly control myself any longer. But it will soon be all right again back here with Kat and Albert. This is where I belong.** Just kind of that, absence, kind of, he didn't really *belong*. He wasn't really fitting with normal society he kind of *belonged* on the front lines, this. They kind of find it now, the soldier, just as a person.

Lily: I think part of it is also, yeah I think part of it is the clarity, maybe. And another thing is that he is now, I think he's, it's just realization of a lot of things. Like, I think going back home makes him realize that even if he's seen so many things, he *does* want to have some sort of a life. Which there's a, there's a, a, paragraph, I'm not sure what page it's on, *but* he did say that he wants to have that, but at the same time, he doesn't quite feel like he belongs in, in a regular society anymore. And I think that also being home, where things have not changed that much, and it's a comfort to him. Then he goes back to the front. It's like the *fear* has become paralyzing again, maybe similar to how it might have been when he first started, coming to the front.

Mica: Do you really think he would have, um, made this, you know, this change, would he have, come to this clarity, or started to think about things in this way had he not gone home? Like would it have happened eventually? Or was it just—

Grace: I'm, I'm still a little muddy about what the clarity is. Are you, Mica?

Mica: Well, um, we talked about, Todd and Allen talked about, he is starting to think about what's going on, and, um, he related that to when he went home and he had come to think about it a little bit. And so do we think that, I'm having a hard time with this question. Do we think that he would have come to this eventually anyways? Or if it was only because he went home that he started to think about what was going on and--

Todd: Well, I think it cleared his thoughts. I think he has to go home as a comparison. Just standing through the war he said, oh, I hate it here. Then like, then leaving it, he then remembers, like he realizes what like *Albert* meant to him, and he just kind of, he knew that they had that special bond with Kat and things, but I think he really emphasized when he came back, saying, wow, I really miss you guys, and you guys would have died without me.

Mica: Do you think the leave was an important trigger, for bringing back emotions and things?

Grace: And so, so, is he clear-- is his clarity limited to, clarity about where he belongs, his, his camaraderie, the importance of his camaraderie with those men? …

Emma: I don't think so.

Lily: Then why does he say … [xxx] and that?

Emma: Because his clarity isn't in his *thoughts* about war right now, because he was thinking about it and he got *lost*, so—

Lily: I'm not sure, well, I was saying that, though clarity might be part of it, but it also could trigger other things in him, because what I *did* notice is he is scared again. He's, really, really paralyzingly scared again, and we see that.

Todd: I think that's when he starts thinking about death.

Lily: Yeah.

Todd: That's what he always avoided, and now he's suddenly thinking about death. Like going home-- I think that was part of that trigger-- like watching his mother suffering. He has that new emotional *guilt* that is now kind of pestering him.

Art: It made him soft.

Grace's insistence that her students more clearly say what they mean by 'change' and 'clarity' sets a tone of academic seriousness in this exchange. Grace repeats her question several times in different ways. She starts with a Checking-In move, which asks, 'Does everyone agree?' Her second question begins to suggest the level of her interest in having the nature of Paul's change thoroughly explored. Hearing that Mica is ready to move on with a question about the role Paul's return home has played in inspiring this new clarity, Grace tries to interest Mica in previous question by asking whether Mica shares her lack of clarity on that point. Grace positions herself as a confused conversant, requiring a few extra moments of everyone's time.

Mica does not seem inclined to give them to her. She responds with one vague sentence, "Well, um, we talked about, Todd and Allen talked about, he is starting to think about what's going on, and, um, he related that to when he went home and he had come to think about it a little bit" and returns to her question, which Todd addresses. Todd's explanation, though, makes it even clearer that the students are speaking about different dimensions of Paul's feelings, and so Grace asks whether what Todd had just said was what everyone else had also meant. Finally, the complex nature of Paul's emotional state has been thrown open as a topic.

As one can see in this excerpt, Grace at times felt the need to intervene in order to clarify whether her students agreed with each other as much as they seemed to think they did. In this example, she asked that everyone articulate more precisely their own under-standings of the character's inner experience. The demand is a challenging one, and as Mica's response to Grace's request suggests, at least one of her students would have preferred to move on. In the end, though, Grace's insistence that her students express their own visions of the protagonist's feelings served to bring contrasting visions of those feelings to the floor.

Similarly, Grace asked her students to work harder at under-standing Allen's question in excerpt 4g. Though Allen's classmates seemed initially disinclined to see intimations of the protagonist's eventual death in a half-empty glass of beer, in struggling with Grace to appreciate Allen's perspective, Rob recalled another possible intimation of that death. Had the author intended either of these? The question is not asked and, in any event, could not be answered with certainty. These students' thoughts remain possibilities to hold in mind as the interpretive work continues.

Through their persistent probing of their students' thinking, Grace and Yale demonstrate that, for them, interpreting a novel together means that people must query each other closely, sometimes repeatedly, and suspend judgment in order to hear what others have to say. It appeared as though many of their students had taken on some of their discursive habits—possibly to make the conversation work in the way their teachers intended or perhaps because those students had also come to find certain of their teachers' discursive moves useful, even possibly engaging.

Opportunities for Learning

Grace and Yale do not introduce interpretive issues, arguments, or claims; nor do they evaluate their students' ideas. Instead, they conceive of their role as one of nurturing and maintaining a scholarly quality of interpretive process—one that is well reasoned, that elicits and entertains thoughts from all students, and that pursues sustainable interpretations of the text's larger meanings through repeated close readings of the text itself. Students are called upon to sharpen and so deepen their thinking and to place their views into relationship with those of their peers, thereby complicating their observations and broadening their theoretical perspectives.

Because only students' thoughts and ideas are available in a student-led discussion, student thinking needs to be taken very seriously. When a classmate is speaking, no part of another student's field of attention is waiting to hear what the teacher will have to say on the topic. Grace's and Yale's students know their teacher will offer few clues as to the contribution's worth; they will have to determine that for themselves. Student claims therefore will often need to be Clarified and Challenged before other class members will willingly integrate them into their own evolving interpretations of the text.

In student-led learning experiences, a student is therefore likely to feel more part of a collective effort to make sense than to feel an individual responsibility to provide it. The lack of teacher evaluation in student-led learning shifts student attention from the goal of imagining what the teacher is looking for based on the character of the teacher's questions and comments to constructing convincing and illuminating possibilities in collaboration with one's peers. Students thereby experience the intellectual rewards and challenges of closely considering a given work, object, or phenomenon of study and of exploring the convergences and divergences between their own and their peers' approach to making meaning.

Again, Piagetian learning theory emphasizes the value of this type of peer discussion for promoting conceptual shifts and realignments. A student who does not feel prepared to answer a teacher's question fully or to challenge a teacher's claim may feel able to expound a bit in response to a peer's query or tentative thought. Students of all ages and all levels of expertise will often also find their classmates' ideas more approachable and engaging than those of the teacher as these ideas will tend to be less resolved and closer in character to their own.

When successful, this continual unearthing of student thoughts and insights generates a rich diversity of interpretive possibility. As we have seen, in order to create such interpretive complexity, teachers will often need to encourage students to query and explore the nuances of their peers' observations and claims. In supporting their students' efforts to place canonical artifacts, such as classic works of literature, into relationship with their own observations and questions, teachers create an intellectual environment within which such artifacts are more likely to become personally meaningful to a greater number of their students. Foundational tools of disciplinary knowledge construction also tend to become more personally meaningful when students are invited to employ those tools in order to understand aspects of the world in their own ways.

By supporting students in uncovering the logic of their own and their peers' reasoning, teachers also teach students to value intellectual transparency, which supports the development of their intellectual authority. Given that any person's organizing conceptual frameworks can only be reconfigured, never entirely replaced, such efforts provide students with valuable opportunities to discern and reconsider the conceptual framing with which they understand and make sense of the world.

Loosening one's hold on one's existing ideas in order to understand anything in a new way can feel uncomfortable for several reasons, one being that the process typically begins with some sense of irreconcilable confusion. A certain quality of interpersonal dynamic is therefore required before students are likely to undertake this kind of learning in a classroom setting. Particularly with secondary students, who have learned to get by in schools when they choose and who can replicate a great deal of language without necessarily understanding it, teachers have to apply themselves if they have their sights set on extending and deepening their students' worldviews.

As can be seen, Grace and Yale approached aspects of their roles somewhat differently. Although they both avoided framing interpretive issues and evaluating interpretive possibilities, a closer look at excerpts of their classroom transcripts reveals differences of tone and content between the two classrooms. We will return to some of these differences at greater length in chapter six when we will be able to compare and contrast the practices of all six participant teachers.

Summary

In student-led negotiations of meaning, students frame their own questions, develop and test their own ideas and propositions, and accept and reject the meanings of others based upon the evidence and reasoning presented as they understand these. They modify their positions, and they influence the positions of others. This is the essential work of any negotiation of meaning, and student-led learning is no different than other collaborative negotiations of meaning in these ways.

To the extent that students master the various challenges of a student-led literary discussion, they learn to identify significant passages, issues, and recurring themes by paying close attention to the text and to the thinking of their classmates. They learn that they and their classmates read novels in different ways and that the novel's text sometimes can and sometimes cannot be seen to support their divergent readings. In cooperatively inhabiting a space dedicated to open knowledge construction, students are also challenged to learn from each other, leading to understandings about how to endure and eventually live constructively with the complexity and uncertainty that characterize collaborative knowledge construction. These lessons are learned as functions of the pedagogical format: if the discussion works, students have learned how to manage largely on their own.

Many educators have come to believe that student-led learning experiences can meaningfully reorganize students' relationships to school learning, leading to more equitable and intellectually generative classroom dynamics. Yet orchestrating student-led learning experiences demands more from a teacher than some observers may realize. Teachers who have not been exposed to this pedagogical form through their own experience as students or within their professional studies can have trouble imagining how to make such an experience work at all, let alone work well.

For it is only by nurturing a sense of intellectual poise and interpersonal interest among the members of one's classroom that one can generate a high quality of intellectual engagement among peers. Shared understandings can only be built when students believe that their teacher and other classroom members are authentically attending to their ideas. Teachers must also assure their students that they will not be abandoned in the midst of an incoherent or partially formed contribution, but that others will support them, if need be, in their efforts to sort out and articulate what they are trying to say.

So significant a transformation of traditional teacher and student roles can only develop with time and study. As with any socially established set of behaviors and guidelines, pedagogical discourse patterns must be learned, and new patterns can feel challenging, perhaps even threatening to some, until classroom members have had a chance to become familiar with them. Professional collaborations and professional development programs can lend invaluable support to teachers who have begun to explore new forms of knowledge construction within their classrooms.

Many teachers seeking to move in this direction may feel more comfortable, at least initially, with co-led learning experiences in which teachers and students share responsibility for framing central issues and questions and for evaluating the ideas and theories that are offered in response to those inquiries. As we will see in the next chapter, co-led learning experiences also provide those interested in distributed knowledge construction processes with a distinctive set of pedagogical possibilities and challenges.

CHAPTER FIVE

Co-Led Learning

In co-led learning experiences, teachers and students work together across all three stages of the knowledge construction process. Rather than only framing an initial challenge, as in student-led learning, the teachers of co-led learning experiences often continue to frame interpretive issues and may also further develop and evaluate student ideas from time to time. Rather than centering most of the discussion on issues that the teacher has framed, as in teacher-led learning, the teachers of co-led learning experiences look to their students to locate many of the matters the class will investigate and to weigh in on the interpretive possibilities that have been generated by their peers.

Co-led learning experiences therefore need to provide students with intellectually generative challenges and with sufficient conceptual and material resources with which to engage those challenges, just as in student-led learning. In co-led learning, teachers work with these challenges and materials alongside their students, scaffolding the collaborative knowledge construction process in response to their students' interests and confusions. Teacher expertise may also be introduced at key junctures in the course of the collaboration.

Rather than positioning students as young scientists or literary scholars, co-led learning experiences position students more as apprentices within the context of a shared cultural enterprise. At times, students may prove able to pursue matters themselves unaided; at other times, students may seek or require explicit instruction or demonstration. Although the extent of teacher direction can vary greatly in co-led learning experiences, the teacher tends to hover near the helm, ready to jump in and steer the course of a conversation or investigation for some period whenever this seems pedagogically valuable.

Much of the contemporary work on creating more dialogic or distributed knowledge construction processes in classrooms would classify as enactments of co-led learning. Many teachers are likely to feel most comfortable with this form, which grants significant interpretive authority to *both* teachers and students. As the pedagogical approach that comprises the vast conceptual middle between the teacher-led and student-led forms, co-led learning is also the most fluid and flexible approach to thinking about one's role as a teacher.

As we have seen, in student-led learning, students are entrusted with the responsibility for framing the group's lines of inquiry and for evaluating their own thoughts and ideas. Grace, who employs student-led learning exclusively during interpretive discussions of literature, mentioned that a couple of colleagues at another school had characterized her practice as "not really teaching." Indeed, discerning the role played by a teacher in student-led learning can be challenging for some, even more so once a group of students has been successfully acculturated to the form. The aim of student-led learning, after all, is to teach students how to construct understandings on their own authority.

In contrast, observers of co-led learning experiences are likely to have little trouble recognizing that teaching is taking place. Yet uninitiated observers may find that co-led discussions feel overly long and roundabout in relation to the amount of "content covered." These differing perspectives can be explained by the differing conceptualizations of pedagogical content involved. Educators who recognize the value of co-led and student-led learning experiences conceptualize content as including experiences with academic ways of thinking and interacting. Rather than primarily sharing and explaining established understandings, these teachers insist that students develop a more practiced relationship with the work and methods of a field.

As I have argued, democratically minded teachers need continually to strive to apprehend their students' current ways of making sense of the world, while also challenging their students to understand and to act upon the world in new ways. Although the balance between these two aspects of the pedagogical relation shifts depending on the nature of the learning experience, both types of awareness always remain in play. When accomplished teachers listen to student ideas, they do so through the lens of what they are hoping their students will learn. When accomplished teachers challenge their students to appropriate new perspectives and material, they seek to meet their students' thoughts and questions in terms their students can appreciate.

This dialectic movement between teacher knowledge and student knowledge becomes most evident and active within co-led learning experiences. Here, teachers navigate what can, at times, feel like unstable ground between the role of group expert on the one hand and fellow learner on the other. The success of a co-led learning experience therefore depends to a considerable extent on how clear a teacher feels about when and why to assume which role and the degree of intellectual and social agility the teacher is able to bring to shifting between the two.

Pedagogical Aims and Means

Magdalene Lampert, a scholar of mathematics education, has long investigated the look and feel of this quality of pedagogical relationship within primary schools and has written probingly of the purposes, challenges, and rewards of this form of learning experience. Lampert speaks of pursuing two agendas simultaneously: supporting her students in appropriating foundational and expert content understandings in mathematics[1] and teaching them how to participate in mathematical discourse. Lampert terms these two sets of understandings "knowledge *of* mathematics, or mathematical content" and "knowledge *about* mathematics, or mathematical practice." Along with other educators who consistently prioritize both types of goals, Lampert emphatically views these two sets of purposes as intertwined.[2]

In one of her considered reflections on the commitments that move her as an educator, Lampert cites Lakatos and Polya, two mathematical scholars, both of whom speak of the intellectual courage and modesty or 'wise restraint' that the practice of mathematical thought requires. Lakatos calls for mathematics teachers to encourage thoughtful speculation as a means of teaching and celebrating the virtues of courage and modesty; Polya places honesty among the "moral qualities" mathematics demands. As Lampert puts it:

From the standpoint of the person doing mathematics, making a conjecture (or what Lakatos call a "conscious guess") is taking a risk; it requires the admission that one's assumptions are open to revision, that one's insights may have been limited, that one's conclusions may have been inappropriate. Although possibly garnering recognition for inventiveness, letting other interested persons in on one's conjectures increases personal vulnerability. Courage and modesty are appropriate to participation in mathematical activity because truth remains tentative, even as the proof of a conjecture evolves.[3]

Lampert notes that neither of the scholars she cites suggests that such personal attributes come readily to professional mathematicians or are commonly achieved. Grown scholars frequently fail to live up to the personal standards Lakatos and Polya propose for their field. Lampert also often discusses her developed appreciation of the complex challenges involved in establishing collaborative classroom discourse capable of fostering honest, courageous, and modest mathematical thought. Yet Lampert's teaching and research have convincingly demonstrated that such values can indeed be taught, even to young children, within a broad range of public school settings.[4]

As Lampert has explained, teachers need to begin by shifting from a stance of 'telling and explaining' to one of 'challenging, demonstrating, and proving.' This shift allows students to experience the look and the feel of mathematical practice as enacted by their teacher as a prelude to participating in mathematical practices themselves. Students are positioned more as interlocutors than as listeners. All claims, whether of the teacher or a student, are supported with evidence and reasoning. This move to *convincing*, rather than simply *telling*, requires that teachers learn how to track their "students' arguments as they wander around in various mathematical terrain and muster evidence as appropriate to support or challenge their assertions, and then support students as they attempt to do the same thing with one another's assertions."[5]

Lampert also talks about the need to provide her students with "structured problems requiring productive thinking."[6] The classroom discussion is then organized by both the character of the problem and the character of her students' intellectual engagements with that problem. Lampert teaches her students to employ the terms 'conditions,' 'conjectures,' and 'revisions,' in lieu of 'answers,' which are either 'right' or 'wrong.' As Lampert characterizes her purposes for students' work:

> Students would make conjectures, I would put them all on the board, and we would discuss them, clarifying the conditions that the person who made the conjecture was assuming, and figuring out as a class which of the conjectures "made sense."[7]

The balance Lampert strikes between teacher and student understandings would seem to suit the work of the upper elementary mathematics classrooms in which she has taught. As can be heard above, Lampert strives to create a discursive space in which she and her students can engage in the practice of mathematical thinking together. Content understandings are then generated through this collaborative effort to interpret the world in mathematical terms.

In addition to considering her disciplinary aims thoughtfully, Lampert has also articulated her aims for her students' social learning. Through classroom anecdotes, Lampert has shared many of the targeted approaches she has designed in order to draw ambivalent, and even resistant, students into the intellectual culture of the classroom.

As Ballenger and other members of the Brookline Teacher Research Seminar have, Lampert speaks of the challenges such students pose as opportunities to rethink her understandings of her teaching and her subject matter. These educators all share a deep commitment to engaging every student and to helping every student grow, a commitment they view as fundamental to a fair and equitable classroom practice. By dramatically reimagining and redistributing the opportunities provided for students to share and to explore their thinking, all of these teachers have sought to upend traditional classroom hierarchies of student performance.

A Collaboration of Not-Quite Equals

As I have noted, of the six participant teachers in this research, two (Randy and Jay) taught in a school that characterized its pedagogy as 'traditional liberal arts,' and three (Yale, Frances, and Grace) taught in a school that considered its pedagogy 'student-centered.' Of this last group, Grace had also studied with Eleanor Duckworth prior to teaching in that school, as had the sixth teacher, Malcolm, who also worked at a private secondary school, but not one with as emphatic a position in relation to degree of "student-centeredness." Both Malcolm and Grace considered Duckworth's work a central influence on their pedagogical beliefs and practices.

It was interesting to see, then, that of these six teachers from these various backgrounds, Jay, a 'traditional liberal arts' teacher, Frances, a 'student-centered' teacher, and Malcolm, a student of Duckworth's, all conducted co-led discussions in their classrooms. This finding suggests that multiple factors influence the ways in which accomplished teachers approach their teaching (assuming they are granted a proper amount of professional autonomy). Again, grounded analyses of classroom discourse are therefore necessary in order to determine the distributions of interpretive authority actually enacted within different teaching practices.

Interpretive Structure

The opening sequences in Frances' two chosen class periods both reflect the balance Frances seeks to achieve between orienting her students in productive directions and opening the floor to their thinking. Opening sequences I observed included having the students write about the interpretive drawings Frances had assigned and having everyone (including Frances) write on a passage that Frances had chosen from two possibilities offered by the students that day. These initial activities tended to generate a lot of collective energy early in the class period. Students came in and would have something specific to focus on and discuss. Here Frances is opening the discussion of the interpretive drawings students had created of the final scene in *The Great Gatsby*.

> **Frances:** … All right, now, what I wanted you to do, ah, take a time out, with your pictures. Let's talk about what, first of all, what it was like to do this. And then what have you figured out? I mean here's Nick, the last scene of the book. He goes back to Gatsby's one more time and, before he does what? What's he gonna do? …

Below, Malcolm, who was teaching *The Sound and the Fury*, by William Faulkner, refers to a topic from the previous day's discussion and another from the previous night's reading. Then he then asks a closed question that pulls students into an engagement with the second of these strands. Malcolm generally began classes with this sort of broad mapping of themes for the day.

> **Malcolm:** Particularly, well, I would like to talk *more* about the relationships, among the characters, similarities and differences, um, that, that started percolating yesterday. And, um, then as you, begin reading, um, or perhaps have finished reading, the novel, ah, we can certainly back to, ah, it's one of the religious [xxx] because he's [xxx] and he also does go to church and hears a sermon about what?

In a similar fashion, Jay, the third to be teaching *The Great Gatsby*, tends to begin class with one or more thematically oriented invitations to interpret the text. In one of his transcripts, Jay asked his students to identify the major symbols of the novel. Below, he outlines three general interpretive strands for the day. Note that, unlike Malcolm, he does not end with a closed question, but leaves his invitation to the students to consider the book's end open. A student, Jimmy, accepts this invitation in the next turn, speaking at some length about his confusions regarding the end of the novel.

> **Jay:** … I'd love it if you just commented on, on, on the ending of the book. How you found the, ah, ending of the book. And then I want to go back to the line of, of a discussion that we started, down, yesterday. And then I have a few things that I'm going to suggest for a re-reading or the beginning of your reconsideration of the book for next Tuesday.

As in the last chapter, I will consider the principal ways in which the framing, developing, and evaluating phases of knowledge construction unfolded in these three classrooms, referring at times to the move types discussed there. I will also code two new types of move in this chapter: Acknowledging and Observing. The first marks a simple acknowledgement of what another person has said; the second offers an observation absent any explicitly interpretive angle. Directing, also shown below, is a teacher move that is not seen in the excerpts treated here; in these classrooms, Directing was typically used to direct students to refer to their books. Below I have outlined the place of all of the move types I have mentioned within the FDE structure. As perhaps will be seen, Acknowledging, Elaborating, and Modifying move types often function both to develop and evaluate to varying degrees.[8]

Framing: *Inviting, Questioning*

Developing: *Answering, Interpreting, Observing // Clarifying, Explaining, Challenging, Justifying // Directing, Checking In // Acknowledging, Elaborating, Modifying*

Evaluating: *Ratifying, Countering*

Once the day's discussion had begun, teachers and students in the co-led discussions employed Challenging and Countering moves in order to open up students' interpretive possibilities as in the student-led discussions. Both types of moves are employed frequently in the following coded excerpt from Frances' classroom. The turns have been numbered to facilitate the discussion that follows.

> ### Excerpt 5a
> 1   **Frances:** So that you're, you're going along with Rebecca's theory of renewal? CLARIFYING [Note: Rebecca nods though the question is not directed to her.] Where's the renewal part? CHALLENGING
>
> 2   **Linda:** In this, in this one it says, um, there are no renewals. Like, he gradually … **had gradually faded. And he had become simply the proprietor of the elaborate roadhouse next-door.** And I was connecting that with, um, the passage about, the city because I interpreted it as, the first time you cross over the bridge, you see this great big city. And you're so impressed. And you think about all the things it has to offer. But then you get in there and realize that it's, really not what you thought it would be. And that's what I sort of see Gatsby as. Like, he has this whole, um, like, um, *reputation* built around him. Like his house. His money. Everything. And then, when Nick was getting to know him, he said he really had nothing to say. … EXPLAINING
>
> 3   **Ana:** And in going along with that, on 69 it says, um **We hadn't reached West Egg Village before Gatsby began leaving his elegant sentences unfinished and slapping himself indecisively on the knee of his caramel-colored suit.** So he's kind of, he can put on like a big show, but … he can't really keep it up. EXPLAINING
>
> 4   **Eddy:** Why does he choke when he says, **Educated at Oxford**, down at the bottom of that page? CHALLENGING [5 sec]
>
> 5   **Rebecca:** Because Oxford is where his family is sort of at. Oxford has been in his family for so many generations. And then, he says that they died. And that's sort of like the past that that's been haunting him ever since. Just like the fact that all his family has died except for him. So I

guess it, he was, he was choking back on tears, I guess, because he was so overcome with *grief* when he mentioned that. JUSTIFYING

6   **Eddy:** It's his family? CLARIFYING/CHALLENGING

7   **Matt:** You think he made such an immediate connection though? Like just, like mentioning Oxford? CHALLENGING

8   **Bill:** You think it's too early even to ask you to think, this is real? Like, he actually went to Oxford and actually won, won that medal? CHALLENGING

9   **Rebecca:** We have a picture. JUSTIFYING

10 **Bill:** But still, if he's got that much money, I think he can fake a picture like that. COUNTERING

11 **Linda:** But it's 1922. Like, he can't really... COUNTERING

12 **Bill:** I mean, what do you do? You get some other people to dress up with a cricket bat, and take a picture. ... I was wondering-- COUNTERING

13 **Frances:** What, what makes you think that? I mean, there must be something else that gives you that idea, Bill. CHALLENGING

14 **Bill:** Well, effectively, he talks about, how like, how absurd his story sounds. JUSTIFYING

15 **Frances:** He who? He who? CLARIFYING

16 **Bill:** Nick. ANSWERING

17 **Frances:** Okay. ACKNOWLEDGING

In each of her first two turns, Frances makes a Challenging move, requesting further evidence for or justification of a student claim. Eddy's, Matt's, and Bill's first turns (6, 7, and 8) are also Challenging moves. Turns that directly oppose another's prior claim, such as student turns 10, 11, and 12, are coded as Countering moves. Both Challenging and Countering moves generally serve to return the floor to the previous speaker in these classrooms, giving that speaker a chance to justify his or her claim. On occasion, though, another student will speak up, offering an argument or textual evidence on the previous speaker's behalf. Unlike a Challenging move, which demands justification or explanation from someone, a Countering move can more easily be ignored or left for later, though in these classrooms, that rarely happened.

As in Yale's student-led discussions, student Challenging and Countering moves often set off extended sequences of uninterrupted student exchanges within the co-led discussions. The coded sequence below from Jay's room provides another example. Again, the novel under discussion is the *The Great Gatsby*, and the discussion centers on Gatsby's character, in this case, on his motivations for throwing his extravagant parties. The brief Acknowledging move Jay makes in the midst of Fredrick's contribution is characteristic of Jay's interactive style.

Excerpt 5b

Doug: I, I think that he wants people to appreciate him, and to love him because, um, he seeks out to be an icon because, you know, he's, he's in this world where there are these iconic figures of wealth and stuff. And he sees that people, uh, *like* these people, and they're *attracted* to them. And, you know, he wants to have these parties where people will just *flock* to him. And if you look back at the schedule, like Edger mentioned, you know there's that, that one *weird*, out of place comment about being better to his parents. And, um, maybe that's what he's looking for. To have better relationships with the people who are around him. And, and you know, he sees wealth and power as a way to achieve that. INTERPRETING

Jimmy: But it seems odd that, I mean, he *throws these parties*, and, and, which would give him an opportunity to, you know, build a relationship. Get *at* them. He just sort of stands and doesn't really take part. You never really see him. He doesn't really even *mingle*, you know, with people. He just sort of stands and watches over. I mean in that way, I guess, people build respect for him and like him. But never to the extent of, being able to even come to his funeral. COUNTERING

Doug: Yeah. ACKNOWLEDGING

Jimmy: So, I mean, I, I know he doesn't strike me as someone who's really just trying to build some sort of network of relationships with many people. He, he, strikes me more as the loner type, personally. ELABORATING

Fredrick: Well, he might still *want to* build relationships, but he just ... I mean, he, he never really worked on, being a people person. I mean, if you look at his list, it's all, it's all like, there's all this self-improvement on it. But I think about like ... he understands about like, practicing etiquette. And of course he learns this smile and gets people to like it. But he doesn't really like learn how to really talk with people very well. Like the first time they see Tom, he just sort of disappeared rather than talk, or anything like that. He sort of, he's, not really a people, a party person. He just sort of = UNFINISHED

Jay: Um-hmm. ACKNOWLEDGING

Fredrick: = stands around and hopes that they'll like him because of his, because he's having the party. Without really getting involved or, having a conversation with people. COUNTERING

Warren: Well he reveals later also that he was throwing the parties with the hope that Daisy = UNFINISHED

Edger: Right, yeah. RATIFYING

Warren: = would saunter in and he would be … and that's, that's almost, that's, ah, why I thought he was, standing up on the marble staircase looking over everything. You know, and if Daisy came in, make a beeline to her. It's, it's sort of like the parties are a way of getting Daisy, not a way of getting *friends,* necessarily. Because he doesn't seem to have a *need* for friends. You know. Nick is the closest friend he has, and that's-- COUNTERING

Fredrick: Um-hmm. ACKNOWLEDGING.

Don: Plus he goes around *asking* people at the parties if they know Daisy. I mean, he's not, he's not exactly like sitting back or anything, just kind of *waiting.* That's, they, they have a purpose. ELABORATING

Al: And he's only friends with Nick, because Nick's friends with Daisy. ELABORATING [Note: a couple of students start to object to this.] That's, that's not the *only* reason. MODIFYING

Jay: Initially, initially. MODIFYING/RATIFYING

The mood in Jay's room generally felt quiet and serious, very much like Grace's room in this way. Students often spoke at length without interruption. A moment or two might pass in silence before Jay would recognize the next speaker. Yet, as in Frances' and Yale's rooms, student Challenging and Countering moves serve to establish points of contention that then organize extended stretches of the conversation.

If a teacher does not choose to resolve such disagreements, students are forced to return to the referenced sections of the text. In the absence of a return to the shared object of study, such disagreements can take on a life of their own, distracting from deeper analyses. This might have happened, for example, in excerpt 5a had Frances not asked Bill to explain what was behind his repeated Challenging and Countering moves to Rebecca. Instead, in turn 13,

Frances employed a Challenging move to draw out the assumptions and understandings that were driving that exchange.

Three of Frances' four turns in that first excerpt also included a Clarifying move, in each case generating another pattern that commonly structured exchanges in all but the teacher-led discussions. As with Challenging and Countering moves, Clarifying moves work to investigate a student's previous contribution, opening it up in a manner that may then inspire subsequent debate.

In the following coded excerpt, for example, Jay uses a Clarifying move in his second turn to query and emphasize an interesting word choice a student has made in response to Jay's prior Inviting move. As with all Clarifying moves, this one requires an Explaining or Answering move, which the student first provides; Jay's move also provides an opening for the student Elaborating move that follows.

Excerpt 5c

Jay: How does the green, how does the green light, um, in *Gatsby's* mind, connect to what we were talking about yesterday? We started talking about the epigraph, and the, ah, Gatsby's attempt to, ah, to win Daisy back. ... INVITING

Don: Well ... well, ah I guess at the end of the book, they kind of seem to suggest that, ah, Fitzgerald seems to suggest like, kind of, the purpose of the green light in the book. And it's on like 189. It says, for he compares it to the Dutch sailors and how they, kind of, saw the, the green of the island, or, of the, oh yeah ... **a fresh green breast of the new world. Its vanished trees, the trees that had made way for Gatsby's house, had once pandered in whispers to the last and greatest of all human dreams**; Ah, I mean, that just kind of ... just kind of the ability to kind of *see* something, you know, kind of in an enchanted way and, just, he kind of-- INTERPRETING

Jay: Seen it in a *what* kind of way? CLARIFYING

Don: I think I might have ... UNFINISHED

Jay: No. It was good. I, I just wanted to be sure I heard it. RATIFYING

Don: Enchanted, I don't know. I kind of threw it out there. ANSWERING But, no, just, just in the way that the Dutch sailors, you know, came through, like, a new world. And, and kind of imagined what other people have not imagined to be *there*. Gatsby in the same way, um, you know, sees this green light as kind of the same thing, the, the new world that he wishes to, to go to. We talked about the [xxx]. How he tries to kind of elevate himself into

the upper class. And, you know, it kind of represents that in a way.
ELABORATING

In the excerpt below, a Clarifying move from Malcolm draws out a contribution that, as an aside spoken while the teacher was also speaking, would likely otherwise have been lost. Bethany's explanation of her toss-off comment touched off considerable debate about whether or not the father in Faulkner's *The Sound and the Fury* found any purpose in life. This discussion lasted for twenty-two student and teacher turns, becoming one of the primary interpretive strands of the class period.

> *Excerpt 5d*
> **Malcolm:** Um, yeah, both of them. Their graves are side by side. The father and Quentin. ANSWERING
>
> **Bethany:** [xx] great. [Note: Bethany has said this while Malcolm was still talking.] INTERPRETING
>
> **Malcolm:** Um … It's great that they are side by side? CLARIFYING
>
> **Bethany:** Yeah. ANSWERING
>
> **Malcolm:** What? CLARIFYING
>
> **Bethany:** Because they're, they're *really different* people, who kind of, died for the same reason, which is … not believing in the point of life anymore. EXPLAINING

In excerpt 5c, Jay asked a student to repeat a word, perhaps to make sure he had heard the word correctly, but certainly also to ensure that the rest of the class heard it as well. Jay's level of attention to his word choice then encouraged Don to elaborate on why he had chosen that word. In the excerpt above, Malcolm used a Clarifying move to highlight a contribution that, as an aside, could easily have been missed altogether. Clarifying moves, then, can accomplish a range of purposes; as a group they invite students to explain and elaborate upon their thinking.

In contrast to Grace and Yale, who avoided evaluating student interpretive possibilities or presenting any such possibilities of their own, teachers in the co-led discussions at times discussed their own interpretive perspectives and also evaluated some portion of their students' interpretive thinking. Across all three classrooms, the use of the IRF sequence was more common and less tentative than in the student-led discussions, although the IRF sequence was not employed to construct interpretive meanings as in Randy's teacher-led discussions. Below, Jay primarily employs the kind of modified IRF sequence that Yale used, with the final Ratification move dropped, to introduce plot details relevant to Tim's interpretation of Gatsby.

Excerpt 5e

Tim: Just again, on the last page about where it says, **Gatsby believed in the green light. The orgiastic future that year by year recedes before us. It eluded us then, but that's no matter. Tomorrow we will run faster.** Well, it seems that, although Nick's saying that, ah, the rest of the people are going to run faster to keep reaching for the future. But it seems that after Gatsby ... well, I mean, he, for the five years he finally gets back to Daisy. But then, after Tom reveals his inadequacies, and Daisy says that she loved Tom at one point. It seems that Gatsby *doesn't* keep reaching out even further. He kind of, he shuts everything down. He goes back and he, he kind of recedes. And it seems that there's that juxtaposition between people who aren't going to give up, and *Gatsby* who senses, senses defeat. And he loses some of his *gusto* for the mission, I guess. INTERPRETING

Jay: When? What's the chronology of that? I mean, how much time is there between ... this receding and his death? INVITING

Tim: I guess it's after ... it all happens pretty quickly I guess after, um, when they're in New York City and, he and Tom get in the argument. And then Tom and Daisy drive off. And, and then they drive back to Long Island. And then Daisy hits Myrtle. INTERPRETING

Jay: Tom. When does he drive off? QUESTIONING

Tim: Um, Daisy and Gatsby drive back. And, um, it just seems that, I guess that probably contributes to it too. ANSWERING

Jay: Then what happens? QUESTIONING Then, then ... that Daisy hits Myrtle? ANSWERING

Tim: Hits Myrtle. ANSWERING [Note: Tim says this at about the same time as Jay.]

Jay: Then what? QUESTIONING

Tim: Um, ah, [8 seconds] UNFINISHED

Warren: Everybody goes back to, their houses. And Gatsby waits in the trees to see if Tom is going to get mad at Daisy. And then she doesn't. So Gatsby goes home. And Nick goes over to Gatsby's house, and they stay up all night just talking. That's when Gatsby tells Nick about Dan Cody. And then,

Nick leaves after breakfast and Gatsby goes to the pool. And when he's in the pool, Wilson comes up and shoots him. ANSWERING

Jay: Um-hmm ... RATIFYING How long does Gatsby *stay* watching ... watching-- QUESTIONING

Mark: Only until, like, four a.m. [Note: several answer with him.] ANSWERING

Student: To see if she'll turn ... like switch on the light. ANSWERING

Don: Yeah. She comes over to the window and looks. And then turns on the light. ANSWERING

Jay: So what's the point at which you ... INVITING

Tim: I, I think you could make an argument that, at the point when she kind of turns off, when she turns off the light and turns away from him, that's kind of like the, a light inside of him turns off, one could say. And it seems kind of like he slinks away. In fact, the [xx] kind of, I wouldn't say sheepishly, but kind of defeated. Because, she was going to turn it on and off if she needed his help. And it seems she turns it off, and he's *resigned* to knowing that there's nothing for him to do then. So he just goes home. INTERPRETING

Below, Malcolm employs the full IRF sequence to introduce the facts of a recent news story that illustrates the legal use of the word 'insane.' This discussion occurs in response to a discussion presented below in excerpt 5h and continues the topic Eddy initiated there by expressing his belief that everyone in the Compson family from *The Sound and the Fury* is "pretty much clinically insane." Malcolm has pushed his students to clarify what they mean to suggest by using this term a couple of times by now. Here, near the end of the class period, Malcolm decides to introduce a legal frame of reference for the word. Malcolm also employs a rarely used move, 'Informing,' which conveys information external to the text and its meanings, and which we have not discussed previously.[9]

Excerpt 5f
Malcolm: Okay, um, so, let's see, you, I don't know, actually it was in the *news* recently, I don't know how much time you have to check the news, um, but you remember a, you might remember, a woman Andrea Yates? QUESTIONING

Several students: Yeah. ANSWERING

Malcolm: Okay, the woman who drowned her five kids in Houston.

INFORMING And um, she, was, what was her defense? QUESTIONING

Erica: She was insane. ANSWERING

Malcolm: She was *insane.* RATIFYING And, what did the court decide? QUESTIONING

Erica: That she wasn't insane. ANSWERING

Malcolm: That she was not insane. RATIFYING Ah, so she's *guilty=* UNFINISHED

Erica: Yeah. RATIFYING

Malcolm: =for her actions and she should be *punished* by the state. INFORMING If she had been found *insane* what's the, what's the *verdict?* QUESTIONING

Eddy: She would have been pardoned. ANSWERING

Malcolm: What? CLARIFYING/CHALLENGING

Erica: She would have been put in an asylum. ANSWERING

Bethany: Yeah. RATIFYING

Malcolm: Okay, and what's the *verdict?* QUESTIONING

Lydia: Involuntary, like manslaughter or something? ANSWERING

Malcolm: If she's, if, if the jury had said she was not, not guilty— QUESTIONING

Erica: Not guilty. ANSWERING

Sandra: She's not guilty? CHALLENGING

Malcolm: By means of insanity. ANSWERING All right, so she's *not* guilty, *because* why? QUESTIONING

Several students: Because she was insane. [Note: simultaneous conversation starts up.] ANSWERING

Malcolm: Because she could *not control* what she was doing. She is not responsible for drowning her five children. Because she could not control it. INFORMING

Sandra: The court *did* decide she was insane. COUNTERING

Malcolm: No they decided she was not insane and she *is* responsible. But now it's just been overturned on appeal. COUNTERING/INFORMING So, do you still want to use the word *insane?* These people are not responsible -- INVITING

Sandra: I think Faulkner would. INTERPRETING

Marty: I think for Quentin. INTERPRETING

As is suggested by the examples presented above, the IRF sequence was employed to different ends in the co-led and student-led discussions than in the teacher-led discussions. In these classrooms, it was used to bring students onto the same page—often literally—regarding some straightforward matter of plot or character development or, in the case of the excerpt above, to introduce an external context that could inform students' use of the term 'insane.' In these classrooms, then, the IRF sequence was principally employed to explore relatively straightforward matters that arose as a result of the students' interpretive work.

These applications of the IRF sequence can be seen to enact the Clarifying, Challenging, and Countering moves discussed earlier, only over a longer series of exchanges. For example, in excerpt 5e from Jay's classroom, Jay employed the IRF sequence as a means of supporting an investigation into Tim's claim. When Tim shares his insight that before he died Gatsby had lost the very drive that had defined him, Jay asks Tim to consider when precisely that would have happened and then supports that inquiry with questions crafted to walk him through the relevant chronology. Essentially, he was asking Tim to elaborate on his answer in the way a Clarifying move would and then supporting him in doing so. Jay's unwillingness to intervene when Tim paused for eight seconds, seemingly unsure of how to respond, also provided an opening for Tim's classmate, Warren, to contribute to the reconstruction of the sequence.

Malcolm's use of the IRF sequence in excerpt 5f can be seen to operate as a means of continuing to Challenge and, ultimately, Counter his students' usage of the word 'insane.' Here Malcolm is, in effect, saying 'you say all these characters are insane, but what about this woman who killed her five children? A jury determined *her* to be sane.' Within this exchange, Malcolm insists that his students think more carefully before employing what he considers to be an important interpretive term.

Participant Frameworks

Qualities of Attention–In the excerpt below, Frances's student, Drew, is explaining his drawing of the final scene in *The Great Gatsby*. The class had begun with all of the students writing about their drawings, which had been assigned the night before, for between five and ten minutes, depending on when each student had arrived. Just as the class discussion was about to begin, Bill had asked Frances whether she had "just ever gotten to the point where you don't have to read [the book] anymore?" and Frances had said, "No. I always read it. Because I always hear something different. You guys always say something that's different that I hadn't thought of before. It's good." Below, well into the ensuing discussion, Frances finds an opportunity to point out something that Bill had seen in the text that she had never noticed before.

Excerpt 5g

Drew: I saw like the *water* as being, it being like what he was trying to reach and where he was, was really important. It was like this huge step. And on 189, he didn't know, or, um, … **he had come a long way to this blue line and his dream must have seemed so close that he could hardly fail to grasp it.** It's like, he's, the water is like the step between him and the green light. And it's, and that it's what's keeping him against it. And the water also is the current that's pushing everything against him. And I also saw like the water, water not just being like what he was paddling against, but like, from his childhood to his adulthood, like, everything that he had to go through to be worthy of Daisy's love. Like, jumping, like, social classes. And just all these struggles. And then, he's still working through the water to get here.

Bill: He dies in the water.

Frances: Oh, hadn't thought of that one. See. I told you. [Note: some student is also saying something inaudible, agreeing with the teacher.]

Eddy: He finds the yacht when he's in the water.

Frances: Yes. And he finds Cody.

Eddy: And that's how he jumps social classes by rowing around in the water.

Frances: [xxx] get on that boat.

Drew: I never made that reference, but that's really good.

Frances: He dies in the water. You're right.

Bill: I would have had him like jumping off the boat. … If I had thought of that earlier, like jumping off and then trying to swim.

Eddy: Yeah.

Bill: And then like drowned.

Drew: I was thinking of like, how the first step that he got off the water was that man that he met, Cody.

Eddy: Yeah, he met Cody.

Frances: Yeah. And that's what, that's what you were saying, wasn't it?

Eddy: Yeah, we're saying.

Frances: Right. Sure.

Rebecca: So we're basically saying, like, the *memories* and trying to get to Daisy is blue, which is water, right? So, and the thing is that he built his house on a blue lawn. So that's what connected that. So he sort of built his house, which we know he got just for Daisy, on memories of her.

Several aspects of this excerpt illustrate the character of Frances' attention to her students' thoughts. One can begin with the assignment itself, which asks students to generate imagery based on their reading of the symbolic language with which Fitzgerald ends his novel. Placing the students' interpretative drawings at the center of the discussion increases the chances that the students will have something to say that Frances has not heard before. It also places them into a position of increased authority. Only they can explain what moved them to represent the symbolism of the text in a particular way.

Secondly, we have the interweaving of contributions from Drew, Bill, Eddy, and Frances, beginning with Bill's remark that Gatsby had died in the water, an apparently spontaneous insight inspired by Drew's discussion of water's larger symbolic role in the scene. This sequence is followed by Frances' observation that she had never thought of Gatsby's dying in water in symbolic terms, after which Eddy notes that water had also been the vehicle of Gatsby's upward mobility. Drew's expression of appreciation either of Eddy's or Bill's comment, or perhaps both, seems to draw Frances's second appreciative remark about Bill's comment, suggesting that she is still marveling at the new angle he has given her on Gatsby's death. This remark, in turn, opens the floor to Bill, who explains how he would have changed his drawing if he had thought of that figurative relationship earlier.

Taken as a whole, this exchange suggests the open quality of interactive interpretive flow that often characterized Frances' classroom. That Frances chose this class period to be transcribed, rather than staying with the other more straightforward interpretive readings of the text, suggests that the work all class members had to do in this session in order to understand each other's interpretive drawings had inspired the sort of collaborative energy that Frances finds most exciting. Her own appreciation of the book's closing scene had been enhanced as a result.

Just after that exchange, Drew returns to the question of Cody, saying, "I was thinking of like, how the first step that he got off the water was that man that he met, Cody." Eddy, who had made this same observation several turns earlier, agrees, prompting Frances to note his prior authoring of that thought. But Eddy does not seem interested in receiving credit for his prior authoring of the notion, given his response to Frances, "Yeah *we're* saying" (emphasis added). With this remark, Eddy seems to suggest that he, Drew, Bill, and the other members of the class are weaving this interpretive strand collectively, a sense that is further strengthened by Rebecca's Summarizing move, which begins, "So *we're* basically saying..." (italics added). Meanwhile, Frances has quickly deferred to Eddy's recasting of the authoring process as collaborative.

Frances' direction to her students to draw the novel's closing scene has demanded that they commit to interpretive visions to share with the class, granting a certain stature to their independent efforts to synthesize prior discussions and extend them in this way. Her clear interest in Bill's new symbolic possibility positions Bill as a valued colleague in this work, implicitly opening this potential role to others at the table. Similarly, her easy deference to Eddy's correction also emphasizes the extent to which Frances thinks of herself as a fellow learner at the table, capable of misstatement and prepared to entertain challenges from others.

The discussions in Malcolm's room divided between a collective reconstruction of the book's action directed by Malcolm as a teacher-led discussion and open exploration of broad issues that the novel raised for his students, such as sanity, the value of life, and the mutual obligations of parents and children. In his interviews,

Malcolm expressed his belief that his students needed his support and direction in order to make sense of the narrative structure of *The Sound and the Fury*. As we will see, Malcolm also felt that he needed to weigh in on certain of the interpretive conclusions of his students.

Throughout the co-led investigations into the issues his students had identified, Malcolm focused on eliciting the logic of his students' reasoning and on challenging them to stay true to the text and to employ language with precision. Below, a single clarifying move by Malcolm sets off an uninterrupted sequence of thirty-four student turns on the topic of whether or not various members of the Compson family, whose story is chronicled in *The Sound and the Fury*, can be considered sane.

> **Excerpt 5h**
>
> **Eddy:** That's just the *genes*. I mean, I think everyone in that family is pretty much clinically insane. [Note: laughter.]
>
> **Malcolm:** You think everyone's insane?
>
> **Dean:** No, the dad seems to be=
>
> **Sandra:** No, I think--
>
> **Dean:** =very, not, not, not insane, really smart, same with Quentin. [Note: Dean keeps talking over Sandra's interruption.]
>
> **Sandra:** You can be really smart and insane at the same time.
>
> **Dean:** [Note: several students start, but Dean takes the floor.] I think, I think he has the best grasp on what's going on of anybody, cause he's not, disillusioned [Note: Sandra tries to interrupt.] by, by wealth or by God or by anything like that, he is--
>
> **Sandra:** No but he's completely disillusioned, he doesn't *believe* in anything anymore. [Note: simultaneous conversation for several seconds.] Do you guys think that that should be the right, like [Note: again, some start talking.] outlook?
>
> **Dean:** Yeah, I think it's depressing.
>
> **Sandra:** Yeah, if you're, if you don't believe in anything, like *objectively*, nothing matters? That can't be healthy.
>
> **Bethany:** He's not saying it's healthy. He's just saying that it's—
>
> **Student:** Healthy, what's healthy?

Sandra: What's healthy, like? [Note: Again simultaneous, unintelligible conversation.] Lack of belief can be perfectly healthy, but belief in *anything*? Like belief in like, family or morals or, like, anything being worth trying for?

Eddy: I mean, he believes in alcoholism.

Bethany: Yeah. [Note: laughter.]

Sandra: I don't think he *does*, I think he's just drinking—

Dean: I think he's addicted. I don't think that he really drinks for any particular reason.

Sandra: Yeah.

We know that Malcolm feels personally invested in the outcome of this exchange as we have already read part of his response to his students' reasoning in excerpt 5f. Yet Malcolm allows the discussion between his students to proceed without his intervention. As can be heard, Malcolm's brief Clarifying move has precipitated a cycle of student explanation and justification, propelled also by genuine differences of belief between his students regarding what the term 'sanity' means and which members of the Compson family can therefore fairly be considered insane.

Malcolm and Frances made about twice as many Clarifying moves as the teacher with the next highest count did.[10] Though one needs to consider not only the quantity but also the character of Clarifying moves in order to compare the manner in which they are used across the classrooms, the simple fact that Malcolm asked for his students to repeat and to elaborate upon their contributions so frequently suggests a prioritizing of and interest in their thoughts.

Jay and his students read and interpreted the book together. One issue would evolve into the next. This was similar in nature to the gradual topic development that occurred in Grace's room. Over time, classroom members collaboratively assembled shared understandings of scenes and characters, grappling with any perturbations to that emerging coherence as these arose.

Unlike Grace, though, Jay intervened at times to reign in the interpretive process, perhaps when he felt the group's line of thought was threatening to unravel or go astray. Yet, as we will see below, in the process of directly or indirectly Countering any of their students ideas or claims, both Jay and Malcolm remained attentive to their stated goal of fostering their students' sense of themselves as near-equal participants in the interpretive work of the classroom.

Boundary Tending–Overall, teachers in the co-led discussions were more willing to constrain the interpretive possibilities represented in a student's contribution than were either Grace or Yale. Yet, at the same time, these teachers remained keenly aware of the risks to their students' sense of intellectual agency that they courted at such moments. Their episodes of boundary tending therefore often evidenced an exacting quality of attention to both the character of their students' contributions and to maintaining their students' sense of interpretive standing.

In this excerpt, one of Jay's students, Al, begins an exchange by returning to a matter the class had discussed earlier and modifying the conclusion the class had reached then. In his second turn, Jay frames a question that Al interprets as Countering what Al has just said, and Al immediately begins to back away from his contested claim. In his next two turns, Jay invites Al back into an engagement with this claim, inspiring his renewed consideration of the tension implied by Jay's question.

Excerpt 5i

Al: Well, going back, going back to how we were talking about how, ah, Gatsby sorted of crafted this charm. Um, it seemed to me, though, that the, the one, the one way that, the one detail that he didn't really craft, was, was his, his smile seemed so, like genuine [xxx]. It doesn't seem like that's something that you can, like that's … as far as we see, basically just his most charming feature.

Jay: Umm.

Al: And … it's, but it seems even like *beyond* charming. He says, you know **It's one of four or five rare smiles that you'll ever see in your life.** And that it's not something that you can *craft*, um, necessarily. So it, I don't know. There's kind of a, there seems like there's sort of a natural quality there [x].

Jay: Does it [4 sec] do we *think* … or does, does Nick apparently think, that the smile is genuine in its, in the *understanding* that it, seems to ensue? Remember, he talks about the fact that the smile seems to understand you fully no more than it would … as much as you would want them, or that you would want and so forth. From what real sense of Gatsby, do we sense that he's a great, understander, of human beings? That he's sensitive to the, the emotional lives of others?

Al: No. Ah, yeah, but I guess, yeah. I guess that sort of goes against this character.

Jay: But he didn't, you're suggesting that he didn't *practice* this smile?

Al: No. No. Yeah, I don't know. It doesn't seem like something you can sort of … I don't know. I mean, that's sort of more of Nick's interpretation of, of … *why* it's an attractive smile. Part of it is Gatsby's, like, attempt to show that he understands people well.

Jay: Right. I'm going to work on this smile. That will say to people, 'I understand you' as fully as you would [xxx]. [Note: Joe and Allen chuckle slightly at how unlikely this seems.]

Al: But it also … he also says it sort of instills in you like a … a confidence that you want to have for yourself. Ah, which, but I mean, it seems like Gatsby … I don't know if that's superficial or not. But it, it seems like Gatsby, that, sort of, Gatsby is capable of doing that, while he may not, ah, understand, people all that well, on the other side. It seems like he is able to, sort of … at least, ah, give, give this confidence. I, I guess it could be just, again, superficial. It, it seems like, something that's that's somewhat genuine, so. [6 sec]

Jay: Go back to the list, for a minute. Ah, how old is Gatsby, apparently … when, when he compiles this, this list? Do we have any sense?

Here Al expresses his reservations about one aspect of an understanding the class had generated that Gatsby had crafted his charm. He does not feel that someone can craft so exceptional a smile. In response, Jay makes a classic teacher-led type of move; he designs a question that will direct Al down a particular line of reasoning, in this case, a reconsideration of the authenticity of Gatsby's smile given the way in which it seems to work in the world. He asks, in essence, does the smile express something genuine? Sensing that the answer to this question will, in some sense, defeat his argument, Al begins to concede the point. Jay then returns with a question designed to draw Al out relative to the central logic of *Al's* claim—that no one can achieve such a smile through practice. This move gives Al a chance both to revisit his prior belief that one cannot practice such a smile *and* to Counter Jay's previous challenge by noting that the text Jay cited only speaks to the narrator's understanding of the smile.

Jay further encourages Al by chuckling at how unlikely the notion of practicing a smile capable of exuding understanding seems. In the light of this brief exchange, Al rearticulates his confusion. In some way, the smile seems genuine, in some way, artificial. At this point, Jay moves on, leaving the matter of whether or not Gatsby crafted his smile unresolved—at least for today.

Below, Malcolm's class is discussing the statement by a character, Quentin, that if she is bad, it is the fault of the people who raised her. As can be seen, Malcolm directly Counters Bethany's interpretation that the girl Quentin was trying to hurt another character. This sort of direct teacher Countering move did not occur in the student-led discussions and was rare even in the co-constructed discussions. As can be seen below, Malcolm follows his refutation of Bethany's claim with an invitation to Bethany to rebut his refutation in turn.

Excerpt 5j
Dean: It's, being illogical.

Malcolm: Illogical?

Dean: Yeah, she was trying to … she's, I, I, almost looked at it as a little, a little girl yelling at her parents. Just a temper tantrum.

Bethany: She is just trying to hurt him.

Marty: Well, like—

Malcolm: Hurt *him*?

Bethany: Hurt him.

Malcolm: There is no way to hurt him=

Bethany: I know but she is trying.

Malcolm: =and she knows that.

Bethany: Well. Why else=

Malcolm: She knows that, doesn't she?

Bethany: =why else would she say it?

Malcolm: Why else would she say it?

Dean: That's not true.

Andrew: That is true.

Malcolm: What?

Andrew: Because it's true.

Malcolm: How so?

Andrew: Cause, like, I would call it their, environment. You're going to be a little, like, *bitter* towards, the authority if they're always telling you that you're like the, origin of, like, all their problems, and just being like overbearing.

Malcolm: Didn't you say that yesterday? [Note: This is directed to Bethany.]

Bethany: What?

Malcolm: You just have to hear it *once.*

Bethany: Yeah.

Malcolm: That you're the suffering, you're the cause of the suffering.

Several aspects of this interaction between Malcolm and Bethany seem notable, beginning with the force of Malcolm's refutation. As the word emphasis in "Hurt *him*?" suggests and as his continuation, "There is no way to hurt him and she knows that," confirms Malcolm finds Bethany's interpretation of the character's motives both surprising and insupportable. Even before Malcolm finishes, Bethany offers the justification "I know but she is trying," which is countered by the end of Malcolm's sentence, "and she knows that." Immediately, Bethany begins her challenge to Malcolm to produce a more credible motive, but she is interrupted by Malcolm's invitation to her to contradict him. Bethany, however, simply finishes her sentence, at which point Malcolm redirects her challenge to the class and draws out Andrew's interpretation.

Though Malcolm's abrupt Countering of Bethany's interpretive possibility and Bethany's easy challenge back has something of a collegial feel to it, Malcolm quickly shifts into his more standard teacher role, querying Bethany first and then the class. Indeed, his prompt follow-up, "She knows that, doesn't she?" may indicate a desire on Malcolm's part to balance the force of his previous statement by inviting Bethany to expand on her opposing view. Bethany, though, seems reluctant to reengage. Having been directly refuted by the teacher, she waits to hear what someone else may have to say on the topic. Malcolm's closing move in this exchange, which cites a comment Bethany had made the previous day, may also express his desire to balance his refutation of her claim by emphasizing the value of another of her recent insights.

As in the exchange between Jay and Al in excerpt 5i, this exchange between Malcolm and Bethany suggests Malcolm's awareness of and concern regarding the extent of his authority in this discussion. In both cases, the teachers evaluated a student move—in Jay's case, indirectly, and in Malcolm's case, by directly Countering the claim. In both cases, the teachers then seem moved to attend more closely to student thinking by drawing the students out in some manner—in Jay's, by asking a question that pulled the student back into an engagement with a claim he had seemed prepared to abandon, in Malcolm's case, by inviting the student's opposing argument.

In the following excerpt, Frances exhibits a similar sort of concern for one of her students, Rebecca, who finds herself at odds with a prevailing sense among her classmates that Gatsby had been lying when he claimed to have attended Oxford. This passage picks up five turns after the end of excerpt 5a. As sometimes happens in this classroom, Frances and the students have begun to joke a bit about the matter when Frances seems suddenly to recall Rebecca's divergent position on the issue.

Excerpt 5k

Kyle: He looked at him sideways, and I knew why Jordan Baker had believed he was lying. He heard the phrase, educated at Oxford or swallowed it or choked on it, as though it had bothered him before. So I just, it's really hard to believe someone if they're just choking up on their words. And, Jordan also thinks he is a liar, and he's got some pretty crazy stories.

Frances: Well, what's the next line that he says? That whole next exchange?

Kyle: Yeah. Um, just continue?

Bill: Yes. You're educated at *Oxford*, and you think San Francisco is in the mid-west? [Note: several say "yeah."] Are you kidding?

Frances: [Note: laughing.] That's a little … Ask these guys… [Note: getting serious again.] Rebecca said he was grieving. I mean you, you find him sincere.

Rebecca: Yes, I do.

Frances: Okay. That's okay. I'm just saying, now *watch* that you're finding him sincere, and you can find a reason for him to choke on those words. These guys can find another reason.

Rebecca: Uh-huh.

Frances: Okay. So keep watching how that's set up.

Here Frances has employed her authority to keep Rebecca's claim on the table, casting doubt on Bill's claim just when it had seemed poised to win the day. At this point, the novel is far from over; Frances uses the opportunity both to suggest that Rebecca (and her classmates) should take note of how she is reading Gatsby and to remind the class of their responsibility to keep looking for evidence for their interpretations.

This kind of watchful care-taking seemed characteristic of all three teachers who employed co-led discussions. Given the back and forth that these teachers seek to cultivate between the students' emerging and their more developed interpretations, it is perhaps not surprising that they should be particularly attuned to and concerned about the tensions inherent in moving between these two forms of engagement. At times when these teachers feel they have asserted their perspective too strongly or have discouraged a student from developing his or her own line of thought, they all move quickly to refocus everyone's attention on that student's thinking.

In an interview, Jay spoke of a time he had been asked to substitute for another teacher and had only first read the short story the class would be discussing the night before class. In some ways, Jay felt it easier to achieve the sense of intellectual community he always seeks in his classrooms as he was coming into the discussion just as the students were, without any settled interpretations of the story.

Of the three teachers who orchestrated co-led discussions, Frances seemed most relaxed regarding the lines she drew between her students' interpretive rights and responsibilities and her own: during my observations, she rarely seemed to second-guess the degree of influence she had exerted within a discussion. In part, this may be due to the fact that Frances drew on discussion between the students to settle most matters of contention and generally expressed her views only after the matter had been explored for some time. By turning to ask her students what they thought about a debatable claim, Frances reliably uncovered enough conceptual dissonance to propel the discussion forward. In her final interview, however,

Frances said that she considers this tension between expressing her own interpretive vision and attending to those of her students to be an ongoing issue, one to which she often returns when reflecting on her practice.

Opportunities for Learning

The teachers of co-led discussions all strove to balance the two sets of learning opportunities represented by the teacher-led and student-led teaching approaches. All three of these teachers spoke of the importance *both* of exposure to the teacher's developed perspective *and* of the students having opportunities to frame interpretive issues and to evaluate interpretive possibilities themselves. The three sets of co-led discussions all drew differently upon characteristics of the teacher-led and the student-led models; as a group, they suggest the great diversity of pedagogical possibility that exists between the two ends of this conceptual spectrum.

In all three classrooms, the teacher allowed for extended student contributions to the framing, developing, and evaluating process, while also providing an interpretive safety net of sorts. Students expected their teacher to step in if they touched on a matter close to their teacher's heart, to clarify a complex or confusing matter, or to provide historical or literary background relevant to the discussion underway. Students were given opportunities to engage the text on their terms but were not expected to do all of the framing, developing, and evaluating themselves.

All three of these teachers asked their students to cope with some degree of interpretive indeterminacy, though the degree to which they did so varied. Jay worked alongside his students, sometimes weighting their various interpretive possibilities with an elaboration or modification or a nod of his head and sometimes not evaluating in any way. Certain issues simply remained open, leaving different students in perhaps different relationships to the various interpretive possibilities that had been advanced. Students who were more attuned to and invested in Jay's authority as the teacher may have felt that their interpretive claims could be considered credible if Jay had not challenged or countered them. Others may have felt at greater liberty to develop their own interpretive perspectives.

Malcolm asked the greatest number of Clarifying questions of any of the six teachers; in all cases, Malcolm seemed genuinely interested in his students' thoughts about the characters and what the characters' stories seemed to suggest about Faulkner's perspective on the human condition. As we have seen, Malcolm also pursued the implications of his students' claims at length. These exchanges grew more common as the weeks went by and the students began to feel more in command of the book's narrative structure. By that time, the students seemed eager to engage the text in this manner and would often get quite lively, and at times argumentative, with each other.

In contrast to Frances, Jay and Malcolm seemed to expect students to come eventually to understand the book in at least some of the same ways that they did. While Frances also contributed substantively to the interpretive process in her classroom, she consistently and explicitly held open the possibility that her students might disagree with each other's interpretations and also with hers.

Although all three of these teachers referred to traditional interpretive themes such as the use of symbolism or the construct of the American Dream, Jay, in particular, would use such themes to structure long stretches of the class discussion. Malcolm balanced his expectations that his students would learn to recapitulate the novel's action with open explorations of issues that the students had located in the text. In Malcolm's room, students seemed to seize on these opportunities to engage each other, in contrast to a reluctance they at times seemed to exhibit toward reconstructing the plot.

In his first interview, Malcolm explained that he both wants to hear about the meanings his students find in the text and wants for them to hear about the understandings he has constructed through his study of *The Sound and the Fury* over the years. Something of this sort was said by each of the teachers who employed co-led discussions. Each also wanted to be in a position to ensure that students learned about significant cultural references or classic literary devices. Such disciplinary understandings help to familiarize students with the broader field and may give them a sense of cultural inclusion, as well as providing additional analytic tools.

Summary

Once a teacher assumes a specific role in the knowledge construction process, certain contingencies are set into motion. When a teacher presents questions and frames issues, students move to generating answers and ideas. When a teacher fails to indicate whether or not students' interpretive possibilities seem supportable and interesting, students will begin to evaluate the worth of their own and each other's claims themselves. These are structural issues that organize the character of the learning experiences that are made available.

In co-led learning experiences, the work of making meanings can be distributed between teachers and students in a variety of ways, presenting students with different sorts of challenges. Assuming that the students are being given and are taking advantage of the opportunity to think and to imagine what the text might mean—as they were in all three of these classrooms—students are learning both about the novel in question and about the act of interpretation. To the extent students are asked to enact all three phases of literary interpretation—framing, developing, and evaluating—they are also learning how to interpret a novel themselves.

In order to theorize the pedagogical potential of different co-led discussions, then, it is important to consider the ways in which questions and issues emerge, how interpretive responses are developed in relation to those issues, and the bases upon which some interpretations are found to be more sustainable than others. In particular, it is important to focus on the dynamic roles that teachers and students are assuming in the construction of meaning and how the teachers have communicated their expectations regarding these roles to students.

Transforming traditional classroom roles and relationships into successful co-led learning experiences requires time and study, and the needed experimentation can, like all learning, result in missteps of different kinds. Educators can certainly be excused for any feelings of uncertainty they may have experienced, or continue to experience, as the field has struggled to reconceive and reconfigure the roles teachers might play in advancing their students' learning.[11]

Fortunately, educational theorists and practitioners are beginning to locate the outline of a new pedagogical relation based upon contemporary understandings about learning. In grounding this new conception within the daily realities of classroom life and in elaborating the look and feel of this new conception in relation to a specific discipline and grade level, Magdalene Lampert has contributed greatly to this project. Much about these new forms of learning still remains to be uncovered, studied, and theorized. There is nothing easy or straightforward about enacting even good teacher-led learning, at least not according to those who study such matters.

CHAPTER SIX

Educating for Democracy

The pedagogical possibilities available in any classroom are merely theoretical until students harness them in the interest of their own learning. This reality raises the issue of motivation, which, although central to the act of learning, is rarely granted its due consideration within educational policy debates and school reform discourse. To a large extent, this lack of attention to issues of student motivation derives from the lack of an adequately comprehensive and compelling conception of the purposes of democratic schools. To the extent educators ponder the larger purposes of a democratic education, they will want and need to consider the ways in which schools work to motivate and inspire all involved, particularly the students.

While today's democratic societies do need to concern themselves with the universal inculcation of the sorts of basic competencies that can arguably be evaluated by standardized tests, to organize school reform primarily around this narrow goal constrains everyone's capacity to recall and to imagine the humanizing possibilities of democratic schools. These competencies are also themselves diminished to the extent they are viewed as distinct from the intellectual investigations and collaborations they enable. Facilities with calculating correctly, committing terms and dates to memory, and reading and writing Standard English fluently are more generatively conceived of as aspects—albeit integral aspects—of the greater project of preparing all students to assume constructive and personally meaningful places within their social worlds.

I have focused on the structural distribution of interpretive authority within classrooms because children need to be willing and able to ask and to address their own questions and to arrive at their own conclusions before they are likely to be willing and able to build constructive and meaningful relationships with others. Democratic purposes would therefore suggest that all students be provided with generous opportunities to locate themselves—their talents, fears, hopes, interests, and desires—within the work they do at school. In opening themselves up to such opportunities, children begin to see themselves as members of larger intellectual and social worlds.

As discussed in chapter two, all learning theorists agree that children must be asked and allowed to generate responsive words, actions, and artifacts in classrooms if they are to appropriate the cultural resources they study and truly make these resources their own. One may learn in different ways to different ends, but to *know* anything, we all need to work the implications through and come to terms with those implications ourselves. There will also always be students who need to be heard in their own terms before they are willing to take much of an interest in the perspectives of anybody else, including a teacher.[1]

Constructing meaningful, powerful, and transparent under-standings together within classrooms extends students' intellectual authority into new areas as the natural consequence of the serious and principled quality of human engagement entailed. Students learn to identify matters that move them and experience the satisfaction of achieving desired ends through their shared efforts to address these matters. This can happen in small ways, as a classroom works together to interpret a book, or create a timeline, or recast an equation; and it can happen in large ways when, for example, teachers empower students to look beyond the walls of their school and seek change within their broader community.[2]

The issue of motivation returns us briefly to our vision of classroom communities as complex social systems. As in so many areas of learning research, the capacity of motivation research to inform classroom practice has been hampered by the widespread use of simple, often dichotomous (rather than mutually constituted or dialectic) causal analyses and single factor models. For example, 'achievement goals,' based upon students' desire to learn, were long viewed as distinct from and even opposed to 'performance goals,' based on students' needs for approval and admiration from others. Both types of goals were then also conceptualized as stable influences rather than as dynamic factors linked to learners' often emotionally volatile experiences of academic performances of any kind.[3]

Many learning researchers have therefore sought to isolate and quantify achievement and performance goals in order to study, for example, the potentially debilitating influences of performance goals. Unsurprisingly, performance goals have been found to be useful in some contexts and problematic in others. As many readers will be able to reconstruct from personal experience, an interest in learning can work constructively in concert with an interest in performing well for or impressing others, while too great or unstable an emotional investment in performing for others can unnerve learners and limit their ability to enjoy learning for its own sake. The variables involved, which include the nature of the challenge, the interpersonal character of the classroom, and the learner's personality, among many others, simply cannot be neglected or "held constant" in research designed to inform human action within a fully constituted social world.[4]

While less concerned and capable teachers lean heavily upon their school's institutionalized reward and punishment structure, teachers such as our six participant teachers strive to inspire a pride of accomplishment among their students in relation to the demands of their classrooms. This project can be seen as comprised of at least two moving parts: conveying one's pedagogical aims and expectations clearly, and inspiring students to care about them. These two parts also intertwine: the character of one's expectations will affect the ways in which one attempts to induce one's students to care about them.

In very general terms, any teacher has two types of interpersonal motivation with which to work: a student's desire to please or impress the teacher—possibly as an end in itself, possibly as a path to the approval of others—and the student's desire to please or impress his or her peers. In addition, there is the lure of the intellectual challenge and the potential sense of accomplishment that tackling such a challenge might provide.

Any child's desire to please others springs from a primal need for approval and the sense of human connection it brings; any child's interest in investigating and mastering intellectual challenges likewise springs from a native intellectual curiosity with which we are all born. These are the motivational wellsprings of the socialization process. All responsible educators teach children how to think and act in order to be considered respectable and valued members of their society. Democratically minded educators also help children to understand the ways in which their personal passions, abilities, and outlooks might intersect with that process. In doing so, democratically minded educators are able to lighten their reliance upon institutional authority and the social power schools wield.

Per our dynamic systems model of classrooms, all of these potential motivating forces, whether interpersonal or intellectual, will continually be operating to varying extents, for good or ill (possibly even for good *and* ill in different ways), in any student's relationship with the demands of classroom life. Whether they reflect upon it or not, all teachers employ aspects of their students' interests in learning, achieving, belonging, and impressing and neglect others in accordance with their own understandings of the purposes of school and the grounds of their authority as teachers.

In striving to create meaningful, powerful, and transparent learning experiences for their students, a teacher can activate all of these motivating forces. Such experiences not only afford students opportunities to connect personally to their schoolwork, but also to view these personal connections as essential to the collective work at hand, leading to feelings of personal worth and to more substantive relationships with teachers and peers. As suggested by many of the transcript excerpts, collectively working toward intellectual transparency not only teaches students how to think in academic terms but can also nurture a greater sense of connection between all classroom members, thereby increasing students' attention to, and possibly even acceptance of, their fellow classmates across perceived social differences.[5]

By employing the participant framework lens to study the ways in which a teacher's language positions students in relation to each other, to the teacher, and to the work at hand, one can consider the manner in which a teacher has drawn upon each of these potential motivating forces. Although many aspects of classroom culture and personal identity need to work together to motivate students to engage seriously, different distributions of interpretive authority draw differentially upon these various potential motivators and so, to some extent, foster distinctive motivational dynamics.[6] Theorizing and investigating possible links between differing distributions of interpretive authority and the quality of students' intellectual engagement therefore become potentially useful and interesting, particularly in situations where students are not meeting established goals for their learning.

While an extended consideration of these questions lies beyond the scope of this work, several points can be made about the ways in which our six participant teachers employed the three forms of learning experience to draw upon students' relationships with their teacher, classmates, and the novel itself as motivating forces. Even in private schools—or selective charter schools—where a certain base-line level of academic motivation can generally be assumed, the character of students' learning will depend upon the ways in which a given class inspires a student's personal engagement and reflection.[7] In standard public school classrooms, even basic levels of student motivation cannot always be assumed. Educators who seek to touch the lives of all of their students must therefore learn how to position their students' interests and purposes into relation with their own.

Randy kept discussions lively and fun. He joked around with his students and let them talk together in preparation for sharing their contributions with the class. In his interviews, Randy expressed a commitment to building a sense of camaraderie in the class and having the students enjoy the time they spent together. To inspire their engagement with the novel, Randy deliberately drew on his students' interest in engaging with each other and in pleasing him. Students who were not comfortable sparring, or even joking, directly with Randy may well have felt comfortable tossing a thought or two around with a classmate and then waiting to see whether those thoughts intersected with the thinking of their more verbally self-assured peers.

Randy's efforts to inspire a sense of enjoyable camaraderie among his students no doubt encouraged many of them to follow the interpretive line that he was constructing and so to learn how to see the novel in many of the same ways as Randy does. For students to want to linger with a teacher's line of thought and to place the teacher's thoughts into relationship with their own—rather than simply reiterating a sufficient number of teacher-approved thoughts in a paper or on a test—students need to identify with the teacher's purposes to some extent, and possibly also the teacher. Certainly, students need to be able to follow the teacher's reasoning and find it either personally useful or engaging in some way.

In Grace's and Yale's rooms, students were expected to connect personally with the book and with the thinking of their peers. Student motivation was thought to derive primarily from these two sources. Although students in demanding private schools generally orient toward meeting a teacher's expectations, Grace and Yale strove to give as few indications as possible regarding the lines of inquiry they found compelling or the interpretive possibilities that to them rang true. Both Grace and Yale spoke in their interviews of valuing student-led discussions for their ability to inspire personal and enduring relationships between students and the literary works they interpret.

Student-led discussions also encourage students to assume a greater sense of their own intellectual authority. Through the exchange that unfolded between Alan and Grace regarding the metaphor Alan had found in excerpt 4g, all of Grace's students learned that metaphors are constructed within individual readers' minds and that not everyone will necessarily notice or value the same ones. Grace felt that she had learned many of the tools she employed in cases such as this from Eleanor Duckworth when Grace had studied with her as a Masters student. In particular, Grace said she had learned to trust the integrity of her students' thinking and therefore had grown comfortable pushing her students to work harder to uncover the assumptions, evidence, and reasoning that lay beneath their ideas and claims.

In student-led learning experiences, students are not rewarded with explicit expressions of approval from the teacher for a point well taken or an issue well framed; rather, students earn a teacher's approval by struggling to make sense of the material at hand. For this reason, teachers need to strive continually to support students who are willing to risk sounding uncertain and unclear in order to construct new understandings as they speak. Teachers must repeatedly reaffirm, both explicitly and implicitly, that they trust all of their students to manage the intellectual and emotional challenges that accompany the work of constructing their own understandings and that they, as teachers, can and will support their efforts when students require extra guidance and encouragement to work an issue through.

The co-constructed classrooms all appeared to draw somewhat differently on students' relationship with the teacher, classmates, and the novel. In Frances' room, as in the student-led discussions, the emphasis was primarily on the students' relationship with the novel and their peers. Over the long years during which Frances had worked with Grace and Yale in the 'student-centered' school, literature department faculty members had often discussed how the school's pedagogical identity could and should be represented within their classrooms. These discussions likely encouraged a number of shared and related practices.

While Frances participated more readily across all phases of the interpretive process than did her two fellow faculty members, she explicitly positioned her interpretive perspective as one possibility among the many available. Frances positioned herself as the expert in the room only when she shared literary lenses or relevant history. For example, Frances wanted her students to reflect upon the place of the North American continent within the dreams and imaginations of Euro-American authors, a theme that she saw as informing not only one's reading of *The Great Gatsby*, but also many other works of North American literature.

In Jay's classroom, in contrast, the dynamic appeared to revolve more tightly around Jay: students often glanced over in hopes of gathering a sense of Jay's response to their thoughts. Although Jay did not regularly ratify his students' contributions as Randy did, Jay's quiet acknowledgements—at times spoken in the midst of a student's contribution—served both to encourage and to foreshorten those contributions. With these unobtrusive cues, Jay often seemed to convey not only that he was following and appreciated a student's point, but also whether he felt the student needed to continue talking or perhaps, as with Fredrick in excerpt 5b, had already developed a point adequately. In the course of the two transcripts analyzed for this research, Jay did not explicitly position his students into relationship with each other's thinking by asking whether everyone agreed with what someone had just said or had any more thoughts on that topic, questions that the five other teachers asked from time to time, particularly Frances and Yale.

Malcolm seemed to shift primarily between asking his students to meet his expectations in relation to the plot and character mappings he provided and asking them to engage seriously with each other's thinking. Again, Malcolm saw this balance as due primarily to the difficult reading level of *The Sound and the Fury*. In a manner similar to that of Frances, Malcolm did not present his personal interpretive perspective as entirely authoritative; yet he did hold certain content-based goals for his students. Malcolm wanted his students to demonstrate that they had grasped the complex narrative structure of the novel, for example, and he did not want them to dismiss everyone in the Compson family as insane. Malcolm felt he would be doing his students a disservice to leave this question about the sanity of the characters open to the students' ongoing reflection and consideration. The dynamic in Malcolm's room seemed to shift, then, between a focal attention upon making sense of the book in ways that were important to Malcolm as the teacher and encouraging the students to work collaboratively to interpret the novel themselves.

As these examples illustrate, the co-led form can retain the teacher-led emphasis on inculcating teacher understandings: a student may earn the teacher's explicit approval for various types of performances, depending on a teacher's pedagogical priorities and approach. At the same time, students are afforded extensive opportunities to explore their own observations and questions about the subject matter in conversation with their teacher and peers.

Comparisons and Contrasts among the Six Classrooms

As we have seen, the thinking required in a teacher-led discussion differs from that required in more collaborative forms of classroom knowledge construction. This is not to say that only one or the other can inspire the conceptual reconfigurations that lead to intellectual growth.[8] Yet different pedagogical approaches go about that work differently: they require different kinds of intellectual investments, performances, and risks.

Follow-up interviews clarified that all six participant teachers prioritize hearing from all of their students regularly, though they vary somewhat as to whether 'regularly' means every class period. This variation did not appear linked to the different distributions of interpretive authority; the commitment to universal participation appeared tied to the private school context, where the classes were all small (twelve or thirteen) and demanding. All six teachers have generated strategies that balance private student conferences with public invitations in order to ensure broad student participation, which they all see as essential to the quality of educational experience they seek to provide.

Across the spectrum, all participant teachers were willing to wait ten and, in several cases, up to twenty seconds for students to contribute in the expected manner, be it a response to one of their own framing moves, to another student's, or to provide a new direction for the conversation. Silences of this duration feel long in a group discussion setting and provide everyone with time to reflect upon the expectations before them. Indeed, such silences will likely be experienced as uncomfortable to some in any group of this size and may even be experienced as punitive in certain situations. On the other hand, such pauses provide opportunities for reflection and likely make it easier for some to speak, particularly in classrooms where students are expected to initiate their own turns as they were in the classrooms of Frances, Grace, and Yale.

Students in Malcolm's, Jay's, and Randy's rooms generally raised their hands to speak, though not always. Hand-raising can be seen to support the purposes of teacher-led learning and to work counter to those of student-led learning; students and teachers in co-led discussions may find that that they prefer one or the other of these possibilities for various reasons. For some students, raising one's hand provides a more comfortable means of entering a conversation, particularly a heated one. Others may be less likely to offer spontaneous insights, particularly if those insights feel somewhat uncertain or potentially peripheral.

At a deeper psychological level, students will tend to feel more or less responsibility for the direction of the conversation, depending on how much control they have over it. If students cannot enter the discussion at will, some will focus on positioning themselves to enter the conversation as soon as possible once they have decided to speak.

The need to focus on attracting the teacher's attention accents each student's relationship to the teacher's authority. In contrast, if one is negotiating with peers for speaking time, the demands of timeliness and relevance are placed into one's own hands, and one's judgment in these regards is exposed to the evaluation of one's peers. In such ways, traditions of turn-initiation can be seen to shape the character of student contributions in a class discussion. In any number of significant matters such as this, the co-led form was found to embrace a broader range of pedagogical possibility than either the teacher-led or student-led form.

As we have seen, the character of a teacher's attention to and engagement with students' divergent meanings can vary within all three forms of learning experience. Although all six teachers spoke of their interest in watching how different groups of students had come to understand the same novel over the years, one often heard that quality of interest in Frances' and Grace's questions to individual students. In interviews, both Frances and Grace marveled at some length about the extent to which each class' interpretive labors represented an original piece of intellectual work.

Use of the Text

An overview of the opening moves made in the six classrooms shows the text being positioned differently across the classrooms. The teachers in the student-led discussions provided few guidelines regarding overall interpretive goals or direction for the class period, instead choosing simply to direct students toward the text. In the three co-led discussions, the teachers provided more overall direction for the day's work, often including a thematic framing of some kind. The text was referenced at both the students' and the teacher's initiation. Finally, in the teacher-led discussion, Randy drew the students into an engagement with one or two text passages that he had selected to illustrate a specific interpretive issue or theme.

In Frances' room, students' texts stayed open most of the class period as they did in Grace's and, to a somewhat lesser extent, Yale's rooms. Students learned to reach for the text in Frances' room in order to generate topics, to develop their interpretive notions, and to judge between them. Though Frances might also voice her own opinion on a matter, she would be reading along with her students when she did so and often seemed to be viewing an issue anew based on the present conversation. She frequently wrote in her journal as the class talked and, after several decades, still made fresh marks in her tattered copy of *The Great Gatsby*.

If students have their texts open and are reading out of them, they can respond more authoritatively to each other's questions. Absent this focus on the text's authority, students have little option but to turn to the teacher for interpretive evaluation or to quibble among themselves. For this reason, the expectation that students work to assemble relevant and compelling evidence for their claims can be seen as essential to their convincing enactment of interpretive and, so, intellectual authority.

The differing ways in which Jay and Frances positioned the text seem to relate to other differences between their practices. In addition to directing her students back to the text, Frances continually worked to position each student's thinking into relationship with that of the other students in her classroom. This process encouraged her students to build upon each other's thinking, deemphasizing their relationship to Frances' interpretive vision.

Malcolm's book, *The Sound and the Fury*, is a difficult text for even accomplished readers; it would be interesting to investigate how various teachers approach that one novel—or to have seen how Malcolm might have approached an easier text. Malcolm devoted considerable time to plot development and narrative voice early on, reading long passages of the novel out loud himself. Malcolm felt that, for this novel, his students needed this kind of scaffolding from him. Establishing clarity in regards to the basic action of the book seemed Malcolm's initial, though by no means exclusive, priority. Even in these early stages, Malcolm's extended readings of the text encouraged his students to build directly upon the text's language as they constructed their own interpretations of the novel's meanings.

Use of the IRF Sequence

As noted by other scholars and also seen in this research, the Initiation/Response/Feedback sequence can be employed to different purposes. This diversity of possibility must be considered in any study of intellectual agency and authority in classrooms. All participant teachers other than Grace commonly employed some version of the IRF sequence to various ends.[9] Grace's classroom had a unique evaluative rhythm, which, as discussed, relied heavily upon student Elaborating moves and on Grace's intermittent Clarifying moves, which served to open up issues that Grace felt needed to be more thoroughly addressed.

Yale commonly employed a modified IRF sequence, with no explicit follow-up move, to bring greater clarity to issues that arose in the course of a discussion. In this classroom, if a student answered a closed question incorrectly, several different things might happen. In an interview, Yale said that he often simply turns and asks another student whether he or she agrees. Another student might also volunteer the correct answer. At other times, Yale asks a series of questions that build back up to the missed question or directs everyone's attention to a particular page and has the relevant section read.

Yale does not say a thing about whether his students have read the text correctly, let alone insightfully, yet often points them back to specific sections of the text, pushing them to tease complex matters out themselves. As we have seen, such sequences can, at times, be read as embedding implicit purposes. In broader terms, such sequences serve notice to students that they need to sharpen up and read the text more closely if they are to make credible sense of it in Yale's eyes.

All the teachers of co-led discussions employed the full IRF sequence from time to time to repair inaccurate readings of the text or, in Malcolm's case, to object to what he saw as his students' inappropriate use of the term 'insane.' In all of the co-led discussions, then, IRF sequences were employed to establish basic elements of plot, scene, and character development and to resolve questions that teachers were not willing to leave open.

In Randy's classroom, IRF sequences were used to develop Randy's talking points for the day. Although Randy framed all of the principal interpretive issues the class dealt with, his use of the IRF sequence to begin a class or to redirect a class to a new topic allowed him to hear student's thoughts and observations and to integrate these into the evolving discourse flow. It gave the process a more collaborative and interactional feel.

When a teacher assumes most of the responsibility for constructing content understandings, the teacher will need to take more frequent turns, and these turns will occur regularly with relatively brief sequences of student turns between them. The IRF discourse move pattern will commonly be employed to give students opportunities to share their thoughts and questions while maintaining the arc of the teacher's reasoning.

In contrast, when teachers want students to participate in the framing and evaluating processes, they are less likely to employ IRF sequences. Rather, teachers seeking to reduce their responsibility for classroom knowledge construction will focus on maintaining the integrity of the students' deliberative processes through strategic discourse moves and through continual reminders to reference an object of study or another type of material proving ground.

Agency

All democratic citizens are free to believe as they choose: no one can expect others to accept or defer to his or her claims in the absence of shared assumptions, pertinent evidence or experience, and a cogent line of reasoning. That grown adults often do accept claims based on questionable assumptions, inconclusive experience or evidence, or weak reasoning suggests that educators within too many schools are not being adequately supported in the work of teaching necessary democratic capacities, dispositions, and understandings.

There are many reasons for this: the work is not easy, nor entirely uncontroversial, nor are the resulting capacities, dispositions, and understandings easily isolated and measured. In addition, teachers (like parents) often feel deeply invested in teaching children and adolescents to see the world in the same ways that they do. This is natural and, as I have argued, also necessary *to a point*: children need to appropriate foundational cultural skills and values and to learn how various sorts of experts view the world. Yet democratic students also need to learn how to wrestle with intellectual challenges themselves. As adults, they will be free to think and act as they choose; adults risk losing children's attention and interest when they do not create spaces in which children can learn how to think for themselves, employing cultural tools and resources capable of linking them to the conversations and collaborative endeavors they will encounter in their adult lives.

The philosopher Amy Gutmann makes a related point when she notes that the idea of liberty relies on the possibility of choice, and that choice is not possible in the absence of options. Gutmann therefore agrees that democratic schools should teach about important controversial ideas so that children can begin to learn how to negotiate intellectual conflict and diversity responsibly and also reflect upon what different points of view might mean in terms of their personal commitments and identities.

> The same principle that requires a state to grant adults personal and political freedom also commits it to assuring children an education that makes those freedoms both possible and meaningful in the future. A state makes choice possible by teaching its future citizens respect for opposing points of view and ways of life. It makes choice meaningful by equipping children with the intellectual skills necessary to evaluate ways of life different from that of their parents.[10]

We must prepare children for the thoughtful exercise of their freedom. Those invested in the future of the children in their care, as all responsible educators and parents are, need to lift up the kinds of issues with which those children will certainly need to grapple and then enable them to do so by providing the tools they will need to work together in these areas. As philosopher Maxine Greene has put this:

> It is because of the apparent normality, the givenness of young people's everyday lives that intentional actions ought to be undertaken to bring things within the scope of students' attention, to make situations more palpable and visible. Only when they are visible and "at hand" are they likely to cry out for interpretation. And only when individuals are empowered to interpret the situations they live together do they become able to mediate between the object-world and their own consciousness, to locate themselves so that freedom can appear.[11]

As anyone who has studied or participated in democratic political processes understands, minority viewpoints can be suppressed when these processes focus more on the power of numbers than on the potential contributions of divergent points of view. While democratic decision-making procedures often result in compromise and deference to the will of the majority, such processes can be made more enlightening and satisfying for all by creating spaces within which to entertain the divergent viewpoints of the few. Although transcending the oppressive aspects of majority rule at the national level may feel daunting, within local venues—particularly within school communities—parents and educators should strive to engage with and learn from diverse views and, in doing so, teach children just how generative and rewarding such interactions can be.

In her work about the place of human care and concern in schools, Noddings calls on educators to see and 'care-for' each student on that student's terms, rather than primarily through the filter of their own priorities and expectations. In her argument, Noddings distinguishes between 'caring-for' and 'caring-about:' one cares-about the problems of distant populations; one cares-for people one knows. Noddings had the following to say about this distinction in the preface of the second edition of her classic text on caring within schools:

> In contrast to caring-for, caring-about is characterized by some distance. It moves us from the face-to-face world of direct responsibility into the wider public realm. I contended (and I still believe) that we cannot care-for everyone, but there is a sense in which we can care-about a much wider population …[which] may be thought of as the motivational foundation for justice… However, I stand by my claim that both caring-about and justice may miscarry if we do not follow up to see whether our efforts have produced conditions under which caring-for actually occurs.[12]

Educators need to ask themselves, do the approaches they advocate and enact lead to greater caring-for within our schools and greater school communities? [13]

By creating classrooms within which all students feel that others care-for them as people and so seek to support their personal growth, teachers make it possible for all students to develop and to inhabit a sense of themselves as intellectual agents. By providing for open discursive spaces, where children are invited to articulate what they believe and why, teachers give children the thrill of coming to know their own minds. These exciting and pleasurable achievements become associated, in turn, with the demanding project of learning how to listen to others who think in unfamiliar ways or hold different beliefs about the world.

Authority

The idea of democratic schools poses a number of troubling challenges to traditional understandings of knowledge and authority. While this has always been true, the pedagogical policy issues implied have grown increasingly obvious and urgent over the past thirty years. In large part, this shift has been the result of three interrelated factors: increasing cultural and intellectual diversity among students within classrooms, a shift in educators' views about how best to cope with such diversity, and society's increasing awareness of the central role cultural context plays in the development of all human understanding.[14]

Yet democratic teachers also need to provide clarity and certainty for their students in a number of crucial areas. Not everything is or can be up for negotiation in a democratic classroom. Accountable Talk, an approach to teaching that has been employed and studied within a broad range of diverse classrooms since the early 1990s, provides teachers with one helpful framework for understanding how to institute democratic standards of knowledge construction within classrooms and encourages teachers to rely upon those standards as a clear and compelling basis for their own authority as teachers.

The Accountable Talk framework charges *all* classroom members with the responsibility to consider themselves accountable in three areas: to community, to reason, and to knowledge.[15] As we have seen, a respectful *community* is necessary in order for students to learn how to *reason* in a convincing and transparent manner, which, in turn, is essential to the democratic construction of publically held understandings. By 'responsibility to knowledge,' the framework references both the responsible use of expert knowledge as well as the transparent construction of shared classroom understandings.

Students must be able to trust their teachers to provide established cultural understandings, "facts, written texts or other publicly accessible information," in a balanced and fair-minded manner.[16] Accountable Talk therefore requires many of the same kinds of developed sensibilities from a teacher that student-led and co-led investigations require. This is not surprising as these constructs overlap and inform each other. By investing themselves in the principles and methods of Accountable Talk, teachers can come to feel more authoritative when employing any of the three pedagogical forms that have been discussed here. As the authors say:

> In the classrooms that use Accountable Talk effectively, teachers have been successful at establishing norms and building a discourse culture that involves risk-taking and the explicit modeling and practice of particular talk moves. Over time (and it often takes many months of concerted effort), new forms and norms of discourse are developed and students from widely varying backgrounds begin to listen to one another, build on one another's ideas, and participate productively in complex deliberative practices. As we said earlier, robust academic learning for students of all backgrounds has been documented in these classrooms, across a range of grade levels and subject areas. However, invariably in these cases, there was a strong and authoritative teacher who stood behind the discourse forms and norms of Accountable Talk. Her authority was both institutionally derived and personally earned.[17]

The role of teacher grants institutional authority that can be employed, as we have seen, in different ways. When teachers employ their authority to insist upon democratic standards of knowledge construction from everyone, including themselves, they establish sure grounds from which to insist on particular types of performances from their students. For example, a student's question in excerpt 3d— about how Holden's relationship with Phoebe fit into Randy's assertion that Holden was no longer willing to remain emotionally vulnerable—provided Randy with an opportunity to consider more deeply and to articulate more clearly the basis for his claim. Certainly, as the teacher, Randy can decline to probe his own thinking in this manner, yet by doing so, he misses an opportunity to create greater intellectual transparency for everybody and to increase his own intellectual authority in the process.

Little demonstrates a commitment to achieving intellectual transparency more powerfully than a teacher being willing to work through his or her own thinking in this manner. Students can hardly fail to miss the implications for democratic knowledge construction: *everyone* is a lifetime learner. Nobody speaks transparently all of the time or has learned to view anything from all possible angles. No one ever could. We all can therefore become greater, larger, and more intellectually authoritative people by attending to others' challenges and divergent points of view. As Gutmann says in regards to the contrasting political or theoretical affiliations of students, educators, and parents:

> Democratic education has the potential for being far more ecumenical and effective if it does not insist on teaching students that all moral beings must identify themselves in any single way…Democratic education instead aims to teach understanding and appreciation of liberty and justice for all from multiple perspectives. There are multiple ways of understanding these values, and there are many self-identifications that converge on the idea that individuals the world over are entitled to the liberties and opportunities necessary to live a good life consistent with their own identities and respecting the equal rights of other individuals.[18]

Achieving an intellectually generative learning community increasingly requires that teachers learn to be explicit about their own understandings and the bases for them and learn to listen to their students in new ways. Classroom discussions may need to be devoted to airing divergent understandings that arise in the course of classroom life. Some classroom guidelines and practices may need to be discussed and even formulated collaboratively before everyone will feel as though they understand and are willing to invest themselves in enacting those guidelines and practices.

All children long to see themselves and the world in new ways and to learn how to manage the challenges that matter to them, including how to live in a safe and caring community with their peers. Democratically minded teachers parlay these motivating forces into a deep and abiding interest in building constructive and meaningful relationships with others and in leading intellectually engaged lives.

Desire

If students attend to their teacher's understandings only when they must in order to score and grade well in order to advance socially, students' relationships with teacher understandings—and with the cultural resources those understandings represent—will tend to be cursory and fleeting. Regardless of a student's social background or academic ambitions, school learning will be experienced primarily as a means to a distant and desired end. Today, when time for the physical, emotional, and intellectual exercise of students' creative energies has been crowded out to make room for test preparation within so many students' school days, one cannot help wondering to what extent educational policy makers recognize and appreciate this basic psychological reality, which plays itself out in predictable ways in classrooms across our nation every day.

In liberating intellect from the mere recapitulation and practiced rendering of the previously known, Dewey believed that democratic schools could create unprecedented opportunities for personal expression and therefore for greater cultural innovation and growth. Dewey viewed the personal liberty that democracy confers as one of its primary sources of psychological power and believed that, by learning to harness that power to culturally generative ends, democratic educators stood the best chance of acculturating students from all backgrounds to the demands and promises of democracy as a form of associated living. For Dewey, the terms 'vocation' and 'occupation' both carried this sense of the essential complementarity of personal meaning and social integration that should serve as an ideal for democratic societies and so schools.

> A vocation means nothing but such a direction of life activities as renders them perceptibly significant to a person, because of the consequences they accomplish, and also useful to his associates. The opposite of a career is neither leisure nor culture, but aimlessness, capriciousness, the absence of cumulative achievement in experience, on the personal side, and idle display, parasitic dependence upon the others, on the social side. Occupation is a concrete term for continuity. It includes the development of artistic capacity of any kind, of special scientific ability, of effective citizenship, as well as professional and business occupations, to say nothing of mechanical labor or engagement in gainful pursuits.[19]

Progressives such as Dewey believed that the release and greater realization of all citizens' creative energies would help to build a happier, more satisfying, and therefore more robustly democratic world. Dewey believed that democratic schools, in particular, could support the development of modes of expression and relationship that could transform human experience for rich and poor, intellectuals, managers, and industrial workers alike.

By establishing the conditions for a democratic form of socially rooted, intellectually engaged happiness, educators demonstrate their relevance and worth to their students every day. Such clarity of purpose stands to be particularly valuable within culturally pluralistic school settings where understandings of education may vary among members of the extended school community. By creating the conditions for the kind of engaged happiness that Dewey theorized, educators improve the quality of life for their students in ways that can be readily perceived.[20]

Classrooms in which both teacher and students have ample time to think about matters they find engaging distinguish themselves from the average elementary or secondary classroom in many ways. Students tend to become more self-directed as they have been charged, in many areas, with responsibility for advancing their own learning. Large group discussions can suddenly open up into extended periods of deep reflection. Below, Noddings characterizes such a moment.

> We may have ceased manipulative activity and fallen quiet; we are listening. We are not trying so much to produce a particular product or answer as we are trying to understand, to see. Whereas explanation is controlled, contrived, and constructed, understanding—like joy—comes unpredictably. One moment we are baffled, stymied. Then, suddenly, the light dawns.[21]

In undertaking to realize their talents and desires in relation to the social worlds they inhabit, children rely on the care and guidance of their elders; the psychological grounding these efforts provide can be seen, in turn, as necessary to the children's own development of curious and caring hearts. We know that many efforts at personal fulfillment are thwarted and that many forms of human limitation cause the universal realization of such a vision to remain a distant aim. Yet whenever and wherever teachers support students in mapping and making sense of their own beliefs, commitments, and dreams, they position those young people as fellow democratic citizens who are entitled to guide their lives by their own lights.

Intellectual Authority as the Heart of It All

Intellectual authority represents a specifically democratic construction of authority because the construct entails a dynamic intellectual reciprocity: one must demonstrate a willingness and ability both to express oneself in culturally fluent terms *and* to apprehend the meanings of others. Sounding commanding in the specialized language of one's field does not establish one as intellectually authoritative in the sense we have been discussing here. Intellectual authority can only grow through a developed interest and capacity to make sense of one's world in collaboration with a diverse array of others.

As I have argued, nurturing students' willingness and ability to weigh contrasting perspectives across human differences of all kinds fosters the natural development of democratic values, purposes, and practices. Learning that they, as democratic citizens, are required to carry on in the face of competing claims and commitments, and that there are established means for doing so, leads to students' appropriation of dispositions and capacities that are essential for democratic deliberative processes of every kind.

Inspiring a genuine sense of intellectual reciprocity among any group of students, though, will forever remain challenging work, irretrievably enmeshed in the local characteristics of a learning environment such as the teacher's and students' personalities and the nature of their relationships with the school, each other, and the material. A narrative-based form of research, such as the participant framework analysis, is therefore needed in order to explore these situated relationships and to enable the nuanced characterization and theorizing of these many interpenetrating influences and variables. In this research, the participant framework analysis served to demonstrate that inspiring student agency cannot simply be seen as a matter of enacting a given set of participation guidelines, but must rather be seen as an interpersonal engagement constituted through the interactions of a complex set of human impetuses and influences.

By explicitly supporting students' personal efforts to construct meaning, democratic schools demonstrate the power of their organizing commitments to all, including children from historically marginalized communities and those who may feel alienated for other reasons. By encouraging children to claim their democratic right to disagree in areas where a diversity of views is not only acceptable but actually desirable in an intellectually open society, educators earn the trust of their students and teach them to claim a sense of their own intellectual authority within that society.

When we consider how desperately short of our most basic pedagogical responsibilities to some children our nation has historically fallen, I believe the recent extreme narrowing of educational policy horizons becomes comprehensible, if not acceptable. Regrettably, the increasingly driven and uniform character of practice to which this narrowing continues to lead us constrains the situated creativity and generativity of the very professionals who must carry us forward. These constraints are disproportionately felt, in turn, by the very children who our most troubled schools are intended to serve. I have cited the following words of Maxine Greene before, but I find it appropriate to call upon them again here.

> This book is in no sense the first to try to reawaken the consciousness of possibility. It will not be the first to seek a vision of education that brings together the need for wide-awakeness with the hunger for community, the desire to know with the wish to understand, the desire to feel with the passion to see...Confronting a void, confronting nothingness, we may be able to empower the young to create and re-create a common world—and, in cherishing it, in renewing it, discover what it signifies to be free.[22]

Although this study was located in the field of literary interpretation, the questions it seeks to address about student agency and authority are basic to every pedagogical relation. Have student questions been entertained and in what fashion? Have students' emerging understandings been articulated and their relation to broader understandings explored? Who has ratified what claims and on what basis? It is only by taking questions such as these into actual classrooms that a satisfying range of answers can be characterized and the articulate, responsible, and effective use of democratic pedagogical authority promoted.

Institutionalizing meaningful, powerful, and transparent knowledge construction processes within classrooms can help to humanize and revitalize the shallow and even combative relationships that exist between students and teachers in many schools. When students feel safe to express their confusions and doubts and have been encouraged to listen to and respond thoughtfully to each other, a broader array of student ideas and voices is heard; even students who have come to feel uncertain about their desire or capacity to meet a teacher's expectations may find themselves willing and able to engage. In such slight shifts of orientation, one sees the aims of democracy at work in the world. There have long been and continue to be accomplished teachers creating personally and pedagogically valuable moments such as this within our schools every day. Our society should do more to support their work.

Notes

Introduction

1   See Pace & Hemmings (2007) for a review of the related scholarship; in particular, note discussions of Blau (1974), Mitchell and Spady (1983), and Parsons (1964).

2   See Pace & Hemmings, eds. (2006), including the foreword by Metz, and Metz (1978) on authority as constructed within relationships and as requiring a mutually agreed upon moral framework. As will be developed within this book, democracy as a social and political form provides the needed moral aims and values for the legitimate construction of authority within democratic schools.

3   As discussed further in chapter six, the construct of 'Accountable Talk' provides a practical interpretation of these democratic discourse ideals; see Michaels, O'Connor, & Resnick (2008).

4   Many philosophers' names are by now associated with this shift of perspective on knowledge. In particular, seminal works by Michael Polanyi (1962/58) and Thomas Kuhn (1996/62) are widely referenced.

5   Dewey's most pointed thoughts on this topic can be found in the volume that includes *The School and Society* and *The Child and the Curriculum* (Dewey, 1990), essays that were originally written in 1900 and 1902, respectively.

6   Dewey's classic text *Democracy and Education* (1944/16) provides a comprehensive vision of the moral principles Dewey found basic to democratic life and relations. A text edited by James Gouinlock includes a more focused selection of Dewey's moral writings (Gouinlock, ed., 1994). A. G. Rud, Jim Garrison, and Lynda Stone recently edited a special issue of *Education and Culture* devoted to contemporary interpretations of the implications of Dewey's thought, including his moral thought, for democratic school practice (Rud et al., eds., 2009). See Fishman & McCarthy (2009) for a discussion of Dewey's thought on the role of morality in human happiness.

7   Gutmann, 1999. Many social scientists who consider the quality of democratic discourse and deliberation within the public sphere also speak of the need for citizens to share the dispositions and skills with which we will concern ourselves here. For example, see Anderson, Cissna, & Clune (2003).

8   Noddings, 1992, 2003a, 2003b.

9   Greene, 1988.

10 See Duckworth (2006) and Van Lier (1996) for two contemporary interpretations of the pedagogical significance of Piaget's work.

11 For example, Moll, ed., 1990; Lee & Smagorinsky, eds., 2000. See Mayer (2010) for discussion of the theoretical intersections between the work of Piaget, Vygotsky, and Dewey.

12 Bransford et al., 2000.

13 See Hicks (1995–1996) for an overview of the field's history; Hicks treats most of the field's major figures and all of the central theoretical strands.

14 See, for example, Anyon (1980, 1981) and Mehan (1979).

15 The term 'interpretive authority' has been employed in relation to established expertise within the world of language arts education. I presented my quite different construction of this term in a 2009 article and will elaborate upon it further here.

16 As with any pedagogical approach, any of the three forms can also be enacted to greater or lesser effect in relation to its distinctive capacities.

17 Noddings, 2003b.

18 Early anthropological work in this country focused upon the cultural differences between Native American ways of learning and knowing and the European forms of education that were imposed upon Native American peoples (Au, 1979; Erikson & Mohatt, 1982; Phillips, 1972). One of the earliest volumes to bring together anthropologists, linguists, and educational theorists to study school practice was Cazden et al., eds., 1972. See also, for example, Ashton-Warner, 1963; Gee, 1990, 1992; Halliday & Hasan, 1989; Heath, 1983; Hicks, ed., 1996 (particularly Hick's introduction).

Chapter One—Democratic Ideas about Knowledge

1 O'Connor and Michaels use this phrase 'values, purposes, and practices' to characterize the organizing dimensions of community- and discipline-based literacies (1993, p. 318). My work follows from the understandings these scholars outline regarding the ways in which any community's linguistic practices embed assumptions, aims, and values.

2 Pragmatists differ among themselves in a number of ways; in contrast to Dewey, for example, Richard Rorty (1982) embraced relativism. Gallie (1966) found that Dewey and his close colleague G. H. Mead followed in the more analytically rigorous footsteps of C. S. Peirce, Pragmatism's founder, rather than sharing what Gallie considers the somewhat more sentimental approach of William James (1970).

3 Of course, one's level of enthusiasm for such engagements will always depend upon more than one's philosophical ideals.

4 By this, I do not mean to suggest that hierarchy is antithetical to democratic relations, although hierarchies based exclusively upon power relations certainly are.

5   For example, see Pais, 1982.

6   A brief, readable essay on this perspective can be found in a later collection of Kuhn's essays (Kuhn, 2000, pp. 105–120).

7   Abraham Maslow is most closely identified with this thinking as a result of his early theorizing of a human hierarchy of needs (Maslow, 1970).

8   Much will be said about this perspective in the next chapter; see, for example, Rogoff (2003).

9   As discussed in chapter two, names associated with this work include Carol Lee, Luis Moll, and Lisa Delpit.

10 If only all high-stakes tests would be crafted with this criteria of 'essential to acting and functioning as an educated citizen' in mind. For while state and federal governments can legitimately be seen to possess an interest in educational outcomes, I would argue that all *universal* standards of performance should exclusively test for the very most basic foundational understandings and skills.

11 For example, one contemporary shift in foundational values is reflected by a number of states recently legalizing gay marriage. We now have a situation where a right to gay marriage is lawfully recognized and protected in some states and not others, opening delicate and sensitive questions for some school communities.

12 Kuhn famously theorized that scientific worldviews or 'paradigms' can collapse suddenly and long-established expert theories and methods be therefore abandoned (Kuhn, 1996/62).

13 For a broad and illuminating collection of articles on the politics and pedagogical implications of textbook use, see Castell, Luke, & Luke, eds., 1989.

14 It is important to realize that this has always been true. Democratic educators need to be able to engage with the public about their aims and means, while non-educators need, in turn, to respect the expertise and insight of those who have studied and worked within the field; see Kliebard (1987) for a history of this nation's continuing debates regarding the direction of school practice.

15 For example, see Ravitch's 5/17/2011 entry in *Education Week*'s online blog 'Bridging Differences' written alternately by Diane Ravitch and Deborah Meier in regards to school closings: http://blogs.edweek.org/edweek/Bridging-Differences/2011/05/what_works_best_help_or_punish.html

16 Einstein, for example, did not approve of Heisenberg's uncertainty principle, which has gone on to transform the philosophy of science.

17 See, for example, Bereiter (1994).

18 Berkman & Plutzer (2010).

19 Berkman & Plutzer (ibid).

20   See Nussbaum and Sinatra (2003) for a presentation and discussion of research on the role student debate of contrasting arguments can play in precipitating conceptual change.

Chapter Two—Knowledge Building as Interpretation

1   For elaboration, see Rogoff, 2003, pp. 236–281. In *Naming Infinity*, Graham and Kantor (2009) tell the story of two mathematical discourse communities in France and Russia and the spiritual framework and commitments that gave the Russian community the courage to proceed with investigations that the French scholars had abandoned amidst doubt and criticism.

2   Applebee (1996, p. 5) calls these "knowledge-in-action" traditions.

3   See Howard Gardner's engaging chronicle of the emergence of cognitive psychology (Gardner, 1985). Cognitive scientists drew upon the emerging fields of artificial intelligence, linguistics, and Piagetian developmental psychology to argue that even the systematic logical and mathematical thought that Piaget studied (and around which Western science has been organized) could not be effectively characterized in such rudimentary terms.

4   Bruner, 1990, 1996.

5   Vygotsky explicitly positioned himself in contrast to Piaget's interest in inborn human propensities toward logical and mathematical thought. Vygotsky's focus on the role of words, signs, and symbols in the development of higher forms of human thought was succeeded in Soviet times by a focus on the role of material tools within forms of human action; see Wertsch, et al., 1995.

6   See Bruner, 1996, especially the first chapter (pp. 1–43).

7   See Mayer, 2010, for a discussion of Dewey's more seamless vision.

8   See Bruner's discussion of narrative dimension of science (1996, p. 42).

9   See Wells, 2001, for a recent construction of this concept within classrooms, which Wells calls a 'community of inquirers;' also Palinscar et al., 1993.

10   Rizzolatti et al., 2008.

11   Mayer, 2005; for a contemporary consideration of the qualitatively divergent thought of children, see Gopnik et al., 1999. Piaget was likely the first to gather and analyze natural patterns of children's speech, thereby inspiring methodological innovations in a host of fields. Others interested in the thought and language of children soon followed Piaget into the classroom (see Isaacs, 1929, 1966/30, 1972/33).

12   Piagetian and now Neo-Piagetian research continues to demonstrate the extent to which children reliably reference developmentally distinctive conceptual schemes in all learning (Bransford, Brown, & Cocking, eds., 2000; Driver, 1994; Fischer & Dawson, 2002).

13 Inhelder and colleagues adapted Piagetian method into a form of learning research they called critical exploration (Inhelder, Sinclair, and Bovet, 1974). Most scholars still identify Piagetian method with the development of mathematical and logical thinking as Piaget focused on these areas of thought. As we will see, Duckworth and her students have expanded the method to other subject areas.

14 Kamii, 1985, p. 123; as Kamii also notes in this essay, "Autonomy as the Aim of Education," Piaget most explicitly discussed intellectual agency in relation to moral development. As she goes on to explain, however, the need to access and engage immature thinking on its own terms—as opposed to overlaying that thinking with verbal demonstrations of adult thought—was implicit in all of Piaget's research and theorizing.

15 Chapman, 1988; Vidal, 1987, 1994.

16 As Fischer explains, Piaget's view of learning as an unending elaboration and rethinking of existing intellectual structures is now widely accepted among learning psychologists.

17 Systems theory has been employed to study the structural and functional dimensions of sociological and psychological systems, which are seen as interpenetrating and as self-regulating. Talcott Parsons was an early figure in introducing systems theory to sociology and Ludwig von Bertalanffy an early figure in introducing systems theory to psychology.

18 By the end of his life, Piaget had begun theoretically integrating cybernetics and systems theory in his conception of structuralism, which Piaget continued to revisit in light of emerging understandings (Piaget, 1968).

19 Rose and Fischer, 2009, p. 401.

20 For example, Rose and Fischer (ibid.) discuss a conceptual progression from single cases to mappings to systematic thought that may underlie all areas of conceptual growth: actions, representations, and abstractions.

21 Vygotsky, 1987; see particularly chapter two, pp. 12–57.

22 See Hatano (1993) for one pointed analysis of the ways in which cognitive science, with its (by now often implicit) embrace of Piaget's vision of the independent learner, must be integrated into sociocultural models of learning, which can otherwise risk being seen and interpreted as transmission models of learning.

23 In contrast to Piaget, Neo-Piagetians view school learning and conceptual development as reciprocal forces, each contributing to the development of the other. See Case, Okamoto, Griffen, et al., 1996, especially the introductory chapter by Case, pp. 1–26.

24 Mayer, 2005; see also, the introduction in Feurerstein, Feuerstein, and Falik, 2010, pp. xv–xviii.

25 See, for example, Wertsch, 1985; Daniels, 2001.

26 See Gallagher and Reid, (1981) for an elegant and comprehensive introduction to Piaget's theoretical language and concepts.

27 See Daniels (2001) for a contemporary interpretation of Vygotsky's work for pedagogical purposes and Forman, et al., eds. (1993) for discussion of issues related to the interpretation of sociocultural theory for classroom research. Also, see Rogoff (2003) for an anthropologically oriented overview of the sociocultural developmental perspective.

28 Again, see Vygotsky, 1987, pp. 12–57.

29 See, for example, Kozulin, 1998; Lemke, 1990.

30 Delpit, 1995.

31 See Moll chapter in Lee & Smagorinsky, eds. (2000, pp. 256–268) and Lee (2007).

32 Which is not to say that significant tensions do not exist in this area of practice: a perceived over-emphasis on "non-mainstream" ways of knowing, including the use of students' native languages, can ignite political battles and is currently doing so.

33 Gardner, 1999.

34 Pediatrician and learning theorist Mel Levine (2002) also argues the importance of attending to individual patterns of learning and has developed many practical approaches for recognizing and addressing intellectual differences that can hold children back when educational institutions are not sufficiently sensitive to individual intellectual variety. See also Phillip (2001) for links to the larger democratic polity.

35 Gardner, 2000.

36 Within dynamic systems conceptions, multiple integral elements continually interact, both influencing and being influenced by each other; together these elements constitute one of multiple interrelated and interpenetrating systems. See Bausch, (2001), Laslo, (1996), and Valsiner et al., eds. (2009). Uri Bronfenbrenner's mapping of multiple nested realms of social influences represents an early integration of this thinking in the world of educational theory (Bronfenbrenner, 1989). See Rose & Fischer (2009) for a recent discussion of the construct of 'dynamic structuralism' within the world of developmental learning theory.

37 As Uri Bronfenbrenner, an early proponent of a systems perspective within social-psychology, argued, social scientists need to craft "more complex theoretical paradigms and research designs that are commensurate with the complexities of human beings functioning in human situations"(Bronfenbrenner, 1993, p. 6).

38 Whether or not further research supports this particular claim, comparable chains of diverse dimensions of influence do continually unfold within all

classrooms. See Cofer's chapter in Fogel, King & Shanker, eds. (2008, pp. 128–135); example is discussed on p. 129.

39   Activity theory emerged in response, in part, to Vygotsky's focus on cultural and historical influences on human meaning-making. See Wertsch et al., 1995, particularly chapter one on the historical roots of both strands of scholarship (pp. 37–55); also Sannino, Daniels, & Gutiérrez, eds., 2009.

40   Cazden, John, & Hymes, eds., 1972; Gumperz, 2003.

41   See Adger, 2003.

42   See Lemke, 1990; Olson, 1980; Wells, 1993, 1999, 2001.

43   Shirley Brice Heath's commanding ethnography of two Piedmont communities (1983) was among the earliest works to illustrate the many profound ways in which the divergent and class-based language practices of students' home cultures serve to shape students' relationships with classroom cultures.

44   Au, 1979; Erikson & Mohatt, 1982; Phillips, 1972. See final endnote in the introduction of this book.

45   See introduction by Deborah Hicks in Hicks, ed., 1996, for a more detailed summary of this history.

46   Bronfenbrenner identified multiple psychological processes that shape development, stating that, "research that deals only with one of these processes not only underspecifies the model, but risks overgeneralization of findings and, which is even more fatal for developmental science, can result in oversimplification and distortion of psychological realities" (1993, p. 5).

47   Cazden, John, & Hymes, eds., 1972.

48   Mehan, 1979; in particular read the first chapter (pp. 1–34), which characterizes the limitations of correlational, quantitative, and participant observation research as well as presenting Mehan's methodological aims and means. My work shares Mehan's perspective and commitments as characterized there.

49   See Mehan, 1979, especially pp. vii–xii. In subsequent work, Cazden (2001) has also highlighted Mehan's contribution in identifying the pedagogical structure 'topically related set' (TRS).

50   Again, see Mehan's methodological discussion in his book *Learning Lessons*, (1979, pp. 1–34) where he makes many related points of relevance here.

51   Sinclair & Coulthard, 1975.

52   The sequence is also known as the Initiation/Response/Evaluation or IRE sequence after subsequent scholarship (Mehan, 1979). I use the broader IRF characterization. See Cazden, 1988, 2001; Mehan, 1979; Newman, Griffin, & Cole, 1989; Wells, 1993.

53   Nystrand et al., 1997.

54   O'Connor and Michaels, 1996. O'Connor and Michaels also discuss the theoretical roots of the construct in Goffman (1974, 1981) and Goodwin (1990).

55   O'Connor & Michaels, ibid., p. 64.

56   Again, see Metz, 1978 and Pace & Hemmings, 2007. Also, again, see Mehan's methodological discussion (Mehan, ibid., pp. 1–34).

Chapter Three—Teacher-Led Learning

1   See both Wells (2007) and responsive commentary from O'Connor & Michaels (2007) for recent explication and exploration of the constructs 'dialogic' and 'monologic' within the classroom context.

2   Again, in the case of potentially divisive content such as evolutionary theory, expert understandings can be positioned within a broader conceptual framing that presents them as understandings that scientific experts find convincing. While students can be expected to learn how and why evolutionary scientists have come to agree upon these understandings, they cannot be required to agree with the assumptions that underlie those expert claims. As discussed in chapter two, the contrasting roles of science and religion in a democratic society might be raised and considered.

3   Lemke, 1990, p. 5.

4   Nystrand, 1997.

5   Wells, 1993. This article also appears as a chapter in Wells, 1999.

6   Mayer, 2009. I consider this issue in both structural and contextual terms.

7   Cazden, 2001.

8   Palincsar and Brown, 1984; cited in Cazden, ibid., p. 66.

9   Wells, 1993, p. 2.

10 Wells, ibid., p. 35.

11 There may well be exceptions to this claim. Typically, classroom discussions seek to advance some ways of viewing and understanding the world over others. I concern myself here with these forms of pedagogical discussions.

12 Again, predictable question and answer sequences that require little imagination or creative thought on anyone's part are most commonly found in schools that serve low-income children and in classrooms that serve low-tracked students. Of course, intellectually engaging practice can and does also occur within exceptional schools located in impoverished communities.

13 I refer readers interested in a more comprehensive explanation of my methodology to my 2009 article in *Language and Education* from which some of my methodological discussion here has been adapted.

14 See Goffman, 1974, for a brief characterization of what he termed a 'participation framework' (pp. 1–4), a concept he then develops within the book; see Goffman, 1981, for his discussion of speakers 'animation' of other speakers.

15 'Revoicing' as a term and theoretical construct is introduced in O'Connor & Michaels, 1996.

16   As Lampert has put it, in "interpretive social science, data are treated as text, and the enterprise is to understand its meaning" (Lampert, 1990, p. 36).

17   The transcripts are verbatim renderings of the recordings and so capture the hesitations, repetitions, and interruptions that are characteristic of natural speech. Pauses, word emphasis, and readings of the text were all marked on the transcripts. Commas indicate momentary hitches in the flow of speech. Brief pauses are indicated with an ellipsis; all pauses over 3 seconds were timed and the times bracketed. Emphasized words have been italicized; readings of the text have been rendered in bold-face. Each unintelligible syllable spoken is represented by a single lower-case x.

18   This approach was in part suggested by conversations I had with colleagues Kate Gill and David Eddy Spicer, both of whom have focused in their own research on the contrast between discourse moves that open or sustain conversation and those that close down discourse possibilities (see also Eggins & Slade, 1997).

19   Applebee, 1974, 1993, 1996; Flood and Langer, eds., 1994; Hillocks, 1999; Langer, 1995; Nystrand, 1997; Rosenblatt, 2005. See also chapter one in Probst, 2004, for a brief overview of related history (pp. 1–27).

20   For example, Eco, 1990; see also Morrell (2008) for contemporary discussion of related issues within the context of urban education.

21   All of the quotations cited here are from the first few pages of my first interview with Randy, just after I had completed my audio recordings in his classroom.

22   See endnote 17 above for transcription protocol.

Chapter Four—Student-Led Learning

1   These educators identified with the ideals of what came to be known as Progressive education, of which Dewey was widely considered the intellectual leader. See Westbrook (1991) particularly the first four chapters. For a recent look at Jane Addams founding contributions to this line of thought, see Ellen Lagemann's recently reissued collection of Addams writings on education (1994) and the chapter by Tröler in *Pragmatism and Education* (2005).

2   In Kamii's research, students constructed all of their own mathematical algorithms and other tools and generalizations from an early age. See Kamii, 1985, 1988, 2000.

3   See, for example, online curricular resources at Criticalexplorers.org.

4   Not that scholars have agreed about this. For example, see Eco, 1990.

5   Again, see Applebee, 1974, 1993, 1996; Flood and Langer, eds., 1994; Hillocks, 1999; Langer, 1995; Nystrand, 1997; Rosenblatt, 2005.

6   On the other end of this continuum, foreign language instruction has historically relied on rote memorization to a greater degree than other academic areas due to the high percentage of foundational understandings that must be mastered. Yet,

even foreign language classes can integrate student-led and co-led learning experiences to great pedagogical effect.

7   See Bruner's summary of the conference (Bruner, 1962). Inhelder would go on to collaborate briefly with Bruner at Harvard and to help conceptualize a line of learning research back in Geneva, in part due to questions the American social scientists had asked about speeding and deepening learning (Inhelder et al., 1974). Piaget did not attend and was later known to express a lack of interest in what he called the "American question" about speeding learning.

8   Federally funded research on student-led knowledge construction has actually focused more upon the fields of science and mathematics as economic and military concerns have often caused funding for educational research to be concentrated in these disciplines. See Marshall, Sears, & Schubert, 2000, particularly chapter three (pp. 34–53). For an example of recent related work, see Michaels, Shouse, and Schweingruber, 2008.

9   For example, David Hawkins, a philosopher of science who participated in the restructuring of science curricula in the 1960s, spoke of the value of student-led investigations in surmounting what he termed 'critical barriers' to student understanding (1978, 2002).

10 The teacher's role in student-led learning experiences and the underlying nature of those experiences are also thoughtfully treated by David Hawkins (2002), particularly in chapter four, "I, Thou, and It" (pp. 48–62). Hawkins was the first director of the Elementary Science Study, which developed student-led science investigations in the 1960s.

11 See, for example, Bransford et al., 2000.

12 In contrast, early elementary classrooms more frequently provide contexts for unstructured exploration, such as water tables and peg boards, as students at this level are more commonly seen as profiting from independent investigations of natural and social phenomena.

13 Cazden shares a beautiful example from Magdalene Lampert's work in mathematics, where Lampert correctly surmises that a student who had claimed that 'eight minus a half is four' was employing the term 'eight' as a quantity and the term 'a half' as an operation upon the quantity of eight. See Cazden, 2001, pp. 51–54, and Lampert et al., 1996. Many, including Cazden, continue to reference Lee Shulman's influential 1986 article on the need for what Shulman termed 'pedagogical content knowledge' in this regard; for example, also see Lee, 2007, pp. 109–110.

14 See Ballenger, 1999, especially chapters one and two (pp. 1–14), and the collected works of the Brookline Teacher Researcher Seminar (BTRS), especially the introduction (Ballenger, ed., 2004, pp. 1–11).

15 Ballenger ibid.; see also, Ballenger, 2009.

16 Luis Moll's (Moll, ed., 1990) and Carol Lee's (2007) work helps to define this field.

17 Ballenger, ed., 2004, pp. 6–9.

18 One might mention, for example, the many teachers who have worked with Pat Carini at the Prospect Center in Vermont and those who have helped to construct the pedagogical practice of the famed Reggio Emilio Schools in Italy. See also, Armstrong, 1980.

19 The term 'exploratory talk' was framed and developed by Douglas Barnes in his 1976 book *From Communication to Curriculum.* Neil Mercer and colleagues have since sought to operationalize this useful construct for classroom practice; see Mercer & Littleton (2007), particularly chapters five and six where the scholars share the results of their long-term classroom research program (pp. 57–112). This research into patterns of talk within student small group work implicitly suggests the importance of explicit teacher demonstration of productive patterns of academic talk.

20 See Duckworth, 2001 (ed.), 2005, 2006. All of Duckworth's work is suffused with these values; see, in particular, chapter five in Duckworth, 2006, "The Virtues of Not Knowing" (pp. 63–68).

21 Duckworth originally termed her work 'extended clinical interviewing,' after Piaget's early iterations of his renowned 'clinical method,' later switching to the name employed for the methodological variation developed by the Genevan learning researchers, which Inhelder introduced in her 1974 book with Sinclair and Bovet (Duckworth, 2005; Inhelder, Sinclair, & Bovet, 1974).

22 Mayer, 2005.

23 See also Schneier, 1998; Schneier has employed critical exploration to teach literature to adolescents within public school contexts.

24 Again, see Duckworth, 2006, especially chapter one in this case, "The Having of Wonderful Ideas" (pp. 1–14).

25 Ibid., p. 116.

26 Duckworth's attention to human, as opposed to cultural, diversity has gotten her into trouble with some who feel that a specifically cultural perspective on learning and knowing is essential to all consideration of school practice today, particularly in view of the oppressive influences that children of racial and cultural minorities, particularly African-Americans, have historically had to endure within public schools in the United States. While analysis of these forces certainly provides an essential backdrop to viewing contemporary school practice within this country, educators do also need to work toward a vision of classroom practice that lies beyond the limitations of today's still often ugly social realities (see, for example, Kozol, 1992).

27 As is suggested by the title of Duckworth's edited volume from 2001: *"Tell Me More": Listening to Learners Explain.*

28 My analysis of the three forms of learning experience is based entirely upon the Framing, Developing, and Evaluating move categories, which have been found reliable through standard co-coding procedures. The sub-codes have not been submitted to co-coding procedures and are not integral to my theorizing of the three forms. Again, see Mayer, 2009, for further elaboration of my coding scheme.

29 For example, O'Connor & Michaels, 1993; see discussion on pp. 329–330.

30 Mercer & Littleton, 2007; see endnote 19 above.

31 See Mayer, 2009, for further examples of how all the teachers employed the IRF sequence.

Chapter Five—Co-Led Learning

1 It can be difficult to distinguish between foundational and expert under-standings within the context of elementary, and even secondary, school math. Textbook algorithms provide one example of an 'expert' approach to manipulating foundational mathematical relationships. The import of Lampert's work in relation to the foundational, expert, and personal analysis lies primarily in the emphasis Lampert places on accessing students' personal observations and understandings about mathematical relationships and on having students themselves collaboratively construct meaningful mathematical tools, including algorithms. For example, see discussion in Lampert, 1990, starting on p. 44.

2 Ibid., see discussion starting on page 44. One cannot learn how to participate in mathematical discourse—or any other type of discourse—in the absence of appropriate content.

3 Lampert, 1990, p. 31.

4 Lampert, 1990, 2001; Lampert et al., 1996. Lampert's work by no means stands alone here, although her work has helped to lead the way. For a recent example of related work, see Herbel-Eisenmann & Wagner, 2010.

5 Lampert, 1990, p. 41.

6 Ibid., p. 39.

7 Lampert, 2001, p. 77.

8 Depending on the purpose of the researcher and the character of the transcripts, one may choose to code these three move types as both Developing and Evaluating, at least in certain situations. Elaborating moves, for example, generally imply ratification of a prior claim.

9 Again, see Mayer, 2009, for a more thorough and focused consideration of the coding system.

10   Each teacher's average number of Clarifying moves per class across the two class periods I analyzed were: Malcolm – 28; Frances – 25; Yale – 14; Grace – 11; Jay – 11; and Randy – 3.

11   See, for example, O'Loughlin, 1992. Just in 1998, Schwartz and Bransford felt moved to write what was to become an oft-cited article called "A Time for Telling." In this research article, the authors argued that even university students needed to be given opportunities to construct and recall the appropriate conceptual tools prior to listening to the lecture.

Chapter Six—Educating for Democracy

1   One of the most distressing effects of our current test-driven reform calculus is that many of the adolescents who had felt most uncertain about whether they needed or wanted what schools had to give have only grown more skeptical. Indeed, research suggests that many have left school all together, at times encouraged by educational administrators looking to improve their testing averages by shedding their poorest academic performers.

2   Brian Schultz, for example, has written an inspiring account of the year in which his classroom of fifth-grade students, with his support, took on the challenge of drawing attention to the need to renovate their dilapidated and dysfunctional school building (Schultz, 2008). The year culminated in a Project Citizen award for the students and an invitation for them to address the Center for Civic Education's National Conference.

3   Hidi & Harackiewicz's meta-analysis of motivation research (2000) is well worth a read for any interested in this topic. The scholars provide a clear and wide ranging synthesis of the relevant research and demonstrate the limitations of such models for the development of meaningful theory.

4   Again, there are no formulas: the safest and wisest response to *any* A or B policy question within educational theory will always remain 'it depends upon a number of contextual variables.' (This includes, of course, questions regarding the most pedagogically effective interpretive authority distribution for a given academic context.)

5   Again, see Hidi & Harackiewicz (ibid.) for a helpful discussion on the relationship between personal and situational interest and the potential links between personal goals and situational interest, the latter of which results from engaging learning experiences.

6   As I hope this work has suggested throughout, motivational dynamics will also vary in relationship to a number of other factors, including the personality of the teacher.

7   Of course, all charter schools are selective to the extent a student's acceptance demands exceptional efforts on the part of a parent or guardian.

8   Although see Nussbaum & Sinatra (2003), for example, for research on the role of argumentation in promoting conceptual change.

9   Again, classroom discourse analysis has shown that roughly two thirds of classroom conversation can be characterized by the Initiation/Response/Feedback move sequence (Nystrand et al., ibid.).

10   Gutmann, ibid., p. 30.

11   Greene, ibid., pp. 121–122.

12   Noddings, 2003, pp. xv–xvi.

13   For Noddings, caring-for entails a profound quality of listening and attending to the needs and wishes of the cared-for. See Haroutunian-Gordon & Laverty, eds., 2011, for a special issue of *Educational Theory* devoted to philosophical perspectives on listening. See also Kimball and Garrison, 1996, on hermeneutic listening as a pathway toward personal agency through the development of students' metacognitive awareness.

14   See Au & Raphael (2000) for one thoughtful consideration of related issues.

15   Accountable Talk was created by educational theorists Sarah Michaels, Catherine O'Connor, and Lauren Resnick. See Michaels, O'Connor, and Resnick, 2008; for related work in the field of K-8 science, see Michaels, Shouse, & Schweingruber, 2008.

16   Michaels, O'Connor, and Resnick, ibid., p. 289.

17   Ibid., p. 295.

18   Gutmann, 1999, p. 315.

19   Dewey, 1944/16, p. 307.

20   Again, see Fishman & McCarthy, 2009.

21   Noddings, 2003, p. 145.

22   Original quote can be found in Greene, 1988, p. 23. I cited this passage from Greene in a recent volume of letters assembled as a tribute to her and to her considerable contributions to the field (Lake, ed., 2011, p. 17).

Bibliography

Adger, C.T., (2003). Discourse in Educational Settings, in *The Handbook of Discourse Analysis*, eds. D. Schiffren, D. Tannen, and H. Hamilton. Oxford, UK: Blackwell Publishing.

Anderson, R., Cissna, K. N., & Clune, M. K., (2003). The Rhetoric of Public Dialogue, *Communication Research Trends*, 22 (1) 1–37.

Anyon, J., (1980). Social Class and the Hidden Curriculum of Work, *Journal of Education*, 162(1) 67–92.

Anyon, J., (1980). Social Class and School Knowledge, *Curriculum Inquiry*, 11(1) 3–42.

Armstrong, M., (1980). *Closely Observed Children.* London: Writers and Readers Publishing.

Applebee, A., (1974). *Tradition and Reform in the Teaching of English: A History.* Urbana, IL: National Council of Teachers of English.

Applebee, A., (1993). *Literature in the Secondary School: Studies of Curriculum and Instruction in the United States.* Research Monograph No. 25. Urbana, IL: National Council of Teachers of English.

Applebee, A., (1996). *Curriculum as Conversation: Transforming Traditions of Teaching and Learning.* Chicago: The University of Chicago Press.

Applebee, A & Langer, J., Nystrand, M. & Gamoran, A., (2003). Discussion-Based Approaches to Developing Understanding: Classroom Instruction and Student Performance in Middle and High School English. *American Educational Research Journal*, 40(3) 685-730.

Ashton-Warner, S., (1963). *Teacher.* New York: Simon and Schuster.

Au, K., (1979). Participation structures in a reading lesson with Hawaiian children: Analysis of a culturally appropriate instructional event. *Anthropology and Education Quarterly*, 11, 91–114.

Au, K. H. & Raphael, T. E., (2000). Equity and Literacy in the Next Millennium. *Reading Research Quarterly*, 35(1), 170–188.

Ballenger, C., ed. (2004). *Regarding Children's Words: Teacher Research on Language and Literacy.* New York: Teachers College Press.

Ballenger, C., (1999). *Teaching Other People's Children.* New York: Teachers College Press.

Ballenger, C., (2009). *Puzzling Moments, Teachable Moments: Practicing Teacher Research in Urban Classrooms.* New York: Teachers College Press.

Bausch, K. C., (2001). *The Emerging Consensus in Social Systems Theory.* New York: Kluwer Academic/Plenum Publishers.

Bereiter, C., (1993). Implications of Postmodernism for Science, or, Science as Progressive Discourse. *Educational Psychologist,* 29(1), 3–12.

Berkman, M. & Plutzer, E., (2010). *Evolution, Creationism, and the Battle to Control America's Classrooms.* New York: Cambridge University Press.

Bloome, D. & Greene, J., (1992). Educational contexts of literacy, in Grabe, W., ed., *Annual Review of Applied Linguistics,* 13, 49–70.

Boring, E., (1956). Evolution and American Psychology, in *Evolutionary Thought in America,* S. Parsons, ed. New York: George Braziller, Inc.

Bransford, J. D., Brown, A. L., & Cocking, R. R., eds., (2000). *How People Learn: Brain, Mind, Experience, and School.* Washington, DC: National Research Council, Commission on Behavioral & Social Sciences & Education, Committee on Developments in the Science of Learning Source.

Bronfenbrenner, U., (1989). Ecological Systems Theory. In R. Vasta, (ed.), *Annals of Child Development,* 6, 187–249.

Bronfenbrenner, U., (1993). "The Ecology of Cognitive Development: Research Models and Fugitive Findings." In R. H. Wozniak & K. Fischer, eds., *Development in Context: Acting and Thinking in Specific Environments.* Hillsdale, NJ: Lawrence Erlbaum Associates, Publishers.

Bruner, J. (1962). *The Process of Education.* Lahore: Franklin Publications.

Bruner, J., (1990). *Acts of Meaning.* Cambridge, MA: Harvard University Press.

Bruner, J., (1996). *The Culture of Education.* Cambridge, MA: Harvard University Press.

Case, R. & Edelstein, W., (1993). *The New Structuralism in Cognitive Development: Theory and Research on Individual Pathways.* New York: Karger.

Case, R., Okamoto, Y., Griffen, S., McKeough, et al., (1996). The role of central conceptual structures in the development of children's thought, *Monographs of the Society for Research in Child Development*, 61(5–6, Serial No. 246).

Castell, S., Luke, A., & Luke, C., eds., (1989). *Language, Authority, and Criticism: Readings on the School Textbook*. New York: Falmer Press.

Cazden, C., John, V., & Hymes, D., eds. (1972). *Functions of Language within the Classroom*. New York: Teachers College Press.

Cazden, C., (2001). *Classroom Discourse: The Language of Teaching and Learning*. Portsmouth, NH: Heinemann.

Chapman, M. (1988). *Constructive Evolution: Origins and Development of Piaget's Thought*. Cambridge: Cambridge University Press.

Cornelius, L. L. & Herrenkohl, L. R., (2004). Power in the Classroom: How the Classroom Environment Shapes Students' Relationships with Each Other and with Concepts. *Cognition and Instruction*, 22(4), 467–498.

Corno, L. & Mandinach, E.B., (1983). The Role of Cognitive Engagement in Classroom Learning and Motivation. *Educational Psychologist*, 18, 88–108.

Csikszentmihalyi, M., (1990). *Flow: The Psychology of Optimal Experience*. New York: Harper Perennial.

Daniels, H., (2001). *Vygotsky and Pedagogy*. New York: Routledge.

Darder, A., (1991). *Culture and Power in the Classroom*. Westport, CT: Bergin & Garvey.

Delpit, L., (1995). *Other People's Children: Cultural Conflict in the Classroom*. New York: The New Press.

Dewey, J., (1929). *The Quest for Certainty*. New York: G. P. Putnam's Sons.

Dewey, J., (1930). *Human Nature and Conduct*. New York: Random House.

Dewey, J., (1944). *Democracy and Education*. New York: Free Press. (Original work published 1916.)

Dewey, J., (1990). *The School and Society* and *The Child and the Curriculum*. Chicago: University of Chicago Press. (Original essays published in 1900 and 1902.)

Duckworth, E., (2001). *"Tell Me More": Listening to Learners Explain*. New York: Teacher's College Press.

Duckworth, E. (2005). Critical Exploration in the Classroom. *The New Educator*, 1(4), 257–272.

Duckworth, E., (2006). *"The Having of Wonderful Ideas" and Other Essays on Teaching and Learning.* New York: Teachers College Press (second edition).

Driver, R., (1994). *Making Sense of Secondary Science: Research into Children's Ideas.* London: Routledge.

Eco, U., (1990). *The Limits of Interpretation.* Bloomington, IN: Indiana University Press.

Eggins, S. & Slade, D., (1997). *Analysing Casual Conversation.* London: Equinox.

Erikson, F. & Mohatt, G., (1982). Cultural Organization of Participation Structures in Two Classrooms of Indian Students, in G.D. Spindler, ed., *Doing the Ethnography of Schooling.* New York: Holt, Rhinehart, and Winston.

Faulkner, William, (1990). *The Sound and the Fury.* New York: Random House.

Feurerstein, R., Feurerstein, R. S., & Falik, L. H., (2010). *Beyond Smarter: Mediated Learning and the Brain's Capacity for Change.* New York: Teacher's College Press.

Fischer, K.W. & Dawson, T.L., (2002). "A New Kind of Developmental Science: Using Models to Integrate Theory and Research." *Monographs of the Society for Research in Child Development.* 67(1), 156–167.

Fishman, S. M. & McCarthy, L., (2009). John Dewey on Happiness: Going Against the Grain of Contemporary Thought. *Contemporary Pragmatism,* 8(2), 111–135.

Fitzgerald, F. S., (2004). *The Great Gatsby.* New York: Scribner.

Flood, J. & Langer, J., eds., (1994). *Literature Instruction: Practice and Policy.* New York: Scholastic, Inc.

Flood, J., Lapp, D., Squire, J., & Jensen, J., (2003). *Handbook on Teaching the English Language Arts.* Mahwah, NJ: Lawrence Erlbaum Associates, Publishers.

Fogel, A., King, B. J., & Shanker, S. G., eds., (2008). *Human Development in the Twenty-First Century: Visionary Ideas from Systems Scientists.* New York: Cambridge University Press.

Forman, E. A., Minick, N., & Stone, C. A., eds., (1993). *Contexts for Learning: Sociocultural Dynamics in Children's Development.* New York: Oxford University Press.

Gallagher, J.M. & Reid, D.K., (1981). *The Learning Theory of Piaget & Inhelder.* Monterey, CA: Brooks/Cole Publishing Co.

Gallie, W. B., (1966). *Peirce and Pragmatism.* New York: Dover Publications.

Gardner, H., (1985). *The Mind's New Science.* New York: Basic Books.

Gardner, H., (1999). *Intelligence Reframed: Multiple Intelligences for the 21st Century.* New York: Basic Books.

Gardner, H., (2000). *The Disciplined Mind: Beyond Facts and Standard Tests, The K-12 Education That Every Child Deserves*: New York: Penguin Books.

Gee, J. P., (1990). *Social Linguistics and Literacies: Ideology in Discourses.* New York: Falmer.

Gee, J. P., (1992). *The Social Mind: Language, Ideology, and Social Practice.* New York: Bergin & Garvey.

Goffman, E., (1974). *Frame Analysis: An Essay on the Organization of Experience.* New York: Harper and Row.

Goffman, E., (1981). *Forms of Talk.* Philadelphia: University of Pennsylvania Press.

Goodwin, M.H., (1990). *He-Said-She-Said: Talk as Social Organization among Black Children.* Bloomington, IN: Indiana University Press.

Gopnik, A., Meltzoff, A. N. & Kuhl, P. K., (1999). *The Scientist in the Crib: Minds, Brains, and How Children Learn.* New York: William Morrow & Co.

Gouinlock, J., ed., (1994). *The Moral Writings of John Dewey.* New York: Prometheus Books.

Graham, L. & Kantor, J., (2009). *Naming Infinity: A True Story of Religious Mysticism and Mathematical Creativity.* Cambridge, MA: Harvard University Press.

Greene, J. & Harker, J., eds., (1988). *Multiple Perspective Analyses of Classroom Discourse.* Norwood, NJ: Ablex.

Gutmann, A., (1999). *Democratic Education.* Princeton: Princeton University Press.

Halliday, M.A.K. & Hasan, R., (1989). *Language, Context, and Text: Aspects of Language in a Social-Semiotic Perspective.* Oxford: Oxford University Press.

Haroutunian-Gordon, S. & Laverty, M. J., eds., (2011). Symposium: Philosophical Perspectives on Listening. *Educational Theory*, 61(2), 117–219.

Hatano, G., (1993). Time to Merge Vygotskian and Constructivist Conceptions of Knowledge Acquisition, in E. Forman, N. Minick, & C. A. Stone, eds., *Contexts for Learning: Sociocultural Dynamics in Children's Development* (pp. 153–166). New York: Oxford University Press.

Hawkins, D., (1978). Critical Barriers to Science Learning. *Outlook*, 29, 3–23.

Hawkins, D., (2002). *The Informed Vision: Essays on Learning and Human Nature*. New York: Algora Publishing.

Heath, S. B., (1983). *Ways with Words: Language, Life, and Work in Communities and Classrooms*. New York: Cambridge University Press.

Herbel-Eisenmann, B. & Wagner, D., (2010). Appraising Lexical Bundles in Mathematics Classroom Discourse: Obligation and Choice. *Educational Studies in Mathematics*, 75, 43–63.

Hickman, L. A., (2009). A Symposium on John Dewey at 150: His Relevance for a Globalized World. *Educational Theory*, 59(4), 375–378.

Hicks, D., (1995–1996). Discourse, Learning, and Teaching. *Review of Research in Education*, 21, 49–95.

Hicks, D., ed., (1996). *Discourse, Learning and Schooling*. Cambridge, UK: Cambridge University Press.

Hidi, S. & Harackiewicz, J. M., (2000). Motivating the Academically Unmotivated: A Critical Issue for the 21st Century. *Review of Educational Research*, 70(2), 151–179.

Hillocks, G., (1999). *Ways of Thinking, Ways of Teaching*. New York: Teachers College Press.

Hymes, D., (1974). *Foundations in Sociolinguistics: An Ethnographic Introduction*. Philadelphia: University of Philadelphia Press.

Inhelder, B., Sinclair H., & Bovet, M. (1974). *Learning and the Development of Cognition*. Cambridge, MA; Harvard University Press.

Issacs, S. (1929). [Review of *The Language and Thought of the Child, The Child's Conception of the World,* and *Judgment and Reasoning in the Child*]. *Pedagogical Seminary and Journal of Genetic Psychology*, 36, 597–607.

Issacs, S. (1966/1930). *Intellectual Growth in Young Children*. New York: Schocken Books.

Issacs, S. (1972/1933). *Social Development in Young Children*. New York: Schocken Books.

James. W., (1970). *Pragmatism and Four Essays from The Meaning of Truth*. New York: The World Publishing Company. (Original essays written in 1907 and 1909.)

Kamii, C., (1985). *Young Children Reinvent Arithmetic: Implications of Piaget's Theory*. New York: Teachers College Press.

Kamii, C., (1988). *Number in Preschool and Kindergarten*. Washington, DC: National Association for the Education of Young Children.

Kamii, C., (2000). *Young Children Continue to Reinvent Arithmetic: Implications of Piaget's Theory*. New York: Teachers College Press.

Kimball, S. & Garrison, J., (1996). Hermeneutic Listening: An Approach to Understanding in Multicultural Conversations. *Studies in Philosophy and Education*, 15, 51–59.

Kliebard, H. M., (1987). *The Struggle for the American Curriculum 1893–1958*. New York: Routledge.

Kozol, J., (1992). *Savage Inequalities: Children in America's Schools*. New York: Harper Collins.

Kozulin, A., (1998). *Psychological Tools: A Sociocultural Approach to Education*. Cambridge, MA: Harvard University Press.

Kuhn, T. S., (1996/62). *The Structure of Scientific Revolutions*. Chicago: University of Chicago Press.

Kuhn, T. S., (2000). *The Road since Structure*. Chicago: University of Chicago Press.

Lake, R., (2011). *Dear Maxine: Letters from the Unfinished Conversation with Maxine Greene*. New York: Teachers College Press.

Lampert, M., (1990). When the Problem is Not the Question and the Solution is Not the Answer: Mathematical Knowing and Teaching. *American Educational Research Journal*, 27(1), 29–64.

Lampert, M., (2001). *Teaching Problems and the Problems of Teaching*. New Haven, CT: Yale University Press.

Lampert, M., Rittenhouse, P. & Crumbaugh, C., (1996). Agreeing to Disagree: Developing Sociable Mathematical Discourse. In D. R. Olson & N. Torrance, eds., *The Handbook of Education and Human*

Development: New Models of Learning, Teaching and Schooling, pp. 731–764. Cambridge, MA: Blackwell.

Langer, J., ed., (1992). *Literature Instruction: A Focus on Student Response*. Urbana, IL: National Council of Teachers of English.

Langer, J., (1995). *Envisioning Literature: Literary understanding and literature instruction*. New York: Teachers College Press.

Lazlo, E., (1996). *The Systems View: A Holistic Vision for Our Time*. Cresskill, NJ: Hampton Press.

Lee, C. D., (2007). *Culture, Literacy, and Learning: Taking Bloom in the Midst of the Whirlwind*. New York: Teachers College Press.

Lee, C. & Smagorinsky, P., eds., (2000). *Vygotskian Perspectives on Literacy Research: Constructing Meaning through Collaborative Inquiry*. Cambridge: Cambridge University Press.

Lee, O. & Anderson, C.W., (1993). Task Engagement and Conceptual Change in Middle School Science Classrooms. *American Educational Research Journal*, 30(3), 585–610.

Lemke, J.L., (1990). *Talking Science: Language, Learning, and Values*. Norwood, NJ: Ablex.

Levine, M., (2002). *A Mind at a Time*. New York: Simon & Schuster.

Marshall, J. D., Sears, J. T., & Schubert, W. H., (2000). *Turning Points in Curriculum: A Contemporary American Memoir*. Upper Saddle River, NJ: Merrill.

Mayer, S. J., (2005). The Early Evolution of Jean Piaget's Clinical Method. *History of Psychology*, Vol. 8, No. 4, 362–382.

Mayer, S. J., (2006). Analyzing Agency and Authority in the Discourse of Six High School English Classrooms. Harvard University: Unpublished dissertation.

Mayer, S. J., (2009). Conceptualizing Interpretive Authority in Practical Terms. *Language and Education*, 23(3) 199–216.

Mayer, S. J., (2010). Dewey's Dynamic Integration of Vygotsky and Piaget, in G. Goodman, ed., *Educational Psychology Reader: The Art and Science of How People Learn*, pp. 103–118. New York: Peter Lang.

Maslow, A. H., (1970). *Motivation and Personality*, (second edition). New York: Harper and Row.

Mehan, H., (1979). *Learning Lessons: Social Organization in the Classroom*. Cambridge, MA: Harvard University Press.

Mercer, N. & Littleton, K., (2004). *Dialogue and the Development of Children's Thinking: A Sociocultural Approach.* New York: Routledge.

Metz, M. H., (1978). *Classrooms and Corridors: The Crisis of Authority in Desegregated Secondary Schools.* Berkeley: University of California Press.

Michaels, S., O'Connor C. & Resnick, L. B., (2008). Deliberative Discourse Idealized and Realized: Accountable Talk in the Classroom and in Civic Life. *Studies in Philosophy and Education, 27,* 283–297.

Michaels, S., Shouse, A.W., & Schweingruber, H.A., (2008). *Ready, Set, Science! Putting Research to Work in K-8 Science Classrooms.* Board on Science Education, Center for Education, Division of Behavioral and Social Sciences Education. Washington, DC: The National Academies Press.

Mitchell, D. & Spady, W., (1983). Authority, Power, and the Legitimation of Social Control. *Educational Administration Quarterly,* 19(1), 5–33.

Moll, L., ed., (1990). *Vygotsky and Education: Instructional Implications and Applications of Sociohistorical Psychology.* New York: Cambridge University Press.

Morgan, N. & Saxton, J., (1991). *Teaching, Questioning, and Learning.* London: Routledge.

Morrell, E., (2008). *Critical Literacy and Urban Youth: Pedagogies of Access, Dissent, and Liberation.* New York: Routledge.

Newman, D., Griffin, P., & Cole, M., (1989). *The Construction Zone: Working for Cognitive Change in School.* Cambridge, UK: Cambridge University Press.

Noddings, N., (2003a). *Caring: A Feminine Approach to Ethics and Moral Education* (second edition). Berkeley: University of California Press.

Noddings, N. (2003b). *Happiness and Education.* New York: Cambridge University Press.

Noddings, N., (2005). *The Challenge to Care in Schools: An Alternative Approach to Education.* New York: Teachers College Press.

Nussbaum, E. M. & Sinatra, G. M., (2003). Argument and Conceptual Engagement. *Contemporary Educational Psychology,* 28, 384–395.

Nystrand, M., (1997). *Opening Dialogue: Understanding the Dynamics of Language and Learning in the English Classroom*. New York: Teachers College Press.

Nystrand, M. & Gamoran, A., (1991). Instructional Discourse, Student Engagement, and Literature Achievement. *Research in the Teaching of English*, 25(3), 261–290.

O'Connor, M.C., (2001). "Can any Fraction be turned into a Decimal?" A Case Study of a Mathematical Group Discussion. *Educational Studies in Mathematics*, 46, 143–185.

O'Connor, M.C. & Michaels, S., (1993). Aligning Academic Task and Participation Status through Revoicing: Analysis of a Classroom Discourse Strategy. *Anthropology and Education Quarterly*. 24(4), 318–335.

O'Connor, M.C. & Michaels, S., (1996). Shifting Participant Frameworks: Orchestrating Thinking Practices in Group Discussion, in D. Hicks, ed., *Discourse, Learning, and Schooling*, 63–103. New York: Cambridge University Press.

O'Connor, C. & Michaels, S., (2007). When Is Dialogue 'Dialogic'? *Human Development*, 50, 275–285.

O'Loughlin, M., (1992). Rethinking Science Education: Beyond Piagetian Constructivism toward a Sociocultural Model of Teaching and Learning. *Journal of Research in Science Teaching*, 29, 791–820.

Olson, D., ed., (1980). *The Social Foundations of Language and Thought: Essays in Honor of Jerome S. Bruner*. New York: W.W. Norton.

Pace, J. L. & Hemmings, A., eds. (2006). *Classroom Authority: Theory, Research, and Practice*. Mahwah, NJ: Lawrence Erlbaum.

Pace, J. L. & Hemmings, A., (2007). Understanding Authority in Classrooms: A Review of Theory, Ideology, and Research, *Review of Educational Research*, 77(1), 4–27.

Pais, A., (1982). *Subtle Is the Lord: The Science and Life of Albert Einstein*. Oxford, UK: Oxford University Press.

Palinscar, A. M & Brown, A. L., (1984). Reciprocal Teaching of Comprehension-Fostering and Comprehension Monitoring Activities. *Cognition & Instruction*, 1(2), 117–175.

Palinscar, A. M., Brown, A. L., & Campione, J. C., (1993). First-Grade Dialogues for Knowledge Acquisition and Use, in E. A. Forman.

N. Minick, & C. A. Stone, eds., *Contexts for Learning: Sociocultural Dynamics in Children's Development* pp. 43–57. New York: Oxford University Press.

Piaget, J. (1923/1959). *The Language and Thought of the Child.* London: Routledge & Kegan Paul Ltd.

Piaget, J. (1968). *Structuralism.* New York: Harper Torchbooks.

Phillip, C., (2001). *Socrates Café: A Fresh Taste of Philosophy.* New York: Norton.

Philips, S., (1972). Participant Structures and Communicative Competence: Warm Springs Children in Community and Classroom, in C. Cazden, V. John, & D. Hymes, eds., *Functions of Language in the Classroom.* New York: Columbia Teachers Press.

Polanyi, M., (1962/58). *Personal Knowledge: Towards a Post-Critical Philosophy.* Chicago: Chicago University Press.

Polman, J., (2004). Dialogic Activity Structures for Project-Based Learning Environments. *Cognition and Instruction*, 22(4), 431–466.

Probst, R. E., (2004). *Response and Analysis: Teaching Literature in Secondary School.* Portsmouth, NH: Heinemann.

Remarque, E. M., (1996). *All Quiet on the Western Front.* New York: Fawcett Books.

Rizzolatti, G., Fogassi, L., & Gallese, V., (2008). Mirrors in the Mind, in *The Jossey-Bass Reader on the Brain and Learning*, pp. 12–19. San Francisco: John Wiley & Sons.

Rogoff, B., (2003). *The Cultural Nature of Human Development.* New York: Oxford University Press.

Rorty, R., (1982). *Consequences of Pragmatism.* Minneapolis: University of Minnesota Press.

Rose, L. T. & Fischer, K., (2009). Dynamic Development: A Neo-Piagetian Approach, in U. Müller, J. Carpendale & L. Smith, (eds.), *The Cambridge Companion to Piaget.* New York: Cambridge University Press.

Rosenblatt, L., (2005). *Making Meaning with Texts.* Portsmouth, NH: Heinemann.

Rud, A. G., Garrison, J., & Stone, L., eds., (2009). John Dewey at 150: Reflections for a New Century, in a special issue of *Education and Culture*, 25(2).

Salinger, J. D., (1985). *The Catcher in the Rye.* New York: Bantam.

Sannino, A., Daniels, H., & Gutierrez, K. D., eds., (2009). *Learning and Expanding with Activity Theory*. New York: Cambridge University Press.

Schneier, L. (1998). Apprehending Poetry, in E. Duckworth, ed., *"Tell Me More:" Listening to Learners Explain*, pp. 42–78. New York: Teachers College Press.

Schwartz, D. & Bransford, J., (1998). A Time for Telling. *Cognition &Instruction*, 16(4), 475–522.

Shuy, R.W., (1981). Topic as the Unit of Analysis in a Criminal Law Case, in ed., D. Tannen, *Georgetown University Roundtable on Languages and Linguistics 1981*. Washington, DC: Georgetown University Press.

Spady, W. & Mitchell, D., (1979). Authority and the Management of Classroom Activities, in D. Duke, ed., *Classroom Management* (pp. 75–115). Chicago: University of Chicago Press.

Sinclair, J. M., & Coulthard, R. M., (1975). *Towards an Analysis of Discourse*. London: Oxford University Press.

Tabek, I. & Baumgartner, E., (2004). The Teacher as Partner: Exploring Participant Structures, Symmetry, and Identity Work in Scaffolding. *Cognition and Instruction*, 22(4), 393–429.

Tröhler, D., (2005). Modern City, Social Justice and Education. Early Pragmatism as Exemplified by Jane Addams, in D. Tröhler & J. Oelkers, eds., (2005). *Pragmatism and Education*, pp. 69–93. Rotterdam: Sense Publishers.

Valenzuela, S., (1999). *Subtractive Schooling: U. S.-Mexican Youth and the Politics of Caring*. Albany: State University of New York Press.

Valsiner, J., Molenaar, P., Lyra, M. & Chaudhary, N., eds., (2009). *Dynamic Process Methodology in the Social and Developmental Sciences*. New York: Springer.

Van Lier, L., (1996). *Interaction in the Language Curriculum: Awareness, Autonomy & Authenticity*. Essex: Longman Group Limited.

Vidal, F. (1987). Jean Piaget and the Liberal Protestant Tradition. In M.G. Ash & W. R. Woodward (Eds.), *Psychology in Twentieth-Century Thought and Society*, pp. 271–294. Cambridge University Press.

Vidal, F. (1994). *Piaget Before Piaget*. Cambridge and London: Harvard University Press.

Vygotsky, L., (1978). *Mind in Society.* Cambridge, MA, Harvard University Press.

Vygotsky, L., (1987). *Thought and Language.* (Kozulin, A., trans.) Cambridge, MA: MIT Press.

Weber, M., (1964/1925). *The Theory of Social and Economic Organization.* (A. M. Henderson & T. Parsons, trans.)New York: Free Press.

Wells, G., (1993). Reevaluating the IRF sequence: A proposal for the articulation of theories of activity and discourse for the analysis of teaching and learning in the classroom. *Linguistics and Education,* 5, 1–38.

Wells, G., (1999). *Dialogic Inquiry: Towards a Sociocultural Theory and Practice of Education.* Cambridge: Cambridge University Press.

Wells, G., ed., (2001). *Action, Talk, and Text: Learning and Teaching through Inquiry.* New York: Teachers College Press.

Wells, G., (2007). Semiotic Mediation, Dialogue, and the Construction of Knowledge. *Human Development,* 50, 244–274.

Wertsch, J., ed. & trans., (1981). *The Concept of Activity in Soviet Psychology.* New York: M.E. Sharpe.

Wertsch, J., (1985). *Vygotsky and the Social Formation of the Mind.* Cambridge, MA: Harvard University Press.

Wilkenson, L., ed., (1982). *Communicating in the Classroom.* New York: Academic Press.

Index

A

activity theory, 43

accountable talk, 170-171

Adger, Carolyn Temple, 185n.

agency: intellectual, 6-7, 87-88, 94, 145, 167-169, 183n., 192n.

Anderson, Rob, 179n.

Anyon, Jean, 180n.

Applebee, Arthur, 182n., 187n.

Armstrong, Michael, 189n.

Ashton-Warner, Sylvia, 180n.

Au, Kathryn, 180n., 185n., 192n.

authority: intellectual 2-3, 7, 9, 10-11, 25, 28, 94, 118, 156, 160, 174-177

interpretive, see interpretive authority; pedagogical, 1-2, 54, 170-172

B

Ballenger, Cynthia, 90-92, 127, 188n., 189n.

Barnes, Douglas, 102, 189n.

Bausch, Kenneth, 184n.

Bereiter, Carl, 181n.

Berkman, Michael, 181n.

Bovet, Magali, 183n., 189n.

Bransford, John, 180n., 182n., 188n., 191n.

Bronfenbrenner, Uri, 184n., 185n.

Brookline Teacher Research Seminar, 90-91, 127, 188n.

Brown, Ann, 186n.

Bruner, Jerome, 35-36, 56, 182n., 187n.

C

Carini, Patricia, 189n.

Case, Robbie, 40, 42, 183n.

Cazden, Courtney, 49, 61, 89, 185n., 186n., 188n.

Chapman, Michael, 183n.

Cissna, Kenneth, 179n.

classroom discourse analysis: history of field, 47-54 methodological explication, 63-68, 187n.

Clune, Meghan, 179n.

Cofer, Lynette, 185n.

cognitive science, 35, 44, 182n.

Cole, Michael, 185n.

Coulthard, Malcolm, 50, 185n.

critical exploration, 92-95, 183n., 189n.

D

Daniels, Harry, 184n., 185n.

Dawson, Theo, 182n.

DeCastell, Suzanne, 181n.

Delpit, Lisa, 42, 90, 181n., 184n.

democracy

democratic approaches to knowledge, 13-17

democratic knowledge systems, 7-8

democratization of school practice, 10-11, 82-83, 94, 120, 155-156

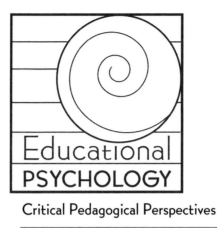

Educational PSYCHOLOGY

Critical Pedagogical Perspectives

Greg S. Goodman, *General Editor*

Educational Psychology: Critical Pedagogical Perspectives is a series of relevant and dynamic works by scholars and practitioners of critical pedagogy, critical constructivism, and educational psychology. Reflecting a multitude of social, political, and intellectual developments prompted by the mentor Paulo Freire, books in the series enliven the educator's process with theory and practice that promote personal agency, social justice, and academic achievement. Often countering the dominant discourse with provocative and yet practical alternatives, *Educational Psychology: Critical Pedagogical Perspectives* speaks to educators on the forefront of social change and those who champion social justice.

For further information about the series and submitting manuscripts, please contact:

Dr. Greg S. Goodman
Department of Education
Clarion University
Clarion, Pennsylvania
ggoodman@clarion.edu

To order other books in this series, please contact our Customer Service Department at:

(800) 770-LANG (within the U.S.)
(212) 647-7706 (outside the U.S.)
(212) 647-7707 FAX

Or browse online by series at:

www.peterlang.com